SOURCE READINGS IN $\mathcal{M}$USIC
HISTORY

SOURCE READINGS IN *Music* HISTORY

OLIVER STRUNK

EDITOR

Revised Edition

LEO TREITLER GENERAL EDITOR

VOLUME 3

The Renaissance

Edited by GARY TOMLINSON

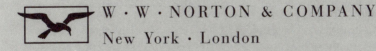

W · W · NORTON & COMPANY
New York · London

The text of this book is composed in Caledonia
with the display set in Bauer Bodoni and Optima.
Composition by the Maple-Vail Book Manufacturing Group
Manufacturing by Maple-Vail Book Manufacturing Group
Book design by Jack Meserole
Cover illustration by Mary Frank

The Library of Congress has cataloged the one-volume edition as follows:

Source readings in music history / Oliver Strunk, editor. — Rev. ed.
    / Leo Treitler, general editor.
        p.   cm.
    Also published in a 7 v. ed.
    Includes bibliographical references and index.
    ISBN 0-393-03752-5
    1. Music—History and criticism—Sources.   I. Strunk, W. Oliver
(William Oliver), 1901–   .   II. Treitler, Leo, 1931–
ML160.S89   1998
780'.9—dc20   94-34569
                                                 MN

ISBN 0-393-96696-8 (pbk.)

W. W. Norton & Company, Inc., 500 Fifth Avenue, New York, N.Y. 10110
http://www.wwnorton.com

W. W. Norton & Company Ltd., 10 Coptic Street, London WC1A 1PU

1 2 3 4 5 6 7 8 9 0

FROM THE FOREWORD TO THE FIRST EDITION OF *SOURCE READINGS IN MUSIC HISTORY*

*T*his book began as an attempt to carry out a suggestion made in 1929 by Carl Engel in his "Views and Reviews"—to fulfil his wish for "a living record of musical personalities, events, conditions, tastes . . . a history of music faithfully and entirely carved from contemporary accounts."[1] It owes something, too, to the well-known compilations of Kinsky[2] and Schering[3] and rather more, perhaps, to Andrea della Corte's *Antologia della storia della musica*[4] and to an evaluation of this, its first model, by Alfred Einstein.

In its present form, however, it is neither the book that Engel asked for nor a literary anthology precisely comparable to the pictorial and musical ones of Kinsky and Schering, still less an English version of its Italian predecessor, with which it no longer has much in common. It departs from Engel's ideal scheme in that it has, at bottom, a practical purpose—to make conveniently accessible to the teacher or student of the history of music those things which he must eventually read. Historical documents being what they are, it inevitably lacks the seemingly unbroken continuity of Kinsky and Schering; at the same time, and for the same reason, it contains far more that is unique and irreplaceable than either of these. Unlike della Corte's book it restricts itself to historical documents as such, excluding the writing of present-day historians; aside from this, it naturally includes more translations, fewer original documents, and while recognizing that the somewhat limited scope of the *Antologia* was wholly appropriate in a book on music addressed to Italian readers, it seeks to take a broader view.

That, at certain moments in its development, music has been a subject of widespread and lively contemporary interest, calling forth a flood of documentation, while at other moments, perhaps not less critical, the records are either silent or unrevealing—this is in no way remarkable, for it is inherent in the very nature of music, of letters, and of history. The beginnings of the Classical

---

1. *The Musical Quarterly* 15, no. 2 (April 1929): 301.
2. *Geschichte der Musik in Bildern* (Leipzig, 1929; English edition by E. Blom, London, 1930).
3. *Geschichte der Musik in Beispielen* (Leipzig, 1931; English edition New York, 1950).
4. Two volumes (Torino, 1929). Under the title *Antologia della storia della musica della Grecia antica al' ottocento*, one volume (Torino, 1945).

symphony and string quartet passed virtually unnoticed as developments without interest for the literary man; the beginnings of the opera and cantata, developments which concerned him immediately and deeply, were heralded and
reviewed in documents so numerous that, even in a book of this size, it has
been possible to include only the most significant. Thus, as already suggested,
a documentary history of music cannot properly exhibit even the degree of
continuity that is possible for an iconographic one or a collection of musical
monuments, still less the degree expected of an interpretation. For this reason,
too, I have rejected the simple chronological arrangement as inappropriate and
misleading and have preferred to allow the documents to arrange themselves
naturally under the various topics chronologically ordered in the table of contents and the book itself, some of these admirably precise, others perhaps
rather too inclusive. As Engel shrewdly anticipated, the frieze has turned out
to be incomplete, and I have left the gaps unfilled, as he wished.

For much the same reason, I have not sought to give the book a spurious
unity by imposing upon it a particular point of view. At one time it is the
musician himself who has the most revealing thing to say; at another time he
lets someone else do the talking for him. And even when the musician speaks
it is not always the composer who speaks most clearly; sometimes it is the
theorist, at other times the performer. If this means that few readers will find
the book uniformly interesting, it ought also to mean that "the changing pat-
terns of life," as Engel called them, will be the more fully and the more faithfully reflected. . . . In general, the aim has been to do justice to every age
without giving to any a disproportionate share of the space.

It was never my intention to compile a musical Bartlett, and I have accordingly sought, wherever possible, to include the complete text of the selection
chosen, or—failing this—the complete text of a continuous, self-contained, and
independently intelligible passage or series of passages, with or without regard
for the chapter divisions of the original. But in a few cases I have made cuts to
eliminate digressions or to avoid needless repetitions of things equally well said
by earlier writers; in other cases the excessive length and involved construction
of the original has forced me to abridge, reducing the scale of the whole while
retaining the essential continuity of the argument. All cuts are clearly indicated,
either by a row of dots or in annotations.

Often, in the course of my reading, I have run across memorable things said
by writers on music which, for one reason or another, were not suited for
inclusion in the body of this book. One of these, however, is eminently suited
for inclusion here. It is by Thomas Morley, and it reads as follows:

> But as concerning the book itself, if I had, before I began it, imagined half the pains
> and labor which it cost me, I would sooner have been persuaded to anything than to
> have taken in hand such a tedious piece of work, like unto a great sea, which the
> further I entered into, the more I saw before me unpassed; so that at length, despair-
> ing ever to make an end (seeing that grow so big in mine hands which I thought to
> have shut up in two or three sheets of paper), I laid it aside, in full determination to

have proceeded no further but to have left it off as shamefully as it was foolishly begun. But then being admonished by some of my friends that it were pity to lose the fruits of the employment of so many good hours, and how justly I should be condemned of ignorant presumption—in taking that in hand which I could not perform—if I did not go forward, I resolved to endure whatsoever pain, labor, loss of time and expense, and what not, rather than to leave that unbrought to an end in the which I was so far engulfed.[5]

OLIVER STRUNK
The American Academy in Rome

5. Thomas Morley, *A Plain and Easy Introduction to Practical Music,* ed. R. Alec Harman (New York: Norton, 1966), p. 5.

FOREWORD TO THE REVISED EDITION

> *Hiding in the peace of these deserts*
> *with few but wise books bound together*
> *I live in conversation with the departed,*
> *and listen with my eyes to the dead.*
> *—Francisco Gómez de Quevedo*
> *(1580–1645)*

The inclusion here of portions of Oliver Strunk's foreword to the original edition of this classic work (to which he habitually referred ironically as his *opus unicum*) is already a kind of exception to his own stricture to collect in it only "historical documents as such, excluding the writing of present-day historians." For his foreword itself, together with the book whose purpose and principles it enunciates and the readings it introduces, comes down to us as a historical document with which this revision is in a conversation—one that ranges over many subjects, even the very nature of music history.

This principle of exclusion worked for Strunk because he stopped his gathering short of the twentieth century, which has been characterized—as Robert Morgan observes in his introduction to the twentieth-century readings in this series—by "a deep-seated self-consciousness about what music is, to whom it should be addressed, and its proper role within the contemporary world." It is hardly possible to segregate historian from historical actor in our century.

For the collection in each of the seven volumes in this series the conversation begins explicitly with an introductory essay by its editor and continues with the readings themselves. The essays provide occasions for the authors to describe the considerations that guide their choices and to reflect on the character of the age in each instance, on the regard in which that age has been held in music-historical tradition, on its place in the panorama of music history as we construct and continually reconstruct it, and on the significance of the readings themselves. These essays constitute in each case the only substantial explicit interventions by the editors. We have otherwise sought to follow Strunk's own essentially conservative guidelines for annotations.

The essays present new perspectives on music history that have much in common, whatever their differences, and they present new perspectives on the music that is associated with the readings. They have implications, therefore, for those concerned with the analysis and theory of music as well as for students of music history. It is recommended that even readers whose interest is focused on one particular age acquaint themselves with all of these essays.

The opportunity presented by this revision to enlarge the book has, of course, made it possible to extend the reach of its contents. Its broader scope reflects achievement since 1950 in research and publication. But it reflects, as well, shifts in the interests and attitudes that guide music scholarship, even changes in intellectual mood in general. That is most immediately evident in the revised taxonomy of musical periods manifest in the new titles for some of the volumes, and it becomes still more evident in the introductory essays. The collections for "Antiquity and the Middle Ages" have been separated and enlarged. What was "The Greek View of Music" has become *Greek Views of Music* (eight of them, writes Thomas J. Mathiesen), and "The Middle Ages" is now, as James McKinnon articulates it, *The Early Christian Period and the Latin Middle Ages*. There is no longer a collection for "The Classical Era" but one for *The Late Eighteenth Century*, and in place of the epithet "The Romantic Era" Ruth Solie has chosen *The Nineteenth Century*. The replacements in the latter two cases represent a questioning of the labels "Classic" and "Romantic," long familiar as tokens for the phases of an era of "common practice" that has been held to constitute the musical present. The historiographic issues that are entailed here are clarified in Solie's and Wye Jamison Allanbrook's introductory essays. And the habit of thought that is in question is, of course, directly challenged as well by the very addition of a collection of readings from the twentieth century, which makes its own claims to speak for the present. Only the labels "Renaissance" and "Baroque" have been retained as period designations. But the former is represented by Gary Tomlinson as an age in fragmentation, for which "Renaissance" is retained only *faute de mieux*, and as to the latter, Margaret Murata places new emphasis on the indeterminate state of its music.

These new vantage points honor—perhaps more sharply than he would have expected—Strunk's own wish "to do justice to every age," to eschew the "spurious unity" of a "particular point of view" and the representation of history as a succession of uniform periods, allowing the music and music-directed thought of *each* age to appear as an "independent phenomenon," as Allanbrook would have us regard the late eighteenth century.

The possibility of including a larger number of readings in this revision might have been thought to hold out the promise of our achieving greater familiarity with each age. But several of the editors have made clear—explicitly or implicitly through their selections—that as we learn more about a culture it seems "more, not less distant and estranged from ours," as Tomlinson writes of the Renaissance. That is hardly surprising. If the appearance of familiarity has arisen out of a tendency to represent the past in our own image, we should hardly wonder that the past sounds foreign to us—at least initially—as we allow it to speak to us more directly in its own voice.

But these words are written as though we would have a clear vision of our image in the late twentieth century, something that hardly takes account of the link, to which Tomlinson draws attention, between the decline of our confidence about historical certainties and the loss of certainty about our own identities. Standing neck-deep in the twentieth century, surrounded by uncountable numbers of voices all speaking at once, the editor of this newest selection of source readings may, ironically, have the most difficult time of any in arriving at a selection that will make a recognizable portrait of the age, as Morgan confesses.

Confronted with a present and past more strange and uncertain than what we have been pleased to think, the editors have not been able to carry on quite in the spirit of Strunk's assuredness about making accessible "those things which [the student] must eventually read." Accordingly, this revision is put forward with no claim for the canonical status of its contents. That aim has necessarily yielded some ground to a wish to bring into the conversation what has heretofore been marginal or altogether silent in accounts of music history.

The sceptical tract *Against the Professors* by Sextus Empiricus, among the readings from ancient Greece, is the first of numerous readings that run against a "mainstream," with the readings gathered under the heading "Music, Magic, Gnosis" in the Renaissance section being perhaps the most striking. The passage from Hildegard's *Epistle* to the prelates of Mainz in the medieval collection is the first of many selections written by women. The readings grouped under the reading "European Awareness of Other Musical Worlds" in the Renaissance collection evince the earliest attention paid to that subject. A new prominence is given to performance and to the reactions of listeners in the collection from the Baroque. And the voices of North American writers and writers of color begin to be heard in the collection from the nineteenth century.

There is need to develop further these once-marginal strands in the representation of Western music history, and to draw in still others, perhaps in some future version of this series, and elsewhere—the musical cultures of Latin America for one example, whose absence is lamented by Murata, and the representation of the Middle Ages in their truly cosmopolitan aspect, for another.

This series of books remains at its core the conception and the work of Oliver Strunk. Its revision is the achievement of the editors of the individual volumes, most of whom have in turn benefited from the advice of numerous colleagues working in their fields of specialization. Participating in such a broadly collaborative venture has been a most gratifying experience, and an encouraging one in a time that is sometimes marked by a certain agonistic temper.

The initiative for this revision came in 1988 from Claire Brook, who was then music editor of W. W. Norton. I am indebted to her for granting me the privilege of organizing it and for our fruitful planning discussions at the outset. Her thoughts about the project are manifested in the outcome in too many ways to enumerate. Her successor Michael Ochs has been a dedicated and active editor, aiming always for the highest standards and expediting with expertise the complex tasks that such a project entails.

Leo Treitler
Lake Hill, New York

CONTENTS

III   MUSIC AND RELIGIOUS REFORM

IV   MUSIC, MAGIC, GNOSIS

V   WRITINGS ON POLYPHONIC PRACTICE

VI GLIMPSES OF OTHER MUSICAL WORLDS

NOTES AND ABBREVIATIONS

Footnotes originating with the authors of the texts are marked [Au.], those with the translators [Tr.].

Omitted text is indicated by five spaced bullets (• • • • •); three spaced bullets (• • •) indicate a typographical break in the original.

References to other volumes in this series are indicated as follows:

SR   Oliver Strunk, ed., *Source Readings in Music History*, rev. ed., Leo Treitler, ed. (New York: W. W. Norton, 1997)

SR 1 Oliver Strunk, ed., *Source Readings in Music History*, rev. ed., Leo Treitler, ed., vol. 1: *Greek Views of Music*, Thomas J. Mathiesen, ed. (New York: W. W. Norton, 1997)

SR 2 Oliver Strunk, ed., *Source Readings in Music History*, rev. ed., Leo Treitler, ed., vol. 2: *The Early Christian Period and the Latin Middle Ages*, James McKinnon, ed. (New York: W. W. Norton, 1997)

Years in the common era (A.D.) are indicated as C.E. and those before the common era as B.C.E.

THE RENAISSANCE

INTRODUCTION

*T*o write history is to strike at each moment a balance between continuity and revision. The Renaissance portrayed in the readings gathered here is both different from the one Oliver Strunk represented in his original *Source Readings in Music History* and also much in touch with it. At one level, the continuities are obvious enough. Strunk's primary concern was to exemplify the writings on music theory and practice that paralleled what he saw as the musical mainstream of the period, namely vocal polyphony. His most important secondary concerns were to give a glimpse of courtly society and the place of music in it, and to locate music in (mainly northern European) movements of religious reform. These broad themes, and many of the specific readings that embodied them for Strunk, have retained a prominent place in my revision of his work. More generally, the first two of these themes have continued to play a central role in the deliberations of Renaissance musicologists all told over the last forty years.

But continuities such as these operate here under the aegis of discontinuity, so to speak. They do so because the Renaissance has not grown straightforwardly more transparent over these last decades, despite our having exhumed and interpreted more and more traces of the literate musical cultures of Europe in the fifteenth and sixteenth centuries. Instead the period has taken on new, dark tints which, if not amounting to any total eclipse of our understanding, have at least caused us to see even once-familiar issues in new lights and colorations. From Strunk's day to our own, the Renaissance has grown immensely more problematic; in the same historiographic motion it has come to seem a culture more, not less, distant and estranged from ours. In the readings collected here, I have hoped to capture some of this complexity and distance.

Our sense of estrangement reflects in part our present-day concerns and the general shift in late twentieth-century intellectual life away from historical certainties toward a defamiliarization of ourselves and those whose histories we write. But it responds also to the traces of a fifteenth- and sixteenth-century European past. These convey an extraordinary ferment of recovery, discovery, and reform, and also the ambivalence and uncertainty attendant on it. Indeed, if there is any unifying thread that extends across European elite perceptions from, say, 1400 to 1600, it is probably the growing sense of the disunity and even disarray of knowledge that had once seemed more tractable and comprehensible. The Renaissance, we might say, forms a coherent historical epoch mainly through its sense of a breakdown of coherence. The estrangement of Renaissance culture, then, is not only a question of our historical relation with it but also of its relation to itself.

We may follow this self-estrangement in the three watchwords I have used above to capture the period. By *recovery* I allude to what has seemed to many the singular triumph of the thinkers of the period: the retrieval of a huge body of ancient thought, unearthing the achievement of Greek and Roman Antiquity in substantially the quantity and form we have today. This project of recovery, often referred to as "humanism" (the term also has useful broader applications in recent historical writing on the Renaissance), exerted a widespread and varied destabilizing force on European elite culture. In the first place, the new and expert philology that sprang up with the accelerating recovery brought many accepted beliefs into question—as when, to mention an exemplary instance, Lorenzo Valla proved the Donation of Constantine, the document on which the Pope's temporal power was founded, to be an eighth-century forgery. Such philology fostered a new awareness of historical contingency and change in languages, thought, and societies. In this way, whatever particular familiarities and connections with the ancient past it affirmed, it carried large and unsettling implications of cultural discontinuity and relativism.

In the second place, the sheer variety of newly accessible ancient authorities threatened once-stable structures of knowledge. For example, the imposing amalgam of Aristotelian and scriptural doctrine that scholastic thinkers had created in the twelfth and thirteenth centuries was challenged by the late fifteenth-century recovery of Plato and the ancient Neoplatonists; the new bodies of thought required that new compromises be struck between Christian and pre-Christian doctrine. Likewise, full knowledge of the ethical dimensions of ancient oratory that came with the full recovery especially of Cicero and Quintilian encouraged new conceptions of the polis and of political action. It also fostered a reorientation within educational curricula in which grammar, rhetoric, history, and ethics—the lightly regarded siblings of logic in the *studia humanitatis,* or "humanities"—could claim some of the prestige traditionally accorded the quadrivium of mathematical arts (arithmetic, geometry, astronomy, and music).

These broad tendencies played themselves out in musical culture as well. Increased philological expertise deepened knowledge of ancient music, often with contradictory results. Thus Heinrich Glarean's humanistic studies aided his overhaul of ecclesiastical modal theory and his application of it to polyphony, but Girolamo Mei's more extensive research into ancient music showed the accepted connection of ancient *tonoi* to modern modes to be misconceived and led him to question altogether the expressive efficacy of polyphony. The revival of Platonic and Neoplatonic philosophy encouraged a mathematical approach to harmonic proportions and temperaments, mainly derived from Boethius, that we might be tempted to see as musical rationalism or, in some of its forms, empiricism. But this mathematicism embodied a view of numbers different from ours; it was associated with views of magic, astrology, and mystical gnosis in which music played a central role (see section IV below). New oratorical modes of political engagement created a context that exacerbated distinctions between practice and its rationalization—what we tend today to call theory. These distinctions would concern and vex the writers of the time that we label music theorists (they are, for example, Pietro Aaron's starting point in the excerpt below [pp. 137–50] and a touchstone for Gioseffo Zarlino [pp. 158–84]).

Most important and most generally, the heightened esteem of grammar, rhetoric, history, and ethics helped exacerbate the dualism of the position that music had long occupied in Western structures of knowledge. In the fifteenth and sixteenth centuries, music did not give up its affiliations with the other mathematical arts: indeed, as I have said, the Neoplatonic resurgence could not help but reaffirm, in what we might call its "harmonic idealism," a transcendant mathematicism behind musical practice. But now the ties of music to the expressive and persuasive arts of poetry and rhetoric took on a novel ideological potency. Music was pulled with a new vigor in two different directions; it was, so to speak, estranged from itself. Its essential and uneasily reconcilable bonds both to pragmatic expressive force, on the one hand, and to idealized number, on the other, were set in an opposition more strenuous than they had known in the preceding centuries.

The readings collected here betray again and again the newly felt importance of music's affiliations with the humanities. They do so in their alignment of song with poetry and oratory, their detailing of the relations between words and notes, their frequent emphasis on solo song, their preoccupation with music's suasive force, and their description of the expressive gestures appropriate to individual genres. And they do so, most of all, in rehearsing, at every opportunity, examples of music's ethical powers culled from ancient writings and scripture. This review usually takes the form of an elaborate praise of music, a formula that was repeated so often as to become almost a standard starting point for musical discussion of the period (see section I and elsewhere). But in a late-Renaissance intellectual atmosphere touched by a revival of ancient skepticism and a new Christian fideism, it could also be voiced in negative terms—as a suspicion and denunciation of music's force (Agrippa [pp. 26–30]). Both gestures manifest the centrality of musical ethics in the elite thought of the period.

The fifteenth and sixteenth centuries were also, famously, a period of geographical, technological, and scientific *discovery;* this, too, contributed to the epistemological fragmentation of the era. In the first place, European navigators, soldiers, and missionaries brought back dizzying accounts of unsuspected lands and civilizations in Africa, America, and Asia. It is not too much to say that the distinctively Western project we have come to call ethnography is foreshadowed in such reports. They merged with and played upon the sense of cultural relativism already fostered by humanist historicism. And this sense in its turn made European efforts to familiarize and domesticate newly-known others more difficult. All told, the geographical and cultural discoveries eventually bred a widespread and uneasy fascination among literate Europeans, a fascination revealed in the immense popularity of proto-ethnographic travel narratives in the years around 1600 (witness, among the accounts here, the many editions and translations of Pigafetta (pp. 224–26) and Ricci (pp. 226–30) that quickly emerged).

These reports on other societies usually reserved room for comment on music (see section VI). In this they not only provide us with tantalizing traces of traditions of song, instrumental performance, and dance now mostly lost; they also afford a glimpse of European approaches to non-European others whose legacy we still live with in the quandaries of today's musical ethnography. They form a largely unexamined aspect of European musical estrangement in the era, of the nascent process by which Europeans grew more and more aware of distant, even incomprehensible musical practices in the geographical world around them and the historical world that had preceded them. And, not least, they reveal again the cultural centrality that music had assumed in the perceptions of literate Europeans, a centrality automatically projected onto others.

Meanwhile technologies of astounding novelty and monumental impact appeared. New navigational devices, such as the compass, aided the voyages of exploration, and gunpowder and other weapons technologies were crucial in the subjugation of indigenous peoples and colonization of their lands that usually followed quickly on the heels of discovery. More and more precise measurements of the heavens called into question hallowed ideas of cosmic order; they would receive their most impressive confirmation at the end of the period, when Galileo turned an odd Dutch contraption of tubes and lenses on the stars. And—most decisive technology of all, at least within Europe—from the second half of the fifteenth century on, thousands upon thousands of books printed with movable type poured forth from presses soon dispersed across Europe. This torrent of printed material conveyed the geographical and cultural discoveries, the newly accessible ancient writings, and knowledge of countless other sorts to larger readerships than had ever been reached in the past.

In music the technological difficulties of printing with movable type were solved only somewhat later, around 1500 and in the following decades. But the achievement resulted by the middle of the sixteenth century in a proliferation of printed scores of astounding extent. These vast quantities of music were not produced to answer the needs of only the most elite aristocratic circles. They also reached a growing bourgeoisie and touched its own aspirations to social distinction—touched them, that is, with the aid of oft-repeated admonishments, gleaned from ancient authors such as Plato and Quintilian, that music was an essential part of any "gentleman's" education and ethical formation (see here Zarlino [pp. 15–21], Ronsard [pp. 22–25], Castiglione [pp. 47–52], Peacham [pp. 68–73], and others).

The movements of *reform* that swept Europe throughout the sixteenth century may, finally, be understood in part as a widespread response to the subtle forces of disorientation that arose in a climate of discovery and recovery. The pressing need for reform was most obviously manifested in the religious schisms, strife, and doctrinal debate of the Protestant and Italian Reformations. Song, given its immense and central role in the Catholic liturgy, was inevitably implicated in these struggles (see section III). But we need to remember that reform was not restricted to religious matters. A concern for it pervaded all aspects of life, and we might with some justification speak of reformations of secular society that gained powerful voice in the same decades that saw the first burgeonings of religious reformation. The immense popularity and influence of Castiglione's *Libro del cortegiano* bespeak a perceived need for clear social standards that might separate true (or, in Peacham's word, "compleat") gentlemen and gentlewomen from imposters. (Indeed the anxious discrimination of the genuine from the counterfeit is a topos that recurs with telling frequency in all sorts of connections from the late fifteenth century on—genuine versus sham religious faith, inspired versus contrived poetry, rational versus arbitrary learning and action, "honest" versus "meretricious" courtesans, and so forth.) The codes of behavior advocated by works like Castiglione's were derived from a courtly life of renewed vigor and self-consciousness that characterizes the late Renaissance as a whole. In their advocacy, these books came to enforce the codes on anyone who wished to gain admission to society's upper echelons. In a culture that emphasized music's rhetorical and ethical force, it is no surprise that such works usually saved an important place for a discussion of musical expertise and learning.

Given the new esteem for music's psychological force, it is also no surprise that some writers connected music with a female sexuality thought to be insufficiently controlled, thus renewing an association that had a long history in the West. But, in the context of heated debates on the place of women in elite society that were an important aspect of sixteenth-century social critique, voices opposing this view were also raised. Thus for every Castiglione who treats musical performance as a predominantly male pursuit; for every Bembo who impugns the virtue of young women who learn music; and for every Agrippa who repeats the age-old linkage of music to a misogynist view of effeminacy, there is a Doni who extols at once the virtuosity and the virtue of a female performer, a Stampa who sings her own Petrarchan love lyrics without joining the ranks of Venetian courtesans, and even a Casulana who purposefully infiltrates the male bastion of polyphonic composition and publication.

Which brings us back, finally, to Strunk's polyphonic mainstream. Where, in a rethought Renaissance, do we locate this tradition, whose reflection in theoretical writings formed the backbone of the original Renaissance *Source Readings*? Clearly it too is subject to the increased complexity and estrangement I have outlined here. In the first place we need to qualify thoroughly the central role we have accorded the polyphonic tradition. Writers on music who neither wrote polyphony nor discussed its theory tend to emphasize, as the centerpiece of their musical culture, not polyphony so much as practices of solo song (see Castiglione [pp. 47–52], Cortesi [pp. 38–43]). It is by now clear that these practices thrived not only after the great sixteenth-century efflorescence of printed polyphony but before and during it as well and that, indeed, they over-lapped in complex ways with polyphonic styles and genres. Unlike polyphony, solo song did not need to rely on print technology for its effective and wide-spread dissemination (see Calmeta [pp. 43–47]), so its small part in sixteenth-century musical prints is no reliable gauge of its prevalence. And it is clear also that the novelty of musical styles around 1600 was connected not with any unprecedented emphasis on solo singing but rather with the invention of new dramatic styles (i.e., recitative) within vigorous and deeply rooted solo tradi-tions (see Giustiniani [pp. 74–79]) and also with complex changes in musical practice, taste, and professional institutions that allowed solo-song composers to usurp, for a few decades, the print medium that polyphonists had domi-nated. All this needs to be taken into account even while we note the huge dispersion of printed polyphony across Europe through the late sixteenth cen-tury.

In the second place: monophonic repertories loomed at least as large as polyphonic ones in Reformation debates about music in worship. Thus while a Cirillo or an Agrippa might worry over the propriety of polyphony in the liturgy, major musical efforts of reformers north and south of the Alps concerned monophonic repertories and were aimed at either purging old bodies of liturgi-cal plainsong or creating new ones. Calvin banned polyphony from his church, worked with others to create a collection of melodies for his translated Psalter to be sung in the services, and left polyphonists such as Goudimel to harmonize these melodies for devotional singing at home. The moderate Erasmus permit-ted polyphony in church while cautioning that care must be taken to assure its appropriateness to worship; but a more urgent concern for him was the abuse of sequences, probably monophonic, whose length and complexity deformed the liturgy. Even in the case of Palestrina, the fabled savior of church polyph-ony, the most reliable evidence we have of his reform efforts concerns plainchant, not polyphony (see Pope Gregory XIII [pp. 96–98]). Again, the huge extent of polyphonic sacred repertories is not in question here, and nei-ther is the religious commitment of their composers (see Palestrina [pp. 95–96], Byrd [pp. 100–103]). But we need to understand better that these reperto-ries were not the primary music of worship across the whole of Europe and did not inevitably preoccupy those most intent on sacred musical reform.

In regard to Renaissance music theorists (section V) this reassessment of the old polyphonic mainstream cuts deeper still. Recent work by various musicolo-gists (some of them cited in the annotations to the readings; see especially Tinctoris [pp. 123–29] and Aaron [pp. 137–50]) has greatly complicated our sense of the relation between theoretical writings on polyphony and polyphonic repertories themselves. It is increasingly evident that these writings, especially before the middle of the sixteenth century, were not in any unproblematic sense prescriptive of the polyphonists' compositional practices. Rather, they were something closer to ex-post-facto attempts to rationalize—by extending earlier theoretical systems—burgeoning practices whose novelty occasionally beggared the available vocabulary. Thus the whole discussion of mode in polyphony, at least up through Glarean, can be better understood as the theorists' attempt to match systems of tonality devised for plainchant to polyphony than as the laying-out of a set of precompositional choices that faced the composers themselves. Talk of *musica ficta* and the Guidonian compass of hexachords (see Ramis [pp. 129–36]) likewise represents a groping attempt to comprehend the freedoms of polyphonic practice through tools devised to theorize plainchant. And, most dramatically, Tinctoris's discussion of written and unwritten polyphony and of dissonance treatment reveals his own struggle to come to grips with fluctuating categories of music-making. Reading it suggests that we risk great anachronistic distortion in imposing any stable, reified senses of "counterpoint" or even "musical composition" on polyphonic practices of his time.

This particular sense of estrangement, at least, is greatly lessened by the end of the Renaissance. Zarlino's conceptions of "counterpoint" and "composition" are decisively closer to ours than Tinctoris's (though they too have their surprises). The fundamental change in the enterprise of music theory from 1470 to 1600 may be seen in hindsight as a shift from tentative *description* of what polyphonists were about to confident *prescription* of what one needed to do to be a competent polyphonist. The shift, put differently, is from an attempt to observe and rationalize current practice to an attempt to synthesize all permissible practice in a form that might be conveyed as a method or course of study. Certainly this sense of prescriptive law is the most important general achievement of Zarlino's *Istitutioni harmoniche,* the most influential of late-Renaissance music treatises, and in this his book is not so very different from Castiglione's in approach and tone.

One more word, on the question of retaining Strunk's "Renaissance" as the period designation for this collection. The term shows, at this late date, a mixture of neutrality and historiographic vested interest similar in kind to that built into other period labels historians still use out of convenience and for want of preferable alternatives. It is probably no worse than "Middle Ages" or "Romantic" in its difficulties, and it is a good deal better, I think, than "Baroque" and "Classic." I have avoided the most common alternative to it, "early-modern," for two reasons. First, as the foregoing discussion of estrangement makes evident, I am not happy with the confident continuities and teleologies between the sixteenth and later centuries that the term "early-modern" suggests. Second, "early-modern" may be helpful to those historians whose materials move outside the elite echelons of fifteenth- and sixteenth-century society—the echelons, that is, that have since the middle of the nineteenth century been associated with the term "Renaissance." But such non-elite materials are, for the music historian, exceedingly rare and play little role here (note that even the accounts that follow of music from Mexico, Peru, the Congo, and China speak of elite music-making). This restriction of materials also explains why more neutral and sweeping chronological designations such as "the fifteenth and six-teenth centuries" cannot serve. "Renaissance" continues to be, simply, the best label we have for the particular societal and cultural strands represented in this volume.

•   •   •

Lewis Lockwood, who had begun contemplating this revision before per-sonal concerns induced him to withdraw, corresponded on the project with several leading scholars of Renaissance music, including Allan Atlas, Lawrence Bernstein, the late Howard M. Brown, Jessie Ann Owens, and Claude V. Pa-lisca; this correspondence and Professor Lockwood's notes on it were helpful to me in my planning. I also have consulted with various colleagues on the project; among them, Martha Feldman and Cristle Collins Judd have been particularly helpful (the latter with invaluable assistance concerning section V). Leo Treitler has been a model general editor, patient, attentive, and full of thought-provoking queries. Marina Brownlee, Lance Donaldson-Evans, and Joseph Farrell looked over my translations from Spanish, French, and Latin respectively and saved me from more than one embarrasssing gaffe (all the gaffes left over are my own). I wish also to salute Oliver Strunk himself; though I had read through his Renaissance *Source Readings* more than once before, I never fully appreciated the canniness and intelligence of his choices, transla-tions, and annotations until I remade them. Finally, and by way of closing a circle of sorts, I dedicate this work to a man who had a hand in the first version of *Source Readings* and has had a hand in many fundamental musicological enterprises since: Joseph Kerman.

PRAISES AND DISPRAISES OF MUSIC

1 Johannes Tinctoris

Born around 1435 near the Flemish town of Nivelles, Johannes Tinctoris may have sung under Du Fay at Cambrai Cathedral. In the 1460s he was in charge of the choirboys at the Cathedral of Orleans and studied at the university there. By the early 1470s he had moved to Naples, where he served King Ferdinand and tutored Ferdinand's daughter Beatrice. In 1487 Tinctoris traveled in France and Germany in search of singers for Ferdinand's chapel. He died in 1511, a canon of Nivelles.

Tinctoris's principal writings include the treatise on harmonic proportions here excerpted; the *Terminorum musicae diffinitorium,* the first European dictionary of musical terms, written for his royal pupil before 1476 and published in 1495; the *Liber de natura et proprietate tonorum (Book on the Nature and Character of the Modes),* dedicated in 1476 to his contemporaries Ockeghem and Busnois; and a book on the art of counterpoint, the *Liber de arte contrapuncti,* completed in 1477. The last work is particularly important for its guidelines concerning dissonance treatment in polyphony; it lays the groundwork for many later counterpoint treatises of the Renaissance. And it is particularly intriguing for its distinction between counterpoint sung from written polyphonic scores and counterpoint sung over books of plainchant without written-out parts (for these topics see no. 32 below, pp. 123–29).

In the forewords to his treatises and in remarks scattered through them, Tinctoris reveals himself to be a knowledgeable and shrewd observer of the contrapuntal styles of his day and of the immediately preceding generations. The dedication presented here shows this clearly enough, with its famous remark about the English "fount and origin" of contemporary Continental practices. It also exemplifies a rhetorical gesture—one whose antecedents reach back to ancient models—that would flourish through the Renaissance: the *laus musicae,* or praise of music, a mythological and historical sketch of music's antiquity, nobility, and power.

Proportionale musices
(1473–74)

THE PROPORTIONAL OF MUSIC, BY MASTER JOHANNES TINCTORIS, LICENTIATE IN LAWS, CHAPLAIN TO THE MOST SUPREME PRINCE FERDINAND, KING OF SICILY AND JERUSALEM, BEGINS WITH GOOD OMEN

DEDICATION

To the most sacred and invincible prince, by the divine providence of the King of Kings and Lord of Lords, King of Sicily, Jerusalem, and Hungary,

TEXT: C. E. H. Coussemaker, *Scriptorum de medii aevi . . . nova series* (4 vols., Paris: A. Durand, 1864–76), vol. 4, pp. 153–55. Translation by Oliver Strunk.

Joannes Tinctoris, the least among professors of music and among his chaplains, proffers humble and slavish obedience, even to kissing his feet.

Although, most wise king, from the time of the proto-musician Jubal, to whom Moses has attributed so much, as when in Genesis he calls him the first of all such as handle the harp and organ,[1] many men of the greatest fame, as David, Ptolemy, and Epaminondas (princes of Judaea, Egypt, and Greece), Zoroaster, Pythagoras, Linus the Theban, Zethus, Amphion, Orpheus, Musaeus, Socrates, Plato, Aristotle, Aristoxenus, and Timotheus bestowed such labor upon the liberal art of music that, on the testimony of Cicero,[2] they attained a comprehension of almost all its powers and its infinite material, and although for this reason many of the Greeks believed that certain of these men, and especially Pythagoras, had invented the very beginnings of music; nevertheless we know almost nothing of their mode of performing and writing music. Yet it is probable that this was most elegant, for they bestowed on this science, which Plato calls the mightiest of all,[3] their highest learning, so that they taught it to all the ancients, nor was anyone ignorant of music considered an educated man. And how potent, pray, must have been that melody by whose virtue gods, ancestral spirits, unclean demons, animals without reason, and things insensate were said to be moved! This (even if in part fabulous) is not devoid of mystery, for the poets would not have feigned such things of music had they not apprehended its marvelous power with a certain divine vigor of the mind.

But, after the fullness of time, in which the greatest of musicians, Jesus Christ, in whom is our peace, in duple proportion made two natures one, there have flourished in his Church many wonderful musicians, as Gregory, Ambrose, Augustine, Hilary, Boethius, Martianus, Guido, and Jean de Muris, of whom some established the usage of singing in the salutary church itself, others composed numerous hymns and canticles for that purpose, others bequeathed to posterity the divinity, others the theory, others the practice of this art, in manuscripts now everywhere dispersed.

Lastly the most Christian princes, of whom, most pious King, you are by far the foremost in the gifts of mind, of body, and of fortune, desiring to augment the Divine Service, founded chapels after the manner of David, in which at extraordinary expense they appointed singers to sing pleasant and comely praise to our God[4] with diverse (but not adverse) voices. And since the singers of princes, if their masters are endowed with the liberality which makes men illustrious, are rewarded with honor, glory, and wealth, many are kindled with a most fervent zeal for this study.

At this time, consequently, the possibilities of our music have been so marvelously increased that there appears to be a new art, if I may so call it, whose

1. Genesis 4: 21.
2. *De oratore* 1.3.10
3. *Republic* 401d.
4. Psalm 147:1.

fount and origin is held to be among the English, of whom Dunstable stood forth as chief. Contemporary with him in France were Dufay and Binchois, to whom directly succeeded the moderns Ockeghem, Busnois, Regis, and Caron, who are the most excellent of all the composers I have ever heard. Nor can the English, who are popularly said to shout while the French sing,[5] stand comparison with them. For the French contrive music in the newest manner for the new times, while the English continue to use one and the same style of composition, which shows a wretched poverty of invention.

But alas! I have perceived that not only these, but many other famous composers whom I admire, while they compose with much subtlety and ingenuity and with incomprehensible sweetness, are either wholly ignorant of musical proportions or indicate incorrectly the few that they know. I do not doubt that this results from a defect in arithmetic, a science without which no one becomes eminent, even in music, for from its innermost parts all proportion is derived.

Therefore, to the purpose that young men who wish to study the liberal and honorable art of music may not fall into similar ignorance and error in proportions, and in praise of God, by whom proportions were given, and for the splendor of your most consecrated Majesty, whose piety surpasses that of all other pious princes, and in honor of your most well-proportioned chapel, whose like I cannot easily believe to exist anywhere in the world, I enter, with the greatest facility my powers permit, upon this work, which with appropriateness to its subject I conclude should be called the *Proportional of Music.* If I have ventured in it to oppose many, indeed nearly all famous musicians, I entreat that this be by no means ascribed to arrogance. Contending under the banner of truth, I do not order that my writings should necessarily be followed more than those of others. What in their writings I find correct, I approve; what wrong, I rebuke. If to my readers I seem to carry on this my tradition with justice, I exhort them to put their trust in me; if without justice, let them rather believe others, for I am as ready to be refuted by others as to refute them.

5. Compare Ornithoparcus, *Musice active micrologus* (Leipzig, 1516), 4.8, and Pietro Aaron, *Lucidario in musica* (Venice, 1545), fol. 31.

2 Gioseffo Zarlino

Gioseffo Zarlino was born at Chioggia, not far from Venice, in 1517. From 1541 his teacher was Adriano Willaert, choirmaster at St. Mark's from 1527 to 1562. In 1565, on the departure for Parma of Cipriano de Rore, Willaert's successor, Zarlino fell heir to his old teacher's position, which he occupied until his death in 1590. The *Istitutioni harmoniche,* or *Harmonic Institutes,* his principal work, was first published in 1558 and reprinted in 1562 and 1573. Other writings of his are the *Dimostrationi harmoniche* (1571) and the *Sopplimenti musicali* (1588), this last in reply to the stand taken by Vincenzo Galilei, a rebellious pupil who had attacked Zarlino's teaching on proportions, tuning, and other matters in his *Dialogo della musica antica, et della moderna* (1581; see no. 37 below, pp. 184–89).

In the *Istitutioni harmoniche* Zarlino sought to unite theoretical principles based on natural laws with practical rules for polyphonic composition. Many aspects of his approach are strikingly modern in tone: he grasped the full implications of just intonation and produced classical authority for it, dealt with harmony in terms of the triad rather than the interval, recognized the importance of the fundamental antithesis of major and minor, attempted a rational explanation of the old rule forbidding the use of parallel fifths and octaves, and isolated and described the effects of the false relation (for some of these topics, see no. 36 below, pp. 162–69). Zarlino's contrapuntal precepts were widely dispersed, long-lived, and hugely influential. They crystallized across the seventeenth century into the pedagogy that is still offered today in the "modal counterpoint" classes of many music departments. Zarlino's writings bear witness to the extraordinary range and depth of his reading; appropriately and no doubt with some pride, he recalled in the title *Istitutioni harmoniche* Quintilian's encyclopedic and systematic account of ancient rhetorical theory and practice, the *Institutio oratoria*. Something of Zarlino's ecumenical learning is reflected in the praise of music that follows.

FROM *Istitutioni harmoniche*

(1558)

BOOK 1

CHAPTER 2: ON THE PRAISES OF MUSIC

. . . The writings of ancient philosophers make it clear how much music was celebrated and held to be sacred. The Pythagoreans in particular believed that the world was composed musically, and that the heavens caused harmony in their revolutions, and that our soul is formed according to the same laws, and that it is awakened and its powers vivified by songs and instrumental music. Some Pythagoreans wrote that music was the prince of all the liberal arts, and some called it ἐγκυκλοπαιδέια, or "circle of the sciences," since it embraces (as Plato said) all disciplines.[1] We can see this to be true if we begin with grammar, first of the seven liberal arts, since we hear a great harmony in the proportionate juxtaposition and order of words. And if the grammarian departs

---

TEXT: The facsimile of the edition of 1573 (Ridgewood, N.J.: Gregg Press, 1966), pp. 7–11. Translation by Gary Tomlinson. Zarlino's postils are given here as author's notes.

1. *Laws* 1 [probably 642a; see also 2.654a–b]. [Au.]

from this he brings to our ears a displeasing sound in his phraseology, so much so that we listen to or read with difficulty prose or verse bereft of polished, beautiful, ornate, sonorous, and elegant order. Next, in dialectics, whoever considers the proportions of syllogisms will see that the truth is shown to be far from the false by means of a marvelous harmony greatly pleasing to our ears. The orator also gives marvelous delight to his listeners in his oration by using musical accents and appropriate rhythms. The great orator Demosthenes understood this best of all. He was asked three times what the principal part of oratory was, and three times he responded that enunciation mattered above all else.[2] Gaius Gracchus, a man of utmost eloquence, also knew this, as Cicero[3] and Valerius Maximus[4] relate: whenever he had to speak before the people he kept hidden behind him a servant musician who set the measure or voice or tone of his speech on an ivory flute, in a manner that relaxed him when he grew too excited and aroused him when he flagged.

Next, we can see that poetry is so closely joined with music that whoever would separate the two would be left, as it were, with a body separated from its soul. This is confirmed by Plato, who says in the *Gorgias* that anyone who removed harmony, number, and meter from poetry would be left with commonplace and impoverished speech.[5] Therefore we find that poets have employed the greatest diligence and marvelous artifice in accommodating their words to their verses and laying out the feet according to the requisites of speech. Virgil observed this throughout his *Aeneid,* matching all three sorts of speech found in his poem with appropriately sonorous verse, and doing it with such artifice that he seems to put the things he treats before our eyes by means of the sounds of his words. Thus where he speaks of love we find that he chose words sweet, pleasing, and gracious to the ears; where he needed to sing of wars and to describe naval battles or seafaring deeds or similar things, where the subjects are bloodletting, anger, hatred, vengeance, displeasing sentiments and all things hateful, he chose hard, bitter, and displeasing words that arouse fear in the speaking and hearing of them.[6] ... All this is enough to conclude that poetry would be without any beauty if it were not made of harmonically ordered words.

Beyond this I will not speak of the close relations and similarities of arithmetic and geometry to music; I will say only that if an architect has no knowledge of music (as Vitruvius shows) he will not know how to balance machines, to place vases in theaters, and to arrange well and musically his buildings.[7] Astronomy, likewise, would not be able to judge the good and bad celestial influences

---

2. Related in Quintilian, *Institutio oratoria* 11.3.6.

3. *De oratore* 3 [i.e., 3.225] [Au.] See also Quintilian, *Institutio oratoria* 1.10.27.

4. *Factorum ac dictorum memorabilium libri IX* 8.10[.1] [Au.]

5. 502c.

6. Here follow several examples from the *Aeneid,* the *Georgics,* and the *Eclogues.*

7. *De architectura* 1.1. [Au.] The vases Zarlino mentions were vessels placed, according to Vitruvius, in an arrangement of musical porportion so as to amplify the speech from the stage.

if it were not aided by the fundamentals of harmony. Indeed I will go further: if the astronomer does not understand the concordance of the seven planets and when one is in conjunction or opposition with another, he will never predict future events. Similarly, does not natural philosophy, which takes as its task the rational discussion of the things produced or potentially produced by nature, confess that all things depend on the Prime Mover and are ordered so marvelously that there results in the universe a silent harmony? Thus heavy things take the lowest position, light things the highest, and things of middle weight, according to their nature, a middle place. Moreover, philosophers affirm that the revolving heavens make a harmony, which we do not hear because they revolve too fast, or are too far away from us, or for some other unknown reason. Medicine does not stand far from these subjects, since if the doctor does not understand music how will he mix in due proportion hot things with cold, according to their states? And how will he understand perfectly people's pulses, which the most wise Herophilus orders according to musical proportions?[8]

And to rise even higher among the disciplines, our theology divides the angelic spirits in the heavens into nine choruses and three hierarchies, as Dionysius the Areopagite writes. These gaze perpetually on the Divine Majesty and ceaselessly sing "Holy, holy, holy is the Lord of hosts," as it is written in Isaiah.[9] And not only these, but also the four beasts described by Saint John in his book of Revelations stand before the throne of God and sing the same song. There are also then the twenty-four ancients before the immaculate Lamb, who sing a new song to the highest God with the sound of harps and raised voices.[10] This song is also sung by the harpists playing their harps before the four beasts and twenty-four elders. The Bible is full of these and an almost infinite variety of other things relating to our subject, which in the interest of brevity I will pass over. It is enough to say in supreme praise of music that the Bible, without mentioning other sciences, places music in Paradise, where it is most nobly practiced. And just as happens in the heavenly court, called the Church Triumphant, so in our earthly one, the Church Militant, the Creator is praised and thanked with nothing so much as with music.

But let us leave the superior things aside and return to those produced by nature for the ornament of the world. Here we will see that everything is full of musical concord.[11] ... But if so much harmony is found in celestial and terrestrial things—or, to put it better, if the world was composed by the Creator in such harmony—why should we believe man himself to be bereft of it? And if the soul of the world is (as some say) nothing other than harmony, could it be that our soul is not a cause of all our harmony and harmonically joined with

---

8. The *Anatomica* of Herophilus (4th–3rd century B.C.E.) has not survived. Zarlino takes his information from Martianus Capella, *De nuptiis Philologiae et Mercurii* 9.926–7.

9. *De coelestia hierarchia,* chaps. 7, 8, and 9; Isaias 6. [Au.]

10. Apocalypse [i.e., Revelations] 4, 5, 14, 15, and 19. [Au.]

11. Here follow examples of the musical qualities of the sea, air, earth, rivers, and springs.

the body? This is certainly reasonable to assume, especially since God created man according to the plan of the larger world, called by the Greeks *cosmos* (κὸσμος), that is, "ornament" or "ornate," and made him similar to the world but of lesser quantity, whence he is called *microcosmos* (μικρὸκοσμος), or "small world." So that Aristotle, wanting to show the musical makeup of man, explained very well that the vegetative part of the soul has the same relation to the sensitive, and the sensitive to the intellective, as a triangle has to a rect-angle.[12]

It is thus confirmed that there is no good thing that does not have a musical disposition. And truly music, beyond merely raising our spirits, leads man back to the contemplation of celestial things and has such power that it perfects everything it is joined to. Those people who are gifted in music are truly happy and blessed, as David affirmed saying "Blessed are they that know the joyful sound."[13] On the basis of that authority, the Catholic doctor Hilary, Bishop of Poitiers, speaking of the 65th psalm, was moved to say that music is necessary to Christians, since they find blessedness in its science.[14] Which emboldens me to say that those who do not have knowledge of this science must be numbered among the ignorant.

In ancient times, as Isidore reports, it was no less shameful to be unmusical than to be illiterate.[15] It is no wonder that the most famous and ancient poet Hesiod was excluded from poetic contests, as Pausanius narrates,[16] since he had never learned to play the harp or accompany himself with it. Even The-mistocles, as Cicero reports,[17] was thought less wise and learned after he refused to play the lyre at a symposium. We read also the opposite: how Linus and Orpheus, both sons of gods, were held in great esteem because with sweet song they not only sweetened human souls, so to speak, but those of beasts and birds as well, and, what is more marvelous still, they moved the rocks from their usual places and rivers from their courses. Horace attributes this power also to Amphion, saying:

> Hence too the fable that Amphion, builder of Thebes's
> citadel,
> moved stones by the sound of his lyre, and led them
> whither he would by his supplicating spell.[18]

Perhaps from this example the ancient Pythagoreans learned that musical sounds could soften ferocious animals, and Asclepiades likewise learned that music could quiet discord in the populace and that the sound of the trumpet

---

12. *On the soul* 2.3 [414b]. [Au.]
13. Psalm 88 [i.e. 89:15]. [Au.]
14. Hilary, *Tractatus in LXV psalmum* 1.
15. *Etymologiarum* [i.e., Isidore of Seville, *Etymologiarum sive originum libri XX*] 3.15. [Au.]
16. *Descriptio graeciae* 10 [i.e., 10.7.3]. [Au.]
17. *Tusculan Disputations* 1 [i.e., 1.2.4]. [Au.]
18. *Ars poetica* 11.394–396; trans. H. Rushton Fairclough, *Horace: Satires, Epistles and Ars Poet-ica* (Cambridge, Mass.: Harvard University Press, 1966), 483.

could restore hearing to the deaf.[19] Similarly, Damon the Pythagorean led with music several youths given to wine and pleasure back to a temperate and honest life.[20] Thus they who call music a certain law and rule of modesty speak well, since Theophrastes discovered certain musical modes that quiet perturbed spirits. But Diogenes the Cynic justly and wisely mocked the musicians of his time who had abandoned the customary harmonies and therefore, though they had well tuned harps, had discordant and discomposed souls.[21]

And if we can believe history, all that we have said thus far may seem as nothing, because it is a greater thing to be able to heal the sick than to correct the ways of dissolute youths. Indeed we read of Xenocrates who could restore sanity to the insane with the sound of the organ, or of Thaletas of Crete who expelled the plague with the sound of his harp. And we see today that music can do marvelous things, and that such is the force of sounds and dancing against the poison of the tarantula that in the shortest time those who have been bitten are healed (this is confirmed by experience every day in Apulia, a region in which such animals are abundant).[22] But turning from further secular examples, do we not read in the Bible that the prophet David quieted the evil spirit of Saul with the sound of his harp?[23] Because of this, I believe, this royal prophet ordered that songs and harmonies be used in the temple of God; he knew that they were able to lift the spirits and return people to the contemplation of celestial things.[24] And the prophets, when they wanted to prophesy (Ambrose says, commenting on psalm 118), asked that a good musician begin to play so that spiritual grace, summoned by that sweetness, might enter into them.[25] Eliseus did not want to prophesy to the King of Israel where he might find water for his parched troops until a musician was brought whose singing infused the divine spirit into him; then he foretold everything.[26]

But let us move on, because there are many examples. Timotheus, as St. Basil and many others relate, with music incited King Alexander to combat and then called him back to himself.[27] Aristotle tells in his book *History of Animals*[28] that deer are captured by the singing of hunters and that they delight

---

19. Zarlino took these examples, along with those that follow of Damon, Theophrastes, Xenocrates, and Thaletas, from Martianus, *De nuptiis* 9.923 and 926.
20. The story is usually told not of Damon but of Pythagoras; see, e.g., Quintilian, *Institutio oratoria* 1.10.32, Boethius, *De institutione musica* 1.1, and St. Basil, *To Young Men (Ad adolescentes)* 9.9.
21. See Diogenes Laertius's biographies of the Cynics Diogenes and Menedemus, specifically *Lives of Eminent Philosophers* 6.73 and 104.
22. Alessandro Alessandri [ca. 1461–1523], *Genialium dierum libri sex* 2.16 [Au.] For another early and influential account of this tarantism, see no. 29 below (Ficino), p. 111.
23. 1 Kings [i.e., 1 Samuel] 16. [Au.]
24. 1 Paralipomenon [i.e., Chronicles] 16. [Au.]
25. Ambrose, *In psalmum David CXVIII expositio* 7.26.
26. 4 [i.e., 2] Kings 3. [Au.]
27. Homily 54 *Ad adolescentes.* [Au.] I.e., *To Young Men* 8.7–8; see no. 10 below (Castiglione), pp. 48–49, n. 2.
28. 9.5 [611b]. [Au.]

greatly in the pastoral bagpipe as well as song (which Pliny confirms in his *Natural History*).[29] And so as not to go on any longer about this I will only say that I know people who have seen deer stop and stand attentively listening to the sound of a lyre or lute; and similarly we see everyday birds which, defeated and deceived by harmonic sounds, are captured by bird trappers. And Pliny narrates that music saved Arion from death when he threw himself into the sea; he was carried by dolphins to the shore of the island of Taenarum.[30] But let us set aside many other examples that we could adduce and say a little about good Socrates, master of Plato, who decided when he was old and full of wisdom to learn to play the harp; or about the old Chiron, who included music among the first arts he taught Achilles at a tender age, and who wanted him to play the harp before he dirtied his hands with Trojan blood.[31] Plato and Aristotle do not consider a man well formed who is without music. Indeed they persuade us with many reasons that music should be studied and show that its force in us is very great; and they think it should be taken up in childhood so that it can induce in us a new and good custom that will guide us to virtue and render our souls more capable of happiness.[32] Even the most severe Lycurgus, King of the Lacedaemonians, praised and approved of music among his very harsh laws, since he knew very well that it was most necessary for men and of great help in times of war. His armies, as Valerius tells us, never went to war without being first enflamed and animated by the music of pipes.[33] We still observe that custom in our own time, since of two armies one will not attack its enemy if it is not summoned by the sound of trumpets and drums or of some other musical instruments. And though there do not lack many other examples beyond those given here from which we can learn the dignity and excellence of music, in order not to go on too long, and since what has already been said is sufficient, I leave them aside.

29. 8.32 [i.e., 8.50.114]. [Au.]
30. *Natural History* 9.8 [.28] [Au.] Other sources of this famous story are Herodotus, *History* 1.23 and Plutarch *Moralia* 160e–162b.
31. For Socrates see Quintilian, *Institutio oratoria* 1.10.13–14; for Chiron see ibid. 1.10.30 and pseudo-Plutarch *De musica* 1145d–1146a.
32. *Laws* 3 [700–701]; *Politics* 8.3 [1337b–1338a]. [Au.]
33. *Factorum ac dictorum memorabilium libri IX* 2.1 [i.e., 2.6.2] [Au.] See also Quintilian, *Institutio oratoria* 1.10.15 and pseudo-Plutarch *De musica* 1140c. The Lacedaemonians were the Spartans.

3 Pierre de Ronsard

The great French poet was born in 1524 and died in 1585. Ronsard strived to bring about a rebirth of lyric poetry—in the ancient Greek sense of the term—as a musical expression of the soul in a state of emotion. As this ideal could be achieved only by a close cooperation of music and poetry, Ronsard set all his efforts in this direction. Thus, to the collected poems that appeared under the title *Les amours de Cassandre* (1552–53), he added a musical supplement containing settings of his poems by Marc-Antoine de Muret, Claude Janequin, Pierre Certon, and Claude Goudimel. Considering Ronsard's views on the union of music and poetry, it is not surprising that more than two hundred of his poems were set to music, some of them repeatedly, in the second half of the sixteenth century. There are entire collections of Ronsard's poems in settings by Philippe de Monte, Antoine de Bertrand, and other contemporary composers; and his verses are found in a great number of chanson collections by the composers named above, Orlando di Lasso, Claude Le Jeune, Guillaume Costeley, and others. Ronsard's dedication to Francis II of one such anthology, the *Livre des mélanges* published in 1560 by Le Roy and Ballard, rehearses many ancient examples, by now almost commonplaces, of the powers of music and the esteem in which it was held.

Livre des mélanges
(1560)

DEDICATION

Even, Sire, as by the touchstone one tries gold, whether it be good or bad, so the ancients tried by music the spirits of those who are noble and magnanimous, not straying from their first essence, and of those who are numbed, slothful, and bastardized in this mortal body, no more remembering the celestial harmony of heaven than the comrades of Ulysses, after Circe had turned them into swine, remembered that they had been men. For he, Sire, that hearing a sweet accord of instruments or the sweetness of the natural voice feels no joy and no agitation and is not thrilled from head to foot, as being delightfully rapt and somehow carried out of himself—'tis the sign of one whose soul is tortuous, vicious, and depraved, and of whom one should beware, as not fortunately born. For how could one be in accord with a man who by nature

TEXT: *Oeuvres complètes*, ed. Paul Laumonier (Paris: A. Lemerre, 1914–19), vol. 7, pp. 16–20. Translation by Oliver Strunk. Laumonier gives the text of 1572; Strunk translated the text of 1560, which he restored with the help of Laumonier's note (see n. 7 below, p. 24).

hates accord? He is unworthy to behold the sweet light of the sun who does not honor music as being a small part of that which, as Plato says, so harmoniously animates the whole great universe.[1] Contrariwise, he who does honor and reverence to music is commonly a man of worth, sound of soul, by nature loving things lofty, philosophy, the conduct of affairs of state, the tasks of war, and in brief, in all honorable offices he ever shows the sparks of his virtue.

Now to tell here what music is; whether it is governed more by inspiration than by art; to tell of its concords, its tones, modulations, voices, intervals, sounds, systems, and transformations; of its division into enharmonic, which for its difficulty was never perfectly in use; into chromatic, which for its lasciviousness was by the ancients banished from republics; into diatonic, which was by all approved, as approaching nearest to the melody of the macrocosm; to speak of the Phrygian, Dorian, and Lydian music; and how certain peoples of Greece went bravely into battle inspired by harmony, as do our soldiers today to the sounds of drums and trumpets; how King Alexander was roused to fury by the songs of Timotheus,[2] and how Agamemnon, going to Troy, left on purpose in his house I know not what Dorian musician, who by the virtue of the anapestic foot tempered the unbridled amorous passions of his wife Clytemnestra, inflamed with love of whom Aegisthus could never attain to enjoyment until he had wickedly put the musician to death;[3] to wish further to deduce how all things, as well in the heavens and in the sea as on the earth, are composed of accords, measures, and proportions; to wish to discuss how the most honorable persons of past ages, monarchs, princes, philosophers, governors of provinces, and captains of renown, were curiously enamored of the ardors of music; I should never have done; the more so as music has always been the sign and the mark of those who have shown themselves virtuous, magnanimous, and truly born to feel nothing vulgar.

For example I shall take solely the late King your father,[4] may God absolve him, who during his reign made it apparent how liberally Heaven had endowed him with all graces and with gifts rare among kings; who surpassed, not only in grandeur of empire, but in clemency, liberality, goodness, piety, and religion, not only all the princes his predecessors, but all who have ever lived that have borne that honorable title of king; who, in order to reveal the stars of his high birth and to show that he was perfect in all virtues, so honored, loved, and esteemed music that all in France who today remain well-disposed toward this art, have not, all combined, so much affection for it as he had alone.

You also, Sire, as the inheritor both of his realm and of his virtues, show that you are his son, favored by Heaven, in so perfectly loving this science and its accords, without which nothing of this world could remain whole.

1. The reference is probably to *Timaeus* 90d or 80b.
2. See no. 10 below (Castiglione), pp. 48–49, n. 2.
3. See *Odyssey* 3.267–272, as elaborated by Athenaeus, *Deipnosophists* 1.14, and later scholiasts.
4. Henri II.

Now to tell you here of Orpheus, of Terpander, of Eumolpus, of Arion, these are stories with which I do not wish to burden the paper, as things well known to you. I will relate to you only that anciently the kings most eminent for virtue caused their children to be brought up in the houses of musicians, as did Peleus, who sent his son Achilles, and Aeson, who sent his son Jason, to the venerated cave of the centaur Chiron to be instructed as well in arms as in medicine and in the art of music, the more so as these three professions, joined together, are not unbefitting the grandeur of a prince; and there were given by Achilles and Jason, who were princes of your age,[5] such commendable examples of virtue that the one was honored by the divine poet Homer as sole author of the taking of Troy, and the other was celebrated by Apollonius of Rhodes as the first who taught the sea to endure the unknown burden of ships; and after he had passed the rocks Symplegades and tamed the fury of the cold Scythian Sea, he returned to his country enriched by the noble fleece of gold. Therefore, Sire, these two princes will be to you as patrons of virtue, and when sometimes you are wearied by your most urgent affairs, you will imitate them by lightening your cares with the accords of music, in order to return the fresher and the better-disposed to the royal burden which you support with such adroitness.

Your Majesty should not marvel if this book of miscellanies, which is very humbly dedicated to you by your very humble and obedient servants and printers Adrian Le Roy and Robert Ballard, is composed of the oldest songs that can today be found,[6] because the music of the ancients has always been esteemed the most divine, the more so since it was composed in a happier age, less contaminated by the vices which reign in this last age of iron. Moreover, the divine inspirations of music, poetry, and painting do not arrive at perfection by degrees, like the other sciences, but by starts, and like flashes of lightning, one here, another there, appear in various lands, then suddenly vanish. And for that reason, Sire, when some excellent worker in this art reveals himself, you should guard him with care, as being something so excellent that it rarely appears. Of such men have arisen within six or seven score years Josquin Desprez, a native of Hainaut, and his disciples Mouton, Willaert, Richafort, Janequin, Maillard, Claudin, Moulu, Certon,[7] and Arcadelt, who in the perfec-

5. François II, husband of Mary Queen of Scots, was sixteen years old on January 19, 1560 and died on December 5 of that year. For Chiron and Achilles see no. 2 above (Zarlino), p. 21, n. 31; various ancient writers attest Jason's education with Chiron (see Pauly-Wissowa, *Real-Encyclopädie*, s.v. "Chiron"), but none that I have seen speaks specifically of musical training.

6. The composers most frequently represented are Willaert, Gombert, Lasso, Josquin, Leschenet, Arcadelt, Crequillon, Mouton, Certon, and Maillard.

7. For the remainder of this paragraph the edition of 1572 substitutes the following: "and Arcadelt, and now the more than divine Orlando [di Lasso], who like a bee has sipped all the most beautiful flowers of the ancients and moreover seems alone to have stolen the harmony of the heavens to delight us with it on earth, surpassing the ancients and making himself the unique wonder of our time."

tion of this art does not yield to the ancients, from being inspired by Charles, Cardinal of Lorraine, his Apollo.

Many other things might be said of music, which Plutarch and Boethius have amply mentioned. But neither the brevity of this preface, nor the convenience of time, nor the subject permits me to discourse of it at greater length. Entreating the Creator, Sire, to increase more and more the virtues of Your Majesty and to continue you in the kindly affection which you are pleased to have for music and for all those who study to make flourish again under your sway the sciences and arts which flourished under the empire of Caesar Augustus, of which Augustus may it be God's will to grant you the years, the virtues, and the prosperity.

4 William Byrd

Born in 1543, William Byrd, the foremost polyphonist of Elizabethan England, died at Stondon Massey, Essex, in 1623. Early on he studied with Thomas Tallis, and he assumed the position of organist and choirmaster at Lincoln Cathedral in 1563. Seven years later he was appointed Gentleman of the Chapel Royal in London, where also he served as organist (at first along with Tallis), and where he remained until around 1590. From then on, though he retained membership in the Chapel, he spent less time in London and more and more in Stondon Massey. Perhaps he distanced himself from London to avoid persecution for his recusancy: he remained Catholic in Anglican England throughout his life, seems to have taken part in some pro-Catholic initiatives, and probably escaped punishment on more than one occasion only by virtue of his considerable celebrity.

Composer of numerous English anthems, psalm settings, and consort songs, of three masses, and of a large body of instrumental music for consort and solo keyboard, Byrd nonetheless devoted himself especially to Latin sacred works. These seem to have answered best his religious convictions, and the more or less veiled Catholic protest of many of his early motets gave way to freely declared liturgical intent in the *Gradualia,* a huge collection of Mass Proper settings dating from 1605–7 (see below, no. 28, pp. 100–103).

This excerpt, from Byrd's *Psalmes, Sonets, & Songs of Sadnes and Pietie* of 1588, is in a different vein altogether. Far from the trials of Elizabethan recusancy, it is just as distant from the high-flown classicism of Tinctoris's, Zarlino's, and Ronsard's paeans. Here Byrd gives an earthy and plebeian assessment of music's advantages.

Psalmes, Sonets, & Songs of Sadnes and Pietie

(1588)

FRONTISPIECE

Reasons briefely set downe by th'auctor, to perswade every one to learne to sing.

First, it is a knowledge easely taught, and quickly learned where there is a good Master, and an apt Scoller.

2. The exercise of singing is delightfull to Nature & good to preserve the health of Man.

3. It doth strengthen all parts of the brest, & doth open the pipes.

4. It is a singuler good remedie for a stutting & stammering in the speech.

5. It is the best meanes to procure a perfect pronunciation, & to make a good Orator.

6. It is the onely way to know where Nature hath bestowed the benefit of a good voyce: which guift is so rare, as there is not one among a thousand, that hath it: and in many, that excellent guift is lost, because they want Art to expresse Nature.

7. There is not any Musicke of Instruments whatsoever, comparable to that which is made of the voyces of Men, where the voices are good, and the same well sorted and ordered.

8. The better the voyce is, the meeter it is to honour and serve God therewith: and the voyce of man is chiefely to be imployed to that ende.

Omnis spiritus laudet Dominum.

Since singing is so good a thing
I wish all men would learne to sing.

TEXT: Facsimile of the original frontispiece in *The Collected Works of William Byrd,* ed. Edmund H. Fellowes (20 vols., London: Stainer & Bell, 1937–50), vol. 12, p. xxxiv.

5 Henry Cornelius Agrippa

Skepticism—philosophical doubt as to human capacities to obtain any true or certain knowledge—grew in importance through the sixteenth century and finally found classic expression in works such as Montaigne's *Apology for Raymond Sebond.* In a general fashion, this growth reflects the erosion across the period of once-solid structures of knowledge. More specifically, it was nurtured by three forces: evangelical and Protestant emphasis on faith rather than knowledge or works as the road to salvation; the revival in Neoplatonic circles of certain forms of mystical gnosis dating from Late Antiquity but believed, in the sixteenth century, to be much older; and the recovery of the thought of the ancient Skeptics themselves, especially in the writings of Sextus Empiricus.

In 1530, the first two of these forces joined together in a famous skeptical diatribe by Henry Cornelius Agrippa. (The third force was less prominent; Sextus's works were not first published until 1562 and 1569, and Agrippa's knowledge of ancient Skepticism seems to have been fragmentary and indirect.) *De incertitudine et vanitate scientiarum et artium atque excellentia verbi Dei declamatio (Declamation of the Uncertainty and Vanity of the Sciences and Arts and of the Excellence of the Word of God)*, or *De vanitate*, as it is customarily called, devotes chapters to many different disciplines, doctrines, activities, social classes, and the like, ranging from ethics, religion, and mathematics to juggling, swordplay, and courtiers. In each case Agrippa depicts knowledge as a destroyer of innocence, an ally of sin, and a refuge of falsehood. In place of knowledge he advocates, at the end of his book, unquestioning faith in the scriptures. His chapter on music is typical. It begins with a review, reminiscent of nos. 1–3 above, of claims in favor of music (omitted here) and proceeds to demolish these claims with vitriol and counter-example. Though controversial, *De vanitate* clearly touched a chord dear to many contemporary readers: numerous editions appeared through the later sixteenth and seventeenth centuries, and the work was translated into Italian, English, French, Dutch, and German.

The itinerant scholar, magician, physician, and soldier Agrippa was born in 1486 in or near Cologne. He is also known for his huge treatise on magic, *De occulta philosophia*, drafted over a long period and published in 1533, two years before his death.

FROM *Declamation of the Uncertainty and Vanity of the Sciences and Arts*
(1530)

CHAPTER 17: OF MUSIC

. . . And although men confess that this Art hath much sweetness, yet the common opinion is, and also everyone may see it by experience, that it is the

TEXT: the first English edition: *Of the Vanitie and Uncertaintie of Artes and Sciences*, trans. James Sanford (London, 1569), fols. 28v–30r. A complete edition of this translation has been edited by Catherine M. Dunn (Northridge, Calif., 1974); where signaled below I have profited from her annotations in making my own. For a review of older interpretations of *De vanitate* and a helpful new reading, see Michael H. Keefer, "Agrippa's Dilemma: Hermetic 'Rebirth' and the Ambivalences of *De vanitate* and *De occulta philosophia*," *Renaissance Quarterly* 41 (1988): 614–53.

exercise of base men, and of an unprofitable and untemperate wit, which have no consideration of beginning nor ending, as it is read of Archabius the trumpeter, to whom men were glad to give more to make him cease, than to make him sing. Of which so unreasonable Musicians Horace speaketh:

> It is a fault, a common fault
>   that all our Minstrels use,
> The more you seem to crave a song
>   the more they will refuse.
> Request them not they never cease, etc.[1]

For this cause Music hath ever been wandering here and there for price and pence, and is the servant of bawdry which no grave, modest, honest, and valiant man ever professed: and therefore the Greeks with a common word called them the Artificers of Father Bacchus, or else (as Aristotle sayeth) *Dionisiaci technitae*,[2] that is the artificers of the Baccanalia, which for the most part, were always used to have lewd customs: leading for the most part, an unchaste Life: partly also in Misery, and Poverty, the which breedeth and encreaseth Vices. The Kings of the Persians, and Medes reckoned Musicians among Parasites, and Players, as they which take pleasure of their own doings, and make little account of the Masters. And Antisthenes that wise man, when he heard, that a certain man, called Ismenias, was a very good Trumpeter, he said, He is a Ribald, for if he were an honest man, he would not be a Trumpeter:[3] for as it is said, that is no sober, and honest man's Art, but the practice of Players and idle persons. This did Scipio Aemilianus, and Cato contemn, as far off from the Custom of the Romans. Augustus, and Nero were blamed, because they did over greedily follow Music. But Augustus being reproved did refrain: Nero coveting it more and more, was for this cause had in contempt, and little estimation. King Philip understanding that his Son had sweetly sung in a certain place, he reproved him, saying, art thou not ashamed, that thou knowest to sing so well? It is enough, and too much for a Prince, to have leisure to hear, when other sing.[4] Jupiter singeth not among the Greek Poets, nor soundeth the Harp. Learned Pallas doth detest the Flute. In Homer a Harper playeth, and Alcyone, and Ulysses give ear.[5] In Virgil Iopas doth sing and sound the Harp, Aeneas and Dido do harken.[6] When on a time Alexander the Great did sing, Antigonus his Master rent his Harp asunder, and cast it away, saying: It is now meet for thy age to Rule, and not to Sing.[7] And the Egyptians also, as

1. Horace, *Satires* 1.3.1–3 (see Dunn). I have not been able to locate the story of Archabius.
2. Pseudo-Aristotle, *Problems* 30.10.
3. Plutarch, *Lives, Pericles* 1.5.
4. Ibid.
5. *Odyssey* 8.72–103; it is Alcinous, not Alcyone, who listens with Ulysses (see Dunn).
6. *Aeneid* 1.740–46 (see Dunn).
7. I have not located this anecdote; for Alexander's awareness that music was beneath his station see Plutarch, *Moralia, On the Fortune or the Virtue of Alexander* 2.334c–335a.

Diodorus testifieth, did forbid their young men to learn Music, as that which doth effeminate the minds of men.[8] And Ephorus, (as Polybius witnesseth) said, that it was invented to no other end, but to deceive men.[9] But in very deed what is more unprofitable, more to be despised, and more to be eschewed, than these Pipers, Singers, and other sorts of Musicians? Which with so many, and diverse voices of songs, surpassing the chirping of all Birds, with a certain venomous sweetness, like to the Mermaids, with voices, gestures, and lascivious sounds, do destroy and corrupt men's minds. For the which thing the women of the Ciconians did persecute Orpheus unto the Death, because with his Music he corrupted their men.[10] But if there be any truth in Fables, a hundred eyes had Argus in his head, all which notwithstanding were brought asleep, and put out with the Harmony of one Bagpipe.[11] And yet for this, these Musicians do much boast, as though that they were more able to move the affections, than Rhetoricians are: which be so much misled by their madness, that they affirm moreover the Heavens themselves to sing, yet with voices never heard of any man, except perhaps they have come to the knowledge of those Musicians by means of their *Euouae*,[12] or through Drunkeness, or Dreaming. And yet in the mean season, there hath no Musician descended from Heaven, that hath known all the concordances of voices, and that hath found out all the measures of proportions. And for all that they say, that it is a very perfect Art, and which comprehendeth all Disciplines, and that it cannot be handled without the knowledge of all Learnings: attributing to it besides the force of Divination, whereby the plights of the body, the passions of the mind, the manners of men may thereby be judged. They say moreover, that it is an endless Art, and that it cannot be thoroughly learned with any wit: but that daily according to the capacity of every man, it giveth fresh melody. And therefore Anaxilas sayeth not amiss: By God sayeth he, Music is even like Affricke, it yearly bringeth forth some strange Beast.[13] Anathasius for the vanity thereof did forbid it the Churches: but Ambrose more desirous of Ceremony and Pomp, ordained in the Church the use of singing and playing on the Organs. But Augustine standing in doubt, sayeth in his *Confessions,* that hereof there grew to him a hard doubt:[14] but nowadays the unleeful liberty of Music, is so much used in Churches, that together with the Canon of the Mass, very filthy songs have like tunes in the Organs, and the Divine Service is sung by lascivious Musicians hired for a great stipend, not for the understanding of the hearers, but for the stirring up of the mind: But for dishonest lasciviousness,

8. Diodorus Siculus, *Library of History* 1.81.7 (see Dunn)
9. Polybius, *Histories* 4.20.5–6 (see Dunn); also quoted in Athenaeus, *Deipnosophists* 14.626. Polybius, it should be noted, cites Ephorus's view in order to dismiss it.
10. See especially Ovid, *Metamorphoses* 11.1–66.
11. Ovid, *Metamorphoses* 1.668–721 (see Dunn).
12. A shouted refrain at the Dionysiac orgies (see Dunn).
13. Reported in Athenaeus, *Deipnosophists* 14.623; Anaxilas was a Middle Comedian.
14. 10.33 (see Dunn).

not with manly voices, but with beastly skeeking, while the children bray the Discant, some bellow the Tenor, some bark the Counterpoint, some howl the Treble, some grunt the Bass, and cause many sounds to be heard, and no words and sentences to be understood, but in this sort the authority of judgment is taken both from the ears, and mind.

11

$\mathcal{M}$USIC IN
SECULAR SOCIETY

6 Guillaume Du Fay

From June 1434 to April 1436, Pope Eugenius IV, beset by political and military troubles in Rome, resided in Florence. For the last half of this period, Guillaume Du Fay, the preeminent polyphonist of the mid-fifteenth century, joined him there, serving as singer and master of the papal chapel.

Du Fay's stay in Florence represents a convergence of personalities that is almost irresistible to the historian of Renaissance culture. During these twenty-two months, the composer struck up lasting relations with the banking family of the Medici, whose paterfamilias Cosimo was just then consolidating his control over the city; he composed an isorhythmic motet for the consecration of the cathedral of Santa Maria del Fiore, whose huge crossing Filippo Brunelleschi had just covered with his famous cupola; and he befriended the organist and composer Antonio Squarcialupi, who owned the chief manuscript repository of Italian polyphony from the preceding generations (the so-called Squarcialupi Codex).

Du Fay's ties to the Medici seem to have been especially cordial with Piero and Giovanni, Cosimo's music-loving sons. The composer's only surviving autograph letter, reproduced here, accompanied a gift of music he made to them in the mid-1450s. And as late as 1467 Squarcialupi could write a fulsome letter to Du Fay reporting the great enthusiasm for his music felt not only by Piero but also, now, by his son Lorenzo (later called "the Magnificent"). Perhaps these letters represent an occasional and opportunistic interaction (Squarcialupi sent a poem by Lorenzo, asking Du Fay to set it, while Du Fay may have been angling for patronage with his chansons), or perhaps they signal a more consistent relationship whose other traces are now lost.

Du Fay's surviving works include some of the latest isorhythmic motets, some of the earliest cycles of Mass Ordinaries, and many smaller liturgical works and secular chansons. He was born around 1400, probably near Cambrai, and died there in 1474.

Letter to Piero and Giovanni de' Medici
(1456?)

MAGNIFICENT AND NOBLE SIRS, ALL HUMBLE COMMENDATION BEFORE-HAND!

Since I well know that you have always taken pleasure in song and since, I believe, you have not changed your preferences, I have felt encouraged to send you some chansons which, at the request of some gentlemen of the King's

TEXT: Frank A. d'Accone, "The Singers of San Giovanni in Florence during the 15th Century," *Journal of the American Musicological Society [JAMS]* 14 (1961): 318–19. Translation by Frank A. d'Accone. Reprinted by permission of the American Musicological Society. For a facsimile of Du Fay's letter see David Fallows, *Dufay* (London: J. M. Dent, 1982), illustration 18.

court, I composed recently when I was in France with Monseigneur de Savoye.
I also have some others which I shall send you at another time. In addition, in
this past year I wrote four Lamentations for Constantinople[1] which are rather
good: three of them are for four voices and the texts were sent to me from
Naples. I do not know whether you have them there. If you do not have them,
be so kind as to let me know and I shall send them to you. Furthermore, I am
very much pleased with Francesco Sassetti[2] your representative here, for during the past year I was in need of something at the court of Rome and he
helped me most magnanimously and treated me most graciously for which I
extend my unceasing thanks. I understand that you now have some good people in your chapel at San Giovanni and because of this, if it pleases you, I
should like to send you some of my little things more often than I have done
in the past. I do this also out of my regard for Antonio,[3] your good friend and
mine, to whom I beg you commend me cordially. Magnificent and noble sirs,
if there is something which I can do here for your lordships, please let me
know and I shall do it with all my heart through the aid of our Lord, who I
hope will grant you a good and long life, and at the end paradise.

Written at Geneva, the 22nd of February[4]

> Your humble chaplain and unworthy servant,
> GUILLAUME DU FAY, Canon of Cambrai

1. Du Fay's four-voice "O tres piteulx de tout espoir fontaine / Omnes amici eius" is probably one
   of these laments; the other three are lost. Commentators have often speculated that one of the
   lost works may have been the lament performed at Philip the Good's Feast of the Pheasant in
   1454 (see no. 7 below, pp. 37–38). For arguments against the connection see Fallows, *Dufay*, p.
   287.
2. Francesco Sassetti was a member of a prosperous Florentine family of merchants, manager of
   the Medici bank in Geneva, and humanistic book-hunter. See Fallows, *Dufay*, p. 257.
3. Squarcialupi.
4. The letter bears no year, but it is now generally assigned to 1456; see Craig Wright, "Dufay at
   Cambrai: Discoveries and Revisions," *JAMS* 28 (1975): 175–229; p. 190.

7 Olivier de la Marche

Under a succession of dukes from the House of Valois, the Duchy of Burgundy
sponsored through the fifteenth century one of the most sumptuous courts in all
Europe. The high-water mark of its influence and power came during the reign
of Philip the Good, which lasted almost half a century, from 1419 to 1467.
Philip boasted a large and renowned musical establishment that included Gilles
Binchois, Robert Morton, and other composers. Even Du Fay, who spent most
of his last thirty-five years in Cambrai, a city under the sway of the Burgundian
dukes, seems to have held some sort of appointment that brought him to the
court at least once.

The famous Feast of the Pheasant, held on February 17, 1454, offers an unbridled introduction to the prominence of music in Renaissance court festivities. The feast was served up by Philip at Lille in order to inspire his Knights of the Golden Fleece to undertake a new crusade against the Turks, who had captured Constantinople the year before. Here the feast is described, in one of two surviving accounts, by Olivier de la Marche (ca. 1426–1502), a longtime member of the Duke's retinue and chronicler in his *Memoirs* of events at court. La Marche wrote his *Memoirs* mainly in the 1470s and '80s, well after the events described; they were first published at Lyon in 1562.

FROM *Memoir on the House of Burgundy*
(ca. 1471–92)

The hall where the banquet was held was large and beautifully hung with a tapestry depicting the life of Hercules. . . . In this hall were three covered tables, one medium-sized, another large, and another small. On the medium-sized table there was a skilfully made church with transept and windows, in which there were four singers and a ringing bell. . . . The second table, which was the largest, had on it (most conspicuously) a pastry in which there were twenty-eight living persons playing in turn various instruments. . . . The third table, smaller than the others, had on it a marvelous forest, like a forest of India, in which there were many strange and strangely made beasts that moved by themselves as if alive. . . .

When everyone was seated, in the manner described, a bell rang very loudly in the church on the principal table (it was the first course on that table). After the bell had stopped ringing, three little children and a tenor sang a very sweet chanson. And when they had finished, in the pastry (the first course on the long table, as noted above) a shepherd played a bagpipe in a very novel fashion. Hardly a moment after that there came in through the entrance to the room a horse walking backwards, richly covered with red silk. On it were two trumpeters seated back to back without a saddle. They were dressed in mantles of gray and black silk, with hats and masks; and they led the horse backwards up and down the length of the room, all the while playing a fanfare on their trumpets. To help in this action there were sixteen knights dressed as stablehands.

When this was finished an organ was played in the church and a German cornett was played, very strangely, in the pastry. Then a goblin entered the hall, a greatly disfigured monster with the hairy legs and feet and long talons of a griffin from the waist down and the form of a man above the waist. . . . When

TEXT: *Mémoire sur le maison de Bourgogne*, in *Choix de chroniques et mémoires sur l'histoire de France*, ed. J. A. C. Buchon, vol. 2 (Paris: Société du Panthéon Littéraire, 1842), pp. 490–96. Translation by Gary Tomlinson.

the goblin had departed, those in the church sang and in the pastry were played
a shawm with another instrument; and a bit later four trumpets sounded a
joyous and very loud fanfare. The trumpets were behind a green curtain hung
over a large pedestal at one end of the hall. When the fanfare ended the curtain
was suddenly drawn and a person playing the role of Jason, heavily armed, was
spied on the pedestal. . . . After this mystery play [of Jason], organs in the
church played a motet, and after them three sweet voices in the pastry sang a
long chanson called "Sauvegarde de ma vie."[1]

Later, after the church and the pastry had each played four times, from
the door where the other things had entered there came into the hall a stag,
marvelously large and beautiful, all white with large antlers of gold, and covered, as far as I could tell, with red and green silk. On the stag rode a twelve-
year-old girl dressed in a short robe of scarlet velvet, carrying on her head a
black scalloped hood, and wearing lovely slippers. She held the stag's antlers in
her hands. When she entered the room she began to sing loud and clear the
upper part of a chanson; and the stag sang the tenor, without the participation
of anyone else. The chanson they sang was named "Je ne vey onques le pareille,
etc."[2] While they sang they walked down the chamber in front of the tables
and then returned. This action seemed good to me, and it was well received.
After this beautiful action of the white stag and the child, the singers sang a
motet in the church and in the pastry a lute accompanied two good voices; in
this manner the church and the pastry always did something between the plays.

After this, when those in the pastry had done their duty, on the pedestal
where we had seen the play of Jason the four trumpets heard earlier played
another fanfare. Then the curtain mentioned before was drawn back and Jason
appeared again, richly armed as before. . . . [After this second play] the curtain
was closed, organs were played in the church, and four minstrels in the pastry
played flutes.

Then, high at one end of the hall, a fire-breathing dragon set out; it flew
most of the length of the chamber and then went out, leaving us guessing what
had become of it. After that those in the church sang, and some blind men in
the pastry played hurdy-gurdies. Next, high in the air at one end of the room a
heron flew in. Several people cried out at it, in the manner of falconers; and
immediately a falcon set out from the side of the room, flying round and soar-
ing in circles. And from the other side of the hall another falcon set out; it
attacked with great ferocity and wounded the heron so grievously that it fell in
the middle of the room. After another cry rang out, the heron was presented
to Monsieur the Duke. Then once more there was singing in the church, and
in the pastry three drums were played together.

Next the four trumpets were sounded on the pedestal, and after their fanfare
the curtain was drawn and Jason appeared armed and fortified. . . . At the end

1. Jason was the mythological patron of Philip's Order of the Golden Fleece, founded in 1429.
2. This song might well be related to the three-voice *rondeau* "Je ne vis onques la pareille" that
   has come down to us in various manuscript sources. It is ascribed both to Du Fay and to Binchois.

of this third mystery play the organs in the church were heard and in the pastry they played a *chasse* so vivid it seemed there were little dogs yelping and hunters shouting and trumpets sounding, as if we were in a forest. With that *chasse* the role of the pastry ended.

Such were the secular entertainments of the banquet, and I will leave off speaking of them in order to recount a moving spectacle that seemed to me most special of all. It was this: From the door where all the other things had entered there came with great strides a huge giant, without any artifice that I could see, dressed in a long robe of green-striped silk. On his head he wore a turban in the manner of the Saracens of Granada, in his left hand he held an enormous, old-fashioned mace, and with his right hand he led an elephant draped with silk. On the elephant there was a castle, in which there was a woman dressed like a nun in white satin. Over this she wore a cloak of black cloth, and her head was bound with a white kerchief in the style of Burgundy or of a nun. As soon as she entered the hall and saw the noble company gathered there she said with some urgency to the giant who led her:

> Giant, I wish to stop here,
> because I see a noble company
> that I must speak to.
> Giant, I wish to stop here;
> I want to tell them and warn them
> about something that needs full well to be heard.
> Giant, I wish to stop here,
> for I see a noble company.

When the giant heard the lady speak, he looked at her in great fear, and he did not stop until he came before the table of the Duke. There were gathered many people marveling and wondering who the lady could be. As soon as her elephant had stopped she began a lament with the words written here:

> Alas! Alas! I am saddened,
> woebegone, far from pleasure, tormented,
> desolate, the most unhappy
>   of all!
> Each of you looks and sees me,
> yet none recognizes me;
> you all leave me in these straits
>   where I languish
> as no one living has ever languished before.
> My heart is pressed with bitterness and cruelty,
> my eyes melt and I grow pale,
>   as you can see.
> Hear my plaint, you whom I gaze upon;
> help me without dissembling;
> weep for my woe, for I am the Holy Church,
>   your Mother,
> brought to ruin and bitter sadness,
> trampled by harsh abuse;

and my awful grievances I bear, suffer, endure
    on your behalf.

•   •   •   •   •

O noble Duke of Burgundy,
son of the Church, brother to its children,
hear me, and consider my need!
Let your heart feel the shame,
the grieving remorse that I carry in my breast!
Infidels by hundreds and thousands
triumph in their damnèd land,
where once I was wont to be honored.

And you, powerful and honored princes,
grieve at my pain, weep at my sorrow!

•   •   •   •   •

When I saw this action (that is, of Mother Church), and a castle on the back of so strange a beast, I wondered whether I could fathom what it all meant. I think it must be understood this way: The beast, exceedingly different and strange to us, in leading the lady away signifies that she struggles against many great adversities; in this she plays the role of Constantinople, whose adversities we know well. Her castle signifies Faith. In addition, the armed giant leading her gives us to understand that she fears the arms of the Turks who hunt her and seek to destroy her.

8 Paolo Cortesi

Paolo Cortesi, born in Rome in 1465, grew up in a literary family and by the age of seventeen had assumed a position at the papal court as "scriptor apostolicus." He remained in papal service until 1503, when he retired to a villa near San Gimignano in Tuscany. There he died in 1510.

In the 1490s, Cortesi hosted at his house in Rome a loosely knit academy of aristocratic literati in which music played an important role (see no. 9 below, pp. 44–45). He corresponded with some of the most renowned humanistic scholars of his day, including Ermolao Barbaro and Angelo Poliziano, wrote poems in Italian and Latin, and produced Latin treatises and dialogues on subjects as diverse as astrology and Italian literary history. *Three Books on the Cardinalate,* published at Cortesi's villa in the months after his death, is a handbook of comportment for cardinals—a kind of sacred analogue to Castiglione's *Cortegiano* (see no. 10 below, pp. 47–52). It is written in a relentlessly pure Ciceronian Latin that Poliziano, a more flexible and expert Latin stylist, criticized for its slavish adherence to Cicero's vocabulary. This adherence requires, in Cortesi's discussion of the music appropriate for a cardinal's mealtime, elaborate circumlocutions for modern names of instruments, musical genres, and so forth. Luckily, marginalia in the original edition explain many of these round-about expressions; where needed they are included in this translation in brackets.

Cortesi's musical categories are significant. In instrumental music he describes the different effects of various instruments. He categorizes vocal music in two ways: according to ancient doctrines of the differing effects of Dorian, Phrygian, and Lydian modes; and according to the bifurcated traditions of his own milieu, which separated polyphonic composition of masses and motets by composers such as Josquin, Jacob Obrecht, and Heinrich Isaac from the solo singing of vernacular poetry with instrumental accompaniment. Revealingly, Cortesi finds more compelling effects in the latter tradition than in the former.

FROM *Three Books on the Cardinalate*
(1510)

BOOK 2

... Since at this time those things must be sought after by which a cheerful mood is usually aroused, it may well be inquired whether the pleasure of music should be put to use particularly at this point, inasmuch as many, estranged from the natural disposition of the normal sense, not only reject it [music] because of some sad perversion of their nature, but even think it to be hurtful for the reason that it is somehow an invitation to idle pleasure, and above all, that its merriment usually arouses the evil of lust. On the opposite side, however, many agree to resort to it as to a certain discipline that is engaged in the knowledge of concordance and modes.

Indeed, we are convinced that music should be put to use at this time [after meals] for the sake not only of merriment, but also of knowledge and morals. ... Music must be sought after for the sake of morals, inasmuch as the habit of passing judgment on what is similar to morals in its rational basis cannot be considered to be different from the habit of passing judgment on the rational basis of morals themselves, and of becoming expert in this latter judgment through imitation. Also, since the melodious modes of music appear to imitate all the habits of morals and all the motions of passions, there is no doubt that to be entertained by a temperate combination of modes would also mean to get in the habit of passing judgment on the rational basis of morals. This can

TEXT: *De cardinalatu libri tres* (Castel Cortesiano, 1510), fols. 72v–74v; in Nino Pirrotta, "Music and Cultural Tendencies in Fifteenth-Century Italy," *Journal of the American Musicological Society* 19 (1966): pp. 152–55. Translation by Nino Pirrotta. Reprinted by permission of the American Musicological Society.

also be proved, inasmuch as it is evident that all the habits and motions of the soul are found in the nature of the modes, in which nature the similarity to fortitude, or temperance, or anger, or mildness is exhibited, and it can easily be observed and judged that the minds of men are usually brought to those motions just as they are excited by the action of the modes. Nor can there be any doubt that things resembling each other are forced to be such in fact by the very closeness of their affinity.

But, since the kind of modes to be used is twofold, one that is produced by hand, and a second one consisting in the manner of singing, it must be understood that the senators must be engaged in listening to the kind of sounding things [instruments] in which the criterion in the combination of modes can be found more stable, and the mind is freer in its judgment. Concerning this, one must avoid, in those free moments devoted to music, those genres in which the sense of the ear seems to be stunned, and which are, too, most divergent from the rationale of morals. In this class *barbiti* and *pentades* are usually listed, which offend the discriminating ear with the aggressiveness of their notes and with an inordinate sound.[1] And so, those pneumatic genres [organs] can be more useful to the senators, in which tin pipes are usually assembled as it were in the shape of a castle; the which pipes, while they are made most apt to receive and emit the air, amplify the sounds, repeating them high and low. In touching them Isachius [Isaac of Byzantium], son of the peripatetic Argyropylos, stands out for his regular combination of modes. Those who admire most highly Dominicus Venetus or Daniel Germanus usually in their praise omit the fact that they make intemperate use of quick runs, by which the sense of the ear is filled with variety, but the artful modes cannot be knowingly discerned. Indeed, also those genres [clavichord] can be praised that are made out of wood in the shape of an ancient vase, out of which the pressure of the fingers extracts distinct sounds of strings. Which genres, however, are very far from the gravity of the pneumatic genres, because the percussion on them is sooner released, and ending produces a shorter sound. Most renowned in this genre is the precise agility of Laurentius Cordubensis.

Also in the same group are placed those genres [lutes] which can be considered as resembling certain fast ships, and are judged to have the most delightful impact on the ear; for those sure-fingered proceedings, now repetition, now stopping, now lessening and almost interlacing of sounds, are in the habit of creeping easily into the minds of men with their exquisite sweetness. Which genre, indeed, has been more knowingly revived into artistic perfection by our generation, and is acknowledged as the first genre of playing that can be praised for the way in which it is arranged and put together. They say that it was first established by Balthasar and Joannes Maria, both surnamed Ger-

---

1. The *barbiton* is a classic kithara-like instrument, but I have been unable to find any reference to *pentades;* unless this is a misreading for *pektides,* it is my suspicion, enhanced by Cortesi's outspoken dislike for the instrument, that it might be a Hellenization of *quinterne* or *guinterne,* unusual names (at least in Italy) for the popular guitar. [Tr.]

manus, so that the simple repetition in the high region used by the ancients would be joined by a connection of all single sounds from the lower region, and from the latter a combined symphony would flourish more richly. Before them, in fact, Petrus Bonus Ferrariensis,[2] and those who derived from him, often availed themselves of the repetition in the high region; nor was this mode of harmonizing all the individual sounds yet known, by which the sense of the ear can best be filled with perfect sweetness. Almost the same could be said of the Spanish lyre, were it not that its equal and soft sweetness is usually rejected by the satiety of the ear, and its uniformity is longer than it could be desired by the limits imposed by the ear.

The manner of singing, now, is divided into a tripartite description, according to which one manner is called Phrygian, the second Lydian, and the third Dorian. Phrygian is the one in which the spirits of the listeners are usually distracted by the fiercest straining of notes. Of which kind is that music of which French musicians make use by traditional rule in the palatine chapel on the holidays of Christmas and Easter. The Lydian one can be considered to be of two kinds, one that is called complex and the second simple. Complex is the one in which the souls are induced to weeping and compassion by a mode inflected toward sorrows; such may be considered the one in which the papal *novendilia*[3] or the senatorial *parentalia*[4] is customarily celebrated. Of this lugubrious manner of singing did the nation of the Spaniards always make use. Simple is that manner that results in a rather languid modulation; thus we saw to be inflected those verses of P. Maro, which used to be sung, on suggestion of Ferdinand II of Naples by the poet Caritheus.[5] And finally the Dorian manner is by far more restrained in plain moderation; such, as they say, is to be considered that manner that was established by Saint Gregory in the holy . . . (*aberruncatorium?*) in a stately rule of singing.

Concerning these things, our generation divides and distinguishes the whole manner of singing into propitiatory songs, precentorial songs, and sung poems. Propitiatory songs [masses] are those in which all kinds of modes, mensurations, and imitations are employed, and in which praise is given to the genus of musicians for devising the singing most admirably; hence, not without reason Cardinal Giovanni dei Medici, a knowledgeable man in the learned consideration of musical matters, believes that no one should be included in the number of the most eminent musicians, who is not very conversant with the making of the propitiatory mode. And so, just for this reason, they say that Josquin of France was the one who excelled among many, because more science was put

2. That is, Pietrobono dal Chitarrino, a lutenist-singer active in the mid-fifteenth century especially at the Ferrarese court.
3. Nine days of mourning for the death of a pope. [Tr.]
4. Annual memorial services for dead cardinals. [Tr.]
5. Maro is Publius Vergilius Maro, or Virgil. Caritheus, or (Il) Cariteo, is the poet-singer Benedetto Gareth, a leading literary figure and courtier in the Naples of Ferdinand of Aragon; on his participation in the academic scene there see no. 9 below (Calmeta), pp. 45–46.

by him in the propitiatory genres of singing than is usually put into it by the unskilled zeal of recent musicians. Then, those songs [motets] are called precentorial which, although mixed with the propitiatory singing, can be seen to be supernumerary and ingrafted, since for them there is free option of choice; and for this reason it happens, they say, that those modes all of one kind, on which the propitiatory songs unremittingly insist, are not preserved by them. In this genre Jacob Obrecht is considered great for varied subtlety, but more crude in the whole style of composition, and also he is considered to be the one by whom more of the sharpest agreeableness has been sowed among the musicians than would have been enough for the pleasure of the ear—like, in the field of taste, people who seem to like those things that taste of unripe juice better than sugar. For a similar inclination Heinrich Isaac of France is judged to be most apt to compose such precentorial songs; for, in addition to being much quicker than all the others in pouring forth this genre, his style of composition brightens the singing so floridly that it more than satiates the ordinary capacity of the ear. But, although he is the one who excels among many, nevertheless we know that it happens to be blamed on him that he uses in this genre *catachresis*[6] and repetition of modes more liberally than the most the ear can take without sensing annoyance because of uniformity in what it listens to. Nor are Alexander Agricola, Antonius Brumel, Loyset Compère, Jo. Spataro of Bologna far away from such musical praise; although one of them gets more credit than the other for either art or suavity in composing, and one is more acceptable than the other for his borrowing or novelty of paraphrase, all have expertly practiced in this precentorial genre, from which many things can be transferred for the use of the senator.

Finally, those modes usually listed as modes of sung poems that mainly consist of the measure of the octastics or ternaries.[7] Which genre Francesco Petrarca is said to have first established as he sang his exalted poems on the lute. But of late Seraphinus Aquilanus was the originator of the renewal of this genre, by whom such a controlled conjunction of words and songs was woven that there could be nothing sweeter than the manner of his modes. And so, such a multitude of imitative court singers emanated from him that whatever is seen to be sung in this genre in all Italy appears to be born out of the model of his sung poems and melodic modes. For which reason, it can be rightly said that the motions of the souls are usually appeased and excited with more vehemence by the *carmina* produced in this genre; for, when the rhythms of the words and sentences are combined with the sweetness of the melodic modes, nothing can prevent the audience from being exceedingly moved because of the power of the ear and the song's similarity to the soul. And this

6. Literally, improper use of words. [Tr.]

7. Cortesi's *ocstaticorum aut trinariorum ratio* must refer to two of the most prominent fixed forms of Italian sung poetry around 1500: *strambotti,* stanzas of eight eleven-syllable lines typically rhymed *abababcc;* and *capitoli,* stanzas of three eleven-syllable lines with the interlocking rhyme-scheme of Dante's *terza rima: aba bcb cdc* etc.

usually happens quite often when either vehement motions are represented in the singing by the verses, or souls are exhorted to the learning of morals and knowledge, on which human happiness is dependent.

9 Vincenzo Calmeta

Two of the courtiers who frequented Cortesi's academy in the early 1490s were Vincenzo Colli, called Calmeta (ca. 1460–1508), a poet and literary commentator of some stature, and Serafino Ciminelli, called Aquilano after his city of birth (1466–1500), the most renowned poet-singer of the waning fifteenth century. The two became fast friends, Serafino even living with Calmeta when he temporarily lost the support of his chief patron, Cardinal Ascanio Sforza. They were reunited in the mid-1490s at the glittering Milanese court of Lodovico Sforza ("il Moro"), where the Duchess Beatrice d'Este presided over a self-conscious revival of Italian poetry and oratory.

Serafino's untimely death inspired an outpouring of elegies that were collected in a commemorative volume of 1504, for which Calmeta prepared his brief biography. It also stimulated a rage for Serafino's poetry that saw some twenty editions of it published between 1502 and 1513. These show no glimpse of the musical settings, probably semi-improvised, that Serafino had provided for his words. Perhaps their style is reflected in the music setting several of Serafino's lyrics that survives in manuscript and print from around 1500. Or perhaps the excerpts here from Calmeta's *Life,* along with Cortesi's remarks on Serafino (no. 8 above, p. 42), are some of the broadest hints we have to fill this lacuna. Calmeta's *Life* also sketches a lively picture of professional emulation and competition among the singer-poets of the time.

FROM *Life of the Fertile Vernacular Poet Serafino Aquilano*
(1504)

Serafino Aquilano, descended from a very honorable family, was born in Aquila, a city of Abruzzo, in the year of our salvation 1466, when Paul II sat on the Pontifical Throne and Frederick reigned as Roman Emperor. Before he

TEXT: *Vita del facondo poeta volgare Serafino Aquilano*, in Vincenzo Calmeta, *Prose e lettere edite e inedite*, ed. Cecil Grayson (Bologna: Commissione per i testi di lingua, 1959), pp. 60–77. Translation by Gary Tomlinson.

even had the first rudiments of grammar[1] he was taken to the Kingdom of Naples by an uncle named Paul, who gave him to the Count of Potenza, governing there, to serve as page. This Count was an important prince who, though only in the flower of his youth, was so inclined to every virtue that all in his retinue, imitating their master, competed to see who could embody some new virtue. Amidst this praiseworthy school, with its varied pursuits, Serafino devoted himself to music under the tutelage of a certain Fleming named Guglielmo,[2] a most famous musician at that time. In a few years he made such progress that he excelled every other Italian musician in composing songs. Returning to his homeland of Aquila, where he stayed for three years,[3] he gave himself over to learning all the sonnets, canzoni, and *Trionfi* of Petrarch, which he not only knew extremely well but accompanied so beautifully with music that hearing him sing to his lute surpassed all other harmony. Moved then by a desire to seek his fortune he went to Rome. There he stayed in the house of a Bolognese Jerusalemite Knight named Nestor Malvezzo until he was taken into the service of Cardinal Ascanio Sforza. With him Serafino persevered for three years in anger and annoyance—since, their natures being different, the Cardinal (like most princes, and not unjustly) wanted Serafino to conform to his own ways, while the poet's forceful character suffered unwillingly such subjection.

•   •   •   •   •

It was necessary at that time[4] for Cardinal Ascanio to go to Lombardy, and while in Milan Serafino befriended a notable Neapolitan gentleman named Andrea Coscia, a soldier of Duke Lodovico Sforza, who sang sweetly to the lute in various styles including strambotti of Il Cariteo.[5] Serafino not only took this style from him, adding more polish to it, but devoted himself with such passion and labor to composing his own strambotti that he had the good fortune to win great fame in this style. He fell in love at this time with a woman of questionable virtue named Laura. She was the wife of the Milanese gentleman Pietro da Birago and was a very sweet and graceful singer; in his love for her he composed the airs and words of several strambotti. But, overindulging in such ways, he was seriously wounded in the face one night by an assailant whose identity and motive could not be discovered.

The wound healed after a short time, though it left a large scar, and Serafino returned to Rome with Cardinal Ascanio. Frequenting his usual haunts there, he not only seemed novel but aroused much admiration throughout Rome for having brought a new style of singing and raised the strambotto to a higher level. There flourished at the same time in Rome an academy in the house of

---

1. In 1478. I have taken this and the following dates from the entry "Ciminelli, Serafino," by Magda Vigilante, in the *Dizionario biografico degli italiani*.
2. This is Guglielmo Garnier, friend of Tinctoris and Gafori and active as a music teacher in Naples.
3. 1481–1484.
4. 1490.
5. On Il Cariteo see no. 8 above (Cortesi) p. 41, n. 5.

Paolo Cortesi, a youth so much revered at court for his learning, status, and cordiality that his was rather called a center of eloquence and a refuge of all noble virtues than the mere home of a courtier. Every day a multitude of lofty spirits gathered there: Gianlorenzo Veneto, Pietro Gravina, Bishop Montepiloso, Agapito Gerardino, Manilio, Cornelio,[6] and many other erudite men, in whose shadows other younger men, eager to enlarge their own virtue, also lingered to enjoy themselves. Among vernacular poets the ardors of Aretino were held in greatest esteem, while my own fragments also enjoyed some little praise. Therefore Serafino, who spent more time with me than with anyone else, determined to participate in this academy, which afforded such recreation to its worthy members; thenceforth he often introduced the harmony of his music and wit of his strambotti into the arduous debates of those other literati. This only increased his reputation, as all those wise men strived to write strambotti with more recondite sentiments than his. And even though he had such a hurdle and paragon as Aretino to face, and such friendly emulation as Cortesi's and mine, nevertheless he was inferior to no poet of the present century in this style; what is more, there was a time when anyone who heard a new strambotto attributed it to Serafino no matter who had composed it, not out of ill will but admiration.

Many players and singers saw that Serafino's fame came from the force of his recitation more than from his composing, and that that style delighted princes, wise men, and beautiful women. So they set themselves to imitate him and by learning his airs learned his words as well; therefore in a short time his verses were scattered throughout Italy not only by himself but by many other *citaredi*.[7] But Serafino was not yet content with his Burchiellesque sonnets,[8] his ballate, and his strambotti and determined not only to sniff at but to taste and digest all other styles. During one Carnival season, having decided to leave Cardinal Ascanio, he wrote an eclogue that begins "Tell me, my Menander" in imitation of Jacopo Sannazaro, at that time the leader in bucolic verse. In his eclogue Serafino criticized behind a veil of poetic artifice the greed and other detestable vices of the court at Rome; he recited it during Carnival with the backing of Cardinal Colonna, and with it he aroused new admiration.

•　　•　　•　　•　　•

At that time[9] the governor of Abruzzo was Ferdinand of Aragon, later the second of that name to be King of Naples. News of Serafino's fame reached

---

6. For the identification of these various Roman prelates, church functionaries, literati, and academicians see Calmeta, *Prose e lettere*, ed. Grayson, "Indice de nomi."

7. With this classicizing term, referring to the ancient Greek lyre-like kithara, Calmeta no doubt embraces poets who accompanied themselves either on the lute or on the bowed *lira da braccio*. The latter instrument was also called *viola da braccio;* see no. 10 below (Castiglione), p. 50, n. 11.

8. The reference is to Domenico di Giovanni, called il Burchiello (1404–1449), author of a body of sonnets whose materials range from political satire and literary caricature to virtuosic nonsense-rhymes. His poems were first published in 1475 and reprinted many times over the following centuries.

9. 1493.

him and, being a prince of high ideals endowed with all the graces nature and good fortune can give, he turned his every thought to bringing Serafino to his court. There Serafino remained, in great favor and well rewarded, for three years. In Naples there flourished yet another academy of literati where Jacopo Sannazaro, Attilio Musefilo, Cariteo, and many other learned and perceptive minds gathered under the authority and reverence of Pontano in the Portico Antoniano.[10] But those who were foremost not only in Latin but in vernacular poetry were Sannazaro, Francesco Caracciolo, and Cariteo. Seeing that Serafino soothed with his poems not only common but learned ears as well, and suspecting perhaps that these poems when written down would not bear closer scrutiny, they studied and discussed in various manners his compositions. The result was always a positive verdict, praising Serafino's natural gifts more than his industry.

•   •   •   •   •

Seeing that amorous sonnets were prized, and thinking either that his facility would well enable him to follow that style or that he could with it better enflame the breasts of beautiful young women, Serafino decided to try his hand at some such sonnets in emulation of the ingenious poet Tebaldeo.[11] He won as much renown in these as he had in composing strambotti. I do not deny that they often did not measure up to Tebaldeo's in invention; nonetheless in their disposition they are so well accommodated to their subject matter that they deserve praise for this rather than blame for their weaknesses, if weaknesses they be. Indeed the prince of poets observed this same style of writing, as Macrobius describes at length in his *Saturnalia*.[12] Moreover Serafino's poems and Tebaldeo's cannot tell us whether or not he equalled Tebaldeo in this emulation, since where in the one we find more invention, doctrine, continuity and workmanship, in the other we discern more passion, grace, fullness of verse and natural gift.

•   •   •   •   •

Having attained the age of thirty-five, Serafino died of a pestiferous tertian fever, to the great sadness of the whole Roman court. Receiving the sacraments, he left his body on earth, and his soul returned whence it came on the day of San Lorenzo in the year of our salvation 1500.

---

10. Jacopo Sannazaro and Giovanni Pontano were the leading literary lights of the Neapolitan intelligentsia in the late fifteenth century. Sannazaro is chiefly remembered today for his Italian pastoral romance *L'Arcadia*, which spawned many imitations through the sixteenth century (including Sir Philip Sydney's huge *Arcadia*); Pontano was an expert Latinist who wrote treatises, dialogues, and poems on astrology, philosophy, politics, and other topics. The gathering place of the academy, the "Portico Antoniano," was named after its founder Antonio Panormita (see Giovanni Pontano, *Dialoge*, ed. Hermann Kiefer [Munich: W. Fink, 1984], p. 30).
11. The Petrarchan lyricist Antonio Tebaldeo (1463–1537), active chiefly at Ferrara and Mantua.
12. The reference is to Virgil; see *Saturnalia*, esp. bks. 3–6.

•   •   •   •   •

In reciting his poems he was so passionate and matched the music with the words so judiciously that he moved equally the souls of his listeners, whether wise or mediocre or plebeian or female. And though he competed with many poets, nevertheless he was not of a contentious or evil nature. . . . With this alone I conclude: I believe there never was another poet more successful than he in expressing his thoughts. All his efforts were bent on achieving fame in his lifetime, even if his repute reached only the mediocre and plebeian; and he had the great satisfaction of reaching his goal, giving great account of himself wherever he went. His death was widely lamented by contemporary poets, who thereby saw our age stripped of no small ornament. . . .

10 Baldassare Castiglione

Born in 1478 near Mantua, the descendant of an old and distinguished family, Baldassare Castiglione is one of the most influential figures of Renaissance court life. After an education in the Milan of Ludovico Sforza, he served successively at the courts of Mantua and Urbino (1499–1513) and, as ambassador of Urbino's Duke Francesco Maria della Rovere, at the papal court of Leo X. In 1525 he traveled to Spain as the pope's envoy to the court of Charles V. He died in Toledo in 1529.

Castiglione wrote poetry in Italian and Latin; vivid letters that reveal much about the society in which he moved; and a dramatic eclogue, *Tirsi,* that was staged at Urbino in 1506. His claim to lasting fame, however, rests on *Il libro del cortegiano (The Book of the Courtier).* The on-again off-again genesis of this work began soon after 1508 and ended around 1524. In the following years the book circulated in manuscript, and it was finally published in 1528 with the assistance of Pietro Bembo (see no. 12 below, pp. 54–55). In the *Cortegiano* Castiglione draws in lively dialogues a picture of the ideal courtier, the aristocratic woman, and the relations of courtier and prince. The book professes to be an account of discussions held at the ducal palace in Urbino on four evenings in 1507. The personages depicted are all more or less conspicuous historical figures, including Vincenzo Calmeta and Bembo. In their discussions about music, song, and dance, Castiglione leaves little doubt about the importance these activities assumed at the court of Urbino and in his view of Renaissance courtly society in general. In his specific opinions, Castiglione, like Paolo Cortesi, reserves the highest praise for solo singing with instrumental accompaniment.

FROM *Il libro del cortegiano*
(1528)

BOOK 1

CHAPTER 47

At this they all laughed. And the Count, beginning afresh:

"My lords (quoth he), you must think I am not pleased with the Courtier if he be not also a musician, and besides his understanding and cunning upon the book, have skill in like manner on sundry instruments. For if we weigh it well, there is no ease of labors and medicines of feeble minds to be found more honest and more praiseworthy in time of leisure than it. And principally in courts, where (beside the refreshing of vexations that music bringeth unto each man) many things are taken in hand to please women withal, whose tender and soft breasts are soon pierced with melody and filled with sweetness. Therefore no marvel that in the old days and nowadays they have always been inclined to musicians, and counted this a most acceptable food of the mind."

Then the Lord Gaspar:

"I believe music (quoth he) together with many other vanities is meet for women, and peradventure for some also that have the likeness of men, but not for them that be men indeed; who ought not with such delicacies to womanish their minds and bring themselves in that sort to dread death."

"Speak it not," answered the Count. "For I shall enter into a large sea of the praise of music and call to rehearsal how much it hath always been renowned among them of old time and counted a holy matter;[1] and how it hath been the opinion of most wise philosophers that the world is made of music, and the heavens in their moving make a melody, and our soul framed after the very same sort, and therefore lifteth up itself and (as it were) reviveth the virtues and force of it with music. Wherefore it is written that Alexander was sometime so fervently stirred with it that (in a manner) against his will he was forced to arise from banquets and run to weapon, afterward the musician changing the stroke and his manner of tune, pacified himself again and returned from weapon to banqueting.[2] And I shall tell you that grave Socrates when he was

TEXT: The reprint of the original edition of the translation of Sir Thomas Hoby (London, 1561), as published in *Tudor Translations* 23 (London: D. Nutt, 1900). In his notes Strunk made some use of those of Michele Scherillo's edition of *Il cortegiano* (Milan: U. Hoepli, 1928).

1. Quintilian, *Institutio oratoria* 1.10.9. From here to the end of Chapter 47 Castiglione follows, with many omissions and a few additions, *Institutio oratoria* 1.10.9–33.
2. Variously reported, although not in this form, by Seneca, Dio Chrysostom, Plutarch, and Suidas, the musician being sometimes Xenophantes, sometimes Timotheus, and sometimes Antigen-edes. As told by Castiglione and other writers of his time, the story appears to come ultimately from St. Basil, *To Young Men (Ad adolescentes)* 8.7–8: "Once when he was playing the Phrygian mode to Alexander on his flute, he caused the prince, as it is said, to leap up and rush to his arms in the midst of a banquet, and then, by relaxing the harmony, brought him back again to

well stricken in years learned to play upon the harp.[3] And I remember I have understood that Plato and Aristotle will have a man that is well brought up, to be also a musician; and declare with infinite reasons the force of music to be to very great purpose in us, and for many causes (that should be too long to rehearse) ought necessarily to be learned from a man's childhood, not only for the superficial melody that is heard, but to be sufficient to bring into us a new habit that is good and a custom inclining to virtue, which maketh the mind more apt to the conceiving of felicity, even as bodily exercise maketh the body more lusty, and not only hurteth not civil matters and warlike affairs, but is a great stay to them. Also Lycurgus in his sharp laws allowed music.[4] And it is read that the Lacedemons, which were valiant in arms, and the Cretenses used harps and other soft instruments;[5] and many most excellent captains of old time (as Epaminondas) gave themselves to music; and such as had not a sight in it (as Themistocles) were a great deal the less set by.[6] Have you not read that among the first instructions which the good old man Chiron taught Achilles in his tender age, whom he had brought up from his nurse and cradle, music was one? And the wise master would have those hands that should shed so much Trojan blood to be oftentimes occupied in playing upon the harp?[7] What soldier is there (therefore) that will think it a shame to follow Achilles, omitting many other famous captains that I could allege? Do ye not then deprive our Courtier of music, which doth not only make sweet the minds of men, but also many times wild beasts tame; and whoso savoreth it not, a man may assuredly think him not to be well in his wits. Behold, I pray you, what force it hath, that in times past allured a fish to suffer a man to ride upon him through the tempestuous sea.[8] We may see it used in the holy temples to render laud and thanks unto God, and it is a credible matter that it is acceptable unto Him, and that He hath given it unto us for a most sweet lightening of our travails and vexations. So that many times the boisterous laborers in the fields in the heat of the sun beguile their pain with rude and carterlike singing. With this the unmannerly countrywoman that ariseth before day out of her sleep to spin and card, defendeth herself and maketh her labor pleasant. This is the most sweet pastime after rain, wind, and tempest unto the miserable mariners. With this do the weary pilgrims comfort themselves in their troublesome and long voyages. And oftentimes prisoners in adversity, in fetters, and in stocks. In like

---

his boon companions." Trans. Roy J. DeFerrari and Martin R. P. McGuire in *Saint Basil: The letters* (4 vols., Cambridge, Mass.: Harvard University Press, 1926–34). For the version of Suidas see no. 37 below (Galilei) p. 188, n. 10.

3. Quintilian, *Institutio oratoria* 1.10.13–14.

4. Ibid., 1.10.15.

5. Often reported; see Athanaeus, *Deipnosophists* 14.626.

6. Cicero, *Tusculan Disputations* 1.2.4. See also Quintilian, *Institutio oratoria* 1.10.19.

7. See no. 2 above (Zarlino) p. 21, n. 31.

8. The reference is to Arion's rescue by a musically inclined dolphin; see no. 2 above (Zarlino), p. 21, n. 30.

manner for a greater proof that the tunableness of music (though it be but rude) is a very great refreshing of all worldly pains and griefs, a man would judge that nature had taught it unto nurses for a special remedy to the continual wailings of sucking babes, which at the sound of their voices fall into a quiet and sweet sleep, forgetting the tears that are so proper to them, and given us of nature in that age for a guess of the rest of our life to come."[9]

CHAPTER 48

Here the Count pausing awhile the Lord Julian said:

"I am not of the Lord Gaspar's opinion, but I believe for the reasons you allege and for many others, that music is not only an ornament, but also necessary for a Courtier. But I would have you declare how this and the other qualities which you appoint him are to be practised, and at what time, and in what sort. Because many things that of themselves be worthy praise, oftentimes in practising them out of season seem most foolish. And contrariwise, some things that appear to be of small moment, in the well applying them are greatly esteemed."

BOOK 2

CHAPTER 13

. . . "Methink," answered Sir Frederick, "pricksong[10] is a fair music, so it be done upon the book surely and after a good sort. But to sing to the lute[11] is much better, because all the sweetness consisteth in one alone, and a man is much more heedful and understandeth better the feat manner and the air or vein of it when the ears are not busied in hearing any more than one voice; and beside, every little error is soon perceived, which happeneth not in singing with company, for one beareth out another. But singing to the lute with the ditty[12] (methink) is more pleasant than the rest, for it addeth to the words such a grace and strength that it is a great wonder. Also all instruments with frets[13] are full of harmony, because the tunes of them are very perfect, and with ease a man may do many things upon them that fill the mind with the sweetness of music. And the music of a set of viols[14] doth no less delight a man, for it is very sweet and artificial. A man's breast giveth a great ornament and grace to all these instruments, in the which I will have it sufficient that our Courtier have an understanding. Yet the more cunning he is upon them, the better it is for him, without meddling much with the instruments that Minerva and Alcibiades

---

9. St. John Chrysostom, *Exposition of Psalm XLI.*
10. That is, song from a "pricked" or written score. Castiglione has *il cantar bene a libro sicuramente e con bella maniera.*
11. Castiglione has *il cantare alla viola.* The instrument in question is the *viola* or *lira da braccio,* a bowed instrument favored in Italy around 1500 for the accompaniment of solo song.
12. Castiglione has *il cantare alla viola per recitare.*
13. Castiglione's *tutti gli strumenti di tasti* probably refers to fretted plucked string instruments, as Hoby interprets it, and not keyboard instruments, as modern Italian usage of *tasto* would suggest.
14. Castiglione has *quattro viole da arco.*

refused,[15] because it seemeth they are noisome. Now as touching the time and season when these sorts of music are to be practised, I believe at all times when a man is in familiar and loving company, having nothing else ado. But especially they are meet to be practised in the presence of women, because those sights sweeten the minds of the hearers and make them the more apt to be pierced with the pleasantness of music, and also they quicken the spirits of the very doers. I am well pleased (as I have said) they flee the multitude, and especially of the unnoble. But the seasoning of the whole must be discretion, because in effect it were a matter unpossible to imagine all cases that fall. And if the Courtier be a righteous judge of himself, he shall apply himself well enough to the time and shall discern when the hearers' minds are disposed to give ear and when they are not. He shall know his age, for (to say the truth) it were no meet matter, but an ill sight to see a man of any estimation being old, hoarheaded and toothless, full of wrinkles, with a lute in his arms[16] playing upon it and singing in the midst of a company of women, although he could do it reasonably well. And that because such songs contain in them words of love, and in old men love is a thing to be jested at, although otherwhile he seemeth among other miracles of his to take delight in spite of years to set afire frozen hearts."

Then answered the Lord Julian:

"Do you not bar poor old men from this pleasure, Sir Frederick, for in my time I have known men of years have very perfect breasts and most nimble fingers for instruments, much more than some young men."

"I go not about," quoth Sir Frederick, "to bar old men from this pleasure, but I will bar you these ladies from laughing at that folly. And in case old men will sing to the lute,[17] let them do it secretly, and only to rid their minds of those troublesome cares and grievous disquietings that our life is full of and to taste of that excellence which I believe Pythagoras and Socrates favored in music. And set case they exercise it not at all, for that they have gotten a certain habit and custom of it, they shall savor it much better in hearing than he that hath no knowledge in it. For like as the arms of a smith that is weak in other things, because they are more exercised, be stronger than another body's that is sturdy but not exercised to work with his arms, even so the ears that be exercised in music do much better and sooner discern it and with much more pleasure judge of it than other, how good and quick soever they be, that have not been practised in the variety of pleasant music; because those musical tunes pierce not, but without leaving any taste of themselves, pass by the ears not accustomed to hear them, although the very wild beasts feel some delight in melody. This is therefore the pleasure meet for old men to take in music. The selfsame I say of dancing, for indeed these exercises ought to be left of before age constraineth us to leave them whether we will or no."

15. The auloi (i.e., for Castiglione, wind instruments in general); for the story, see Plutarch, *Life of Alcibiades*.
16. Castiglione has *con una viola in braccio*.
17. Castiglione has *cantare alla viola*.

11 Francis I, King of France

The history of late Renaissance music is also—and fundamentally—a history of print technology and its impact. Beginning in 1501, when Ottaviano Petrucci released in Venice the first volume of music printed from movable type, thousands of collections of masses, motets, frottolas, chansons, madrigals, and other works poured forth from presses across Europe. The sheer volume of music that has come down to us in sixteenth-century prints dwarfs the repertory surviving in fifteenth-century manuscripts and no doubt exceeds the extant corpus from the seventeenth century, when economic decline across much of Europe shrank the music-printing industry along with many other commercial enterprises.

Petrucci's printing method, though it yielded beautiful results, was slow and costly: the staves, notes, and in some cases even the words of vocal works all required separate impressions on each sheet. Andrea Antico, Petrucci's first Italian competitor, chose another labor-intensive method: he did not use movable type at all, but engraved whole pages of music on wooden blocks and printed from them. It was left to Pierre Attaingnant (ca. 1494–1551 or 1552), the first French printer of music from movable type, to perfect a new, less expensive method in which staves, notes, and text could be printed in a single impression. Attaingnant's was the method of choice through the rest of the century.

Attaingnant brought out his first volume of chansons in April 1528; other volumes quickly followed. The next year he was granted a privilege from Francis I copyrighting the contents of his books. When it expired three years later, he petitioned for another, expanded privilege. The King's response was the six-year monopoly on music printing, dated June 18, 1531, that follows.

Royal Privilege for Music Printing to Pierre Attaingnant
(1531)

Francis, by the grace of God King of France, to the magistrates of Paris, bailiffs, seneschals, and to all other justices and officers or their lieutenants, greetings. Having received the humble supplication of our well-loved Pierre Attaingnant, printer-bookseller dwelling in the University of Paris, stating that heretofore no person in this our realm had undertaken to cut, found, and fashion notes and characters for the printing of figural music in *choses faictes* or tablatures for the playing of lutes, flutes, and organs, because of the intricate

TEXT: Daniel Heartz, "A New Attaingnant Book," *Journal of the American Musicological Society* 14 (1961): 22–23. Translation by Daniel Heartz. Reprinted by permission of the American Musicological Society.

conception, long consumption of time, and very great expenses and labors necessary to that purpose, the said suppliant, by protracted excogitation and mental effort and with very great expense, labor, and genius, has invented and brought to light the method and industry of cutting, founding, and printing the said notes and characters both of the said music and *choses faictes* as of the said tablatures for the playing of lutes, flutes, and organs, of which he has printed, has had printed, and hopes in the future to print, many books and quires of masses, motets, hymns, chansons, as well as for the said playing of lutes, flutes, and organs, in large volumes and small, in order to serve the churches, their ministers, and generally all people, and for the very great good, utility, and recreation of the general public. Nevertheless, he fears that after having brought to light his said invention and opened to other printers and booksellers the method and industry of printing the said music and tablatures, these printers and booksellers will similarly wish to attempt printing the said music in *choses faictes* and for the playing of lutes, flutes, and organs. And by this means the said suppliant would totally lose the merit of his labors and the recovery of expenses and investments which he has made and contracted for the invention and composition of the above said characters, unless he is patented and succored by us, having humbly sought our grace. Thus we, having considered these things, do not wish that the said suppliant's labors, application, expenses, and investments in the said affair go unrewarded. May he succeed in it and experience the benefit. From such causes and others stirring us to this we have willed and ordained: we will and ordain that for the time and term of six years to follow, starting with the date of this present day, other than the said suppliant or those having charge from him, may not print nor put up for sale the said books and quires of music in *choses faictes* and tablatures for the playing of lutes, flutes, and organs declared above. We charge and command therefore by these present orders that every person look to the said suppliant's enjoying and fully and tranquilly exercising the ordinance entreated from our present grace. Making strictures and prohibitions to all booksellers and other persons generally, whatever they may be, to print or put up for sale the said books and quires of music and tablature for the said time of six years without the express power and consent of the said suppliant. And this on great penalty to be levied by us and loss and confiscation of said books and quires. To the accomplishment of this all those to whom it may apply are constrained, that they may enforce it with all due ways and reasonable means. For such is our pleasure, all ordinances, restrictions, charges, or prohibitions to the contrary notwithstanding.

Given at St. Germain-en-Laye the eighteenth day of June, the year of grace fifteen hundred thirty-one, of our reign the seventeenth.

By the King, the Cardinal de Tournon, master of the Chapel of the said Seigneur, being present.

Signed
G. HAMELIN

12 Pietro Bembo

Born in Venice in 1470, Pietro Bembo was a humanist scholar, companion of Castiglione at Urbino, longtime literary lion in Padua and Venice, and finally a cardinal at Rome. He exerted a profound and lasting influence on Italian literary and courtly circles of the sixteenth century. His courtly influence sprang from his dialogues *Gli asolani* (*The Asolans,* referring to inhabitants of the town of Asolo, northeast of Venice), first published in 1505. In these dialogues he merged Neo-platonic theories of divine love from the late fifteenth century with an idealized chivalric love that had passed, via the lyrics of Dante and Petrarch, from earlier sources into Italian poetry. (The merger is eloquently summarized in the speech Castiglione had Bembo deliver in the closing pages of the *Cortegiano.*)

Bembo's literary influence emanated especially from his dialogues *Prose della volgar lingua,* first published in 1525. These "writings on the vernacular" exalted the Tuscan Italian of Petrarch (in poetry) and Boccaccio (in prose) as the preeminent Italian literary usages. The doctrines, temperament, and tastes of the *Prose* had an important impact on musical styles as well: they encouraged a decorous, motet-like demeanor and Petrarchan poetic orientation in the mid-century madrigal, an approach most monumentally embodied in Adriano Willaert's collection of madrigals and motets titled *Musica nova.*

Here Bembo writes, in a different and more pragmatic vein, to a daughter he considered overly given to musical pastimes and less than fully attentive to the domestic disciplines that would make her what, by his lights, she should aspire to be: a chaste and obedient wife. Bembo's short letter says much about the forces that circumscribed women's music-making throughout the Renaissance. These forces were complex and ambivalent. Male writers often enough associated women's singing and playing with a debilitating effeminacy or a threatening seductiveness (see for example no. 5 above [Agrippa], p. 29), but at the same time they could turn around and exalt its almost heavenly powers (no. 13 below [Doni], p. 56). Women musicians tended to be cast as either angels or sirens—or sometimes as a strange hybrid of the two.

Published books of letters were common through the sixteenth century; Bembo's began to appear in print in 1548, the year after his death, and saw several editions in the following decades. The present letter was first published in 1552.

Letter to His Daughter Elena
(1541)

I am pleased that you are well, as you relate, and that your brother attends diligently to his studies, which will all redound to his honor and profit. As to

TEXT: Pietro Bembo, *Opere in volgare,* ed. Mario Marti (Florence: Sansoni, 1961), pp. 877–78. Translation by Gary Tomlinson.

your request of me, that I give my blessing to your learning to play the mono-chord, I will explain to you something you are perhaps too young to know: playing music is for a woman a vain and frivolous thing. And I would wish you to be the most serious and chaste woman alive. Beyond this, if you do not play well your playing will give you little pleasure and not a little embarrassment. And you will not be able to play well unless you spend ten or twelve years in this pursuit without thinking of anything else. What this would mean to you you can imagine yourself without my saying more. Therefore set aside thoughts of this frivolity and work to be humble and good and wise and obedient. Don't let yourself be carried away by these desires, indeed resist them with a strong will. And if your companions want you to learn to play for their pleasure, tell them you don't wish to hear them laugh at your shame. Content yourself with writing and cooking; if you do these two pursuits well you will have accomplished much. Thank the Sisters for their prayers for me, for which I am greatly indebted. Stay well, and greet Lucia.

December 10, 1541, Rome

13 Antonfrancesco Doni

Born in Florence in 1513, Antonfrancesco Doni spent most of his mature years in Venice and the Veneto. There (and, for a few years in the 1540s, also in Florence) he pursued a somewhat checkered career as a musician, printer, writer, academician, and general man-about-town. He died in 1574. His *Dialogo della musica* of 1544 joins literary dialogue of the sort exemplified by Castiglione's *Cortegiano* with music printing. Its conversations are punctuated by madrigals and motets sung, in the fiction of the dialogue, by the interlocutors themselves. These characters include two Venetian madrigal composers, Girolamo Parabosco and Perissone Cambio.

Doni's dedicatory letter of the *Dialogo* describes his attendance at the kind of private concert that must have occurred often in aristocratic gatherings. The astoundingly novel music performed at this particular concert would appear in print fifteen years later in Willaert's *Musica nova*. We surmise this because the jealously guarded collection, circulating before its publication, was dubbed *La pecorina* after Polissena Pecorina, the singer Doni heard. Doni singles out the feature of Willaert's "new music" that was most striking to others as well: its extraordinary attention to the diction and declamation of its words.

As for Pecorina, she was a virtuosic participant of Venetian salons and musical circles at least through the 1530s and '40s. She seems to have been, as Doni indicates, a respected aristocrat and not one of the numerous musically gifted courtesans for which some Venetian salons were famous. For Doni, then, music-making by a woman did not carry the stigma Bembo had attached to it in his letter to his daughter. It is ironic that Doni should effectively counter Bembo's view in the context of Willaert's most Bembian musical style.

Dialogo della musica
(1544)

DEDICATION

To Signor Annibale Marchese Malvicino

The music of lutes, instruments, pipes, flutes, and voices made in your house and that of the honorable M. Alessandro Colombo is most worthy, and the viols of San Guido della Porta are a miracle; but if you heard the divine sound I have tasted with the ears of my intellect here in Venice you would be astounded. Here there is a gentlewoman named Polissena Pecorina, wife of a citizen of my hometown, so virtuous and gentle that praises high enough to commend her cannot be found. I heard one night a concert of viols and voices in which she played and sang in the company of other excellent musicians, the flawless master of which was Adriano Willaert. The music, of his invention, in a style never before employed, was so concerted, so sweet, so just, and so miraculously appropriate to the words that I confessed never in my life to have known true harmony until that evening. The man most enthusiastic about such music, most enamored of such compositions, is a gentleman and most excellent spirit also from Florence named Neri Capponi. I was introduced to him by the nobleman Signor Francesco Corboli, and by his grace I felt, saw, and heard this divine music. This Neri spends hundreds of ducats a year on it. He keeps it close to his vest and would not give out a single song even to his father. Here, since I cannot give you that music, I give you this. I am truly sorry not to be able to demonstrate with greater means my friendship for you. Send my infinite regards to Pier'Antonio Burla, Signor Bartolomeo Cossad'occha, and all the other musicians.

April 7, 1544, Venice

Doni the Florentine

TEXT: Antonfrancesco Doni, *Dialogo della musica,* ed. Francesco Malipiero (Vienna: Universal Edition, 1964), p. 5. Translation by Gary Tomlinson. The standard account of the work is James Haar, "Notes on the 'Dialogo della musica' of Antonfrancesco Doni," *Music & Letters* 47 (1966), 198–224.

14 Gaspara Stampa

Across most of Europe, the Petrarchan and post-Petrarchan lyric poetry of the sixteenth century repeatedly plays upon the powers of music, its ability to inspire divine (or other) love, its consolations, and so forth. A theme often repeated was the male poet's praise of his beloved's singing or playing. This typical gender trajectory is reversed in the following sonnets, where it is the female poet who extols her beloved's song, but the deployment of the musical topos is otherwise entirely representative of the lyrics of the period.

Of a sizable group of women poets who achieved fame in the sixteenth century, including Vittoria Colonna, Veronica Franco, Marguerite of Navarre, and Louise Labé, Gaspara Stampa is one of the most gifted. She was born in 1523 in Padua, the daughter of a prosperous jeweler. Her father died in her childhood, and she moved with her mother to Venice. There she came to participate in the city's lively salon culture as both poet and musician. Stampa's *Rime* were first published in 1554, shortly after her premature death in the same year. They constitute a *canzoniere* of Petrarchan profile, celebrating, lamenting, and repenting of her troubled love for Collaltino di Collalto, Count of Treviso.

Two Sonnets
(1554)

HE SINGS WITH SWEETEST HARMONY

In that noble and illustrious company
of Graces who do make you, Count, immortal,
one stands before the rest and spreads her wings:
the most sweet harmony of song.
　　She every bitter, evil care in us
can sweeten, and make light all vile things;
she, when the harsh Euros most assails us,
can quiet waves that just before were rough.
　　Pleasure, laughter, Venus and her Cupids
are seen making the air around serene
wherever her sweet accent echoes forth.
　　And I, if able to remain with you,
would little care to make my return to
the harmony of these celestial choirs.

TEXT: Gaspara Stampa and Veronica Franco, *Rime*, ed. Abdelkader Salza (Bari: G. Laterza, 1913), p. 20. Translation by Gary Tomlinson.

ON THE SAME THEME

She who does not know the heart's sweet rapture,
or how sweetly one forgets all pain,
or how sweetly all desires are calmed,
so that nothing still weighs on the soul,
    Let her come, in all her best good fortune,
one time alone to listen to you, Count,
when you sweeten with your accustomed singing
the earth, the skies, and that which made all nature.
    She'll see, at one sound of your amorous accents
the air grow quiet; and she'll see you stop
the proud waters, the tempests, and the winds.
    And, having seen then all that you can do,
she will believe that tigers, bears, and serpents
Orpheus could have halted with his song.

15 Maddalena Casulana

The roles of women in aristocratic society and public culture were much debated in sixteenth-century Italy and France—if, usually, by men. While women could with some regularity achieve renown as poets and as performing musicians—through institutions of aristocratic prostitution such as Venetian courtesanship but also apart from them (see nos. 13 and 14 above)—it was much rarer for a woman to aspire to a professional, published career in polyphonic composition. In the dedication of the first of her three books of madrigals, Maddalena Casulana signals her awareness of this rarity and of the attitudes largely responsible for it.

Of Casulana's life we know little. She was prominent in the musical circles of Venice and Vicenza from the 1560s to the early 1580s. Already by 1568 her reputation was broad enough to extend beyond the Alps, for in that year Orlando di Lasso conducted an epithalamium of hers in Munich for the wedding of Wilhelm of Bavaria and Renée of Lorraine. Yet, if a report from Perugia in 1582 of a "Casolana famosa" who "sang divinely to the lute" refers to her, she was still young enough at that time to perform in public without censure.

The First Book of Madrigals
for Four Voices

(1568)

DEDICATION

To the Most Illustrious and Excellent Lady Donna Isabella de' Medici Orsina, Duchess of Bracciano

I truly know, Most Illustrious and Excellent Lady, that these first fruits of mine, because of their weakness, will not be able to produce the effect I desire, namely (beyond giving Your Excellency some testimony of my devotion) to expose to the world, insofar as it is given me to do so in the profession of music, the vain error of men who esteem themselves such masters of high intellectual gifts that they think women cannot share them too. In spite of their weakness, then, I have not refrained from publishing them, in the hope that the shining name of Your Excellency, to whom I dedicate them, will light them so brightly that they may enflame another, higher intellect than mine, inciting it to demonstrate clearly in practice what I have only been able to envision in my mind. Therefore, Your Excellency, welcome my candid attempt; and if from such unripe fruit I cannot gain the praise that rewards only virtuous efforts, at least grace me with the prize of your good will, so that I will be reputed most fortunate if not most skilled. I kiss Your Excellency's hand.

Venice, April 10, 1568
Your Excellency's Most Humble Servant, Maddalena Casulana

TEXT: *I madrigali di Maddalena Casulana*, ed. Beatrice Pescerelli (Florence: Leo S. Olschki, 1979), p. 7. Translation by Gary Tomlinson.

16 Charles IX, King of France; Jean-Antoine de Baïf and Joachim Thibault de Courville

The humanist impulse to emulate ancient models led to a number of Renaissance experiments with quantitative verse in modern languages. None of these was more influential than the *vers mesurés à l'antique* and accompanying *musique mesurée* pioneered from 1567 to 1570 by the poet Jean-Antoine de Baïf (1532–1589) and composer Joachim Thibault de Courville (d. 1581). Baïf believed that the fabled ethical effects of ancient music arose from the quantitative measuring of poetic lines and its reflection in musical rhythm. His measured verse in French assigned long or short values to each vowel according to certain orthographic rules; these values were to be conveyed in homophonic musical settings by rhythmic ratios of 2:1. The result in many settings was a freely additive rhythm, little constrained by metrical regularity, whose resonance can be heard in the early seventeenth-century *air de cour* and even in the recitative of later French opera.

Baïf translated the Psalter in measured verse and wrote at least three volumes of *chansonettes mesurées*. In the years after 1575, settings of measured chansons by Courville (of whom only a few works survive), Claude le Jeune, Jacques Mauduit, and others appeared in print. Before that time, Baïf and Courville seem to have jealously guarded their musico-poetic innovations, as the restrictions in the statutes of their Academy of Poetry and Music suggest. The Academy first met at Baïf's home in May 1571. In 1574 it seems to have been transferred, under Henry III, to the Louvre as the Académie du Palais. It was defunct, probably a victim of French religious struggles and political turmoil, by 1584.

Letters Patent and Statutes for an Academy of Poetry and Music
(1570)

LETTERS PATENT

Charles, by the grace of God King of France, greets all present and future subjects. As we always consider it to be of particular importance, following the

TEXT: Frances Yates, *The French Academies of the Sixteenth Century* (London: The Warburg Institute, 1947), pp. 319–22. For Yates's discussion of the Letters Patent and Statutes see pp. 21–27. Translation by Gary Tomlinson.

example of the great and praiseworthy King Francis our ancestor (may God absolve him), to see letters and science flourish throughout our kingdom and likewise in our city of Paris, where there are many men who work on and study them each day; and as the opinion of many great men, including ancient rulers and philosophers, should not be gainsaid, the opinion, namely, that it is of great importance to the morals of the citizens of a city that the music current and heard there should be governed by certain laws, since the souls of most men conform to and behave in accord with it (so that where music is disordered morals are easily depraved, while where it is well ordered men are well chastened); because of these considerations and having seen the request of our Privy Counsel, presented by our dear and good friends Jean-Antoine de Baïf and Joachim Thibault de Courville, relating that for three years now those men have with great study and assiduous labor worked together to advance the French language, bringing both its poetic fashion and the measure and regulation of its music back to those of the ancient Greeks and Romans at the time when their nations flourished; and, as already in the short time they have spent on these matters they have made certain experiments of measured verse set to music, itself measured almost in accord with the laws of the masters of music of that great and ancient age; and as, finally, after this praiseworthy enterprise had reached this point they were not able to think of or find any better way to bring to light their happily successful experiments (desiring as they did not only to gather the fruits of their labors but also, following their first intentions, to multiply the grace God had afforded them) than by establishing in the manner of the ancients an Academy or Company composed both of composers, singers, and instrumentalists and of virtuous listeners to them; which Academy would not only be a school to serve as fertile soil from which one day would come poets and musicians instructed well in their art so as to give us pleasure, but would also profit the public as a whole; and which Academy could not be formed without the listeners subsidizing it through an appropriate fee for the maintenance of themselves and the composers, singers, and instrumentalists, or undertaken without our advice and consent: Let it be known that, having taken this matter under consideration and heard and followed the advice of our dearest and most honored Queen Mother, our most dear and beloved brothers the Dukes of Anjou and of Alençon, the Princes of our blood, and other great and notable counselors, we do now advise in favor of the establishment of the aforementioned Academy or Company. . . . And, as it is our intention that the said Academy should be attended and honored by the most noble men, we have freely accepted and do welcome the title of Protector and First Listener of it, since we wish and intend that all the activities there will be to the honor of God, the aggrandizement of our State, and the ornament of the name of the French People. . . . Such is our pleasure, in testimony of which we have signed this document with our hand and stamped it with our seal. Given at Faux-bourg Saint Germain in the month of November 1570, the tenth year of our reign. Signed CHARLES and, on the reverse, de Neufville for the King.

STATUTES

In order to bring the use of music back to its perfect state, which is to represent words in song made up of harmony and melody, themselves consisting of the choice and well arranged regulation of voice, sound, and concord so as to create the effects required by the sense of the words, constraining, freeing, or enlarging the soul; and in order to revive also the ancient fashion of composing measured verse to accord with song likewise measured according to the art of meter; and in order also that by this means the souls of listeners, accustomed and disposed to music in the very form of their faculties, might arrange themselves so as to be capable of higher knowledge, purging themselves of whatever barbarities may remain in them: we find it appropriate to establish, by pleasure of the King our sovereign master, an Academy or Company made up of musicians and listeners according to the laws and conditions that follow:

Neither the musicians nor the listeners will in any activities of the Academy contravene the public laws of this Realm.

The musicians will be required to sing and recite their measured words and music for two hours every Sunday, according to an order established among them, for the privilege of the listeners registered in the book of the Academy. In this book will be written the names, surnames, and titles of those who subscribe to the Academy, together with the sum they consent to pay; and likewise the names and surnames of the musicians and the conditions under which they are entered, received, and appointed.

None of the musicians will introduce anyone into the Academy without the consent of all the Company.

All the musicians will be required, unless they give a reasonable excuse, to come to the meeting room each day at an appointed time to rehearse the music each of them will have studied separately, which will have been distributed by the two Founders of the Academy, whom the musicians will be obliged to follow and obey in musical matters.

The musicians will swear not to give out any copy of the chansons of the Academy to anyone without the consent of the whole Company. And if one of them should withdraw, he will not be permitted to take away, openly or secretly, any of the books of the Academy or to copy either music or words from them.

No musician will be allowed to withdraw from the Academy without giving two months' prior notice to the Founders, whether the withdrawal is by their consent or because the time the musician agreed to remain in the Academy has expired.

Should one of the musicians fall ill, he will be cared for and treated solicitously until he recovers fully.

If a musician is not approved by the whole Academy for some occasion, he may be relieved of his duties with pay for the time he would have served.

A medallion will be struck carrying an emblem agreed upon by the members of the Academy, which the listeners will wear to gain entry.

If one of the listeners should pass from this life to the next, the heirs of the deceased will be required to return the medallion to the Academy. If this is not done in the months immediately after the death, the heirs will pay one hundred pounds to the treasury of the Academy.

No one will allow another person to enter with him or without him by means of loaning his medallion to him, unless through some special merit he is given the privilege of doing so by the Founders.

During the singing the listeners will not talk or make noise; they will remain as quite as they can until the chanson being performed is finished. While a chanson is being sung neither will they knock on the doors of the room, which will be opened at the end of each chanson to admit listeners.

The listeners registered in the book of the Academy will pay the amount they have agreed to subscribe in semiannual installments, starting and finishing according to the day determined for the start of their attendance.

If a member, after having heard one or two concerts of the Academy, requests a refund of the money he has advanced, it will be returned to him and his name struck from the register. But if he has broken any of the laws of the Academy he will forfeit all the money he advanced.

No listener will touch or pass the barrier setting off the stage, and no one other than the musicians will enter there. Neither will anyone handle the book or the instruments; but, remaining off the stage, they will treat with respect everything that honors and serves the Academy, whether it be its book or its personnel.

If there is a dispute among any of the members of the Academy, musicians or listeners, they will not demand any satisfaction of word or deed within one hundred paces of the house where the Academy will be held.

Admission or refusal of anyone either to be registered in the book of the Academy or to be admitted as a listener ordinary or extraordinary will be at the sole discretion of the Founders.

Whoever breaks any of the above laws, whether musician or listener, will be excluded from the Academy and no longer allowed to enter there and will forfeit any monies paid for the maintenance of the Academy, except when, after the transgression has been repaired, the members of the Academy consent and agree otherwise.

Signed Baïf and Thibault

17 Balthasar de Beaujoyeulx

The *Balet comique de la royne (Ballet-Comedy of the Queen)* was presented at the Louvre on October 15, 1581. It was a high point in the so-called *Magnificences,* a two-week-long series of lavish spectacles sponsored by Henry III to commemorate a royal wedding and, more important, to celebrate his own power and grandeur at a time of religious and political instability. These spectacles involved countless poets, musicians, dancers, jousters, actors, painters, and sculptors, among them the poets Pierre de Ronsard and Jean-Antoine de Baïf and the composer Claude le Jeune. Balthasar de Beaujoyeulx himself (ca. 1535–ca. 1587), of Italian origin, was a dance master and violinist at the French court. He conceived and organized the *Balet comique,* directed the dancers, and wrote the description that was lavishly published a year after the performance. The music for the *Balet comique* was most likely composed by Lambert de Beaulieu, a follower of Baïf and Courville's Academy of Poetry and Music (see no. 16 above, pp. 60–63). The metrical freedoms of the vocal numbers in the commemorative volume reflect the influence of their *musique mesurée à l'antique* and contrast with the foursquare regularity of the instrumental dance music.

The *Balet comique* is noteworthy in its joining of music and dance with a coherent and continuous dramatic storyline. Beaujoyeulx showed his awareness of this novelty in a note to the reader at the beginning of the description. There he justifies, by ancient example and the magnificence of his king, his attempt to "make the balet speak and the comedy sing and resound," merging both in a single "well-proportioned body."

FROM *Le balet comique de la royne*
(1581)

As the nymphs arrived in front of the King, the whole party continued their ballet in two geometrical formations, each different from the other. During their last steps the strings played a very merry strain called la Clochette:

TEXT: The commemorative volume of the event, published in Paris 1582 and in a facsimile edition edited by Margaret M. McGowan (Binghampton, N.Y.: Center for Medieval & Early Renaissance Studies, 1982), fols. 22v–24v, 26v–27r, 30v–34v. Translation by Gary Tomlinson. I have omitted the music for the final chorus here, which is included along with the other musical numbers in the commemorative volume.

LE SON DE LA CLOCHETTE, AUQUEL CIRCE SORTIT DE SON JARDIN

Circe, still hidden in her garden behind a curtain, had hardly heard this music when she burst forth in great anger. Holding her golden wand high in her right hand she went the length of the hall to where the nymphs stood in a crescent formation facing Their Majesties. One after another she touched them with her golden wand, immediately rendering them as immobile as statues. She did the same to the viol players, who could no longer sing or play and indeed remained completely motionless. After that she returned to her garden, with a bold and happy expression one might see on a soldier who had won a glorious victory in some perilous and difficult enterprise. Indeed well might she take pride, having defeated so fierce and grand a courage as that of the nymphs.

When Circe had retired in glory to her garden, from high in the rafters, above the cloud, a great clap of thunder was heard that rumbled and murmured long afterward. When it stopped, suddenly the cloud (which I described before) began little by little to descend. In it was carried and enveloped Mercury, messenger of the god Jupiter, angrily coming to earth to break the spell of the sorceress Circe and deliver the nymphs from their enchantment with the juice of the moly root. Mercury was outfitted just as the poets describe him: dressed in red Spanish satin, painstakingly trimmed with gold, and wearing gilded boots with wings on their heels signifying the agility of his flight. On his head he wore a small, golden cap with wings on both sides. His cloak was of gold and purple cloth, and in his hand he carried the caduceus he once had used to put Argus to sleep for Jupiter.[1] While he descended, this god sang very gracefully the verses given below. He was played by Sir du Pont, a

1. See Ovid, *Metamorphoses* 1.668–721.

gentleman-servant of the King, and accompanied by many honorable musicians.[2]

> I am the messenger of all the gods,
> with winged heels, nimble and changeable,
> who, with his caduceus descended to the Fates
> in the deep abyss to steal away
> and revive dead souls; now that they are
> born again, I once more descend to earth.

> I taught men to obey the law;
> the sciences, arts, and cities come from me;
> among my treasures I grant eloquence;
> and, to heal souls robbed of reason,
> charmed away from virtue by pleasure,
> I carry the excellent root of moly.

> By its power I protected Ulysses, who reached
> the shores of Italy and did not became a swine
> through the enchanted arts of the sorceress Circe;[3]
> Circe who, in a castle she built in France,
> where she charmed the nymphs of the streams in
>   olden times,
> transformed many men into diverse beasts.

> •   •   •   •   •

> I want to expose the art of her illusions;
> I have distilled the moly into water of forgetfulness,
> and by my stronger art would undo hers.
> I know how strong and powerful she is;
> but a great danger gives more pleasure afterwards
> to him who honors the name of a powerful foe.

CHANSON DE MERCURE

Je suis __ de tous __ les dieux le __ com-mun mes - sa - ger Ai -
lé par les __ ta - lons, va - ri - a-ble et le - ger, Qui de ce ca - du-
cée __ à la __ Par-que __ fa - ta - le Dans l'a - bys-me pro -

2. Beaujoyeulx's French here, *accomply de beaucoup d'honorable parties,* is ambiguous. It probably refers to the musical accompaniment of Mercury's song, published in the commemorative volume only in its melody, but it could instead commend the many honorable traits and accomplishments of Sir du Pont himself.

3. For this episode see *Odyssey* 10.274–335.

While Mercury was still in the air, a few feet above the nymphs, he finished his song and sprinkled the moly-root liquor, which he had in a gilded flask, on their heads. He splashed it so far that it reached even the string players who, barely moistened by that water, immediately began playing again; and the nymphs took up their dancing as they had before they were enchanted. Circe, thinking that Mercury had greatly offended her by interfering in her art, determined to show him how much she knew of magic and excercise her power on him and his caduceus as well. Leaving her garden once more, she ran as if in a fury to the middle of the hall; and, passing among that beautiful troupe of dancers as she had before, she touched them and the string players a second time, putting them back into the state from which Mercury had rescued them.

•   •   •   •   •

She approached Mercury, who was still enveloped in the cloud, and raising her golden wand struck him. As soon as he felt the blow he dropped his caduceus and was enchanted, and the cloud carried him motionless to the ground. Circe took him by the hand and led him into her garden, followed by the nymphs, who went gracefully, two by two, with no more movement than what seemed to be granted them by the power of Circe's magic. As they entered her garden they suddenly disappeared, without our being able to tell what had become of them. At that instant the drape that covered the garden of Circe fell away, and we saw clearly the beauty of this delightful garden, glimmering with a thousand torches and lights. We saw also Circe, on a throne at the entrance to her castle, with the trophies of her victory: at her feet, all topsy-turvy, lay Mercury, with no means of moving except by leave and permission of the enchantress. After the curtain was opened a great stag appeared. Leaving the garden it passed in front of Circe, followed by a dog, the dog by an elephant, the elephant by a lion, the lion by a tiger, the tiger by a swine, the swine by other beasts: all men transformed by her sorcery and by the force of her enchantment.

When this act ended, the second entr'acte began at the trellis on the other side of the hall. This new entr'acte was comprised of eight satyrs, seven of whom played flutes and one of whom, Sir de Saint Laurens, singer of the King's Chamber, sang. The harmony of that music was delightful to the King, Queen, Princes, Princesses, and indeed all the audience. Its music was novel in invention and full of gaiety. The satyrs made the round of the hall, continuing their chanson. And at the end of each strophe one of the ensembles in the starry vault above responded, as you can see:

> O Pan, angry Diana
> has left the forest
> along with the woodland nymphs
> who usually trample the grass
> with their dance to the rhythms
> of the sweet harmony of their voices.

•   •   •   •   •

The response of the starry vault:

> Joy and unhappiness,
> fear and hope,
> follow their changeable order
> by an immutable destiny.

18 Henry Peacham

Born around 1576, Henry Peacham studied music in Italy with Orazio Vecchi, probably in 1603–4. He settled in London in 1612 and, apart from the following two years, when he traveled on the Continent, spent the rest of his life there. He had many friends in musical circles, among them the lutenist and composer John Dowland. His most important book, *The Compleat Gentleman,* appeared in 1622 and was reissued in 1626 and 1627. Peacham was an ardent supporter of the royal cause, but his book teaches a more or less Puritan concept of duty. Thus *The Compleat Gentleman* may be called an English Puritan counterpart to Castiglione's *Cortegiano.* Peacham's view of music shows this clearly enough: it is for him an extraordinarily praiseworthy and beneficial activity but should nevertheless not distract us overmuch from "more weighty employments." Peacham's last book was published in 1642, and he died soon thereafter.

FROM *The Compleat Gentleman*
(1622)

OF MUSIC

Music, a sister to Poetry, next craveth your acquaintance, if your genius be so disposed. I know there are many who are *adeo ἄμουσοι* [so far from the

TEXT: The Clarendon Press reprint of the 1634 edition (Oxford, 1906), pp. 96–104. Some of the postils of the original are given here as author's notes.

Muses, so lacking in harmony] and of such disproportioned spirits that they avoid her company (as a great cardinal in Rome did roses at their first coming in, that to avoid their scent he built him an house in the champaign, far from any town) or, as with a rose not long since, a great lady's cheek in England, their ears are ready to blister at the tenderest touch thereof. I dare not pass so rash a censure of these as Pindar doth,[1] or the Italian, having fitted a proverb to the same effect, "Whom God loves not, that man loves not music"; but I am verily persuaded they are by nature very ill disposed and of such a brutish stupidity that scarce anything else that is good and savoreth of virtue is to be found in them. Never wise man, I think, questioned the lawful use hereof, since it is an immediate gift of heaven, bestowed on man, whereby to praise and magnify his Creator; to solace him in the midst of so many sorrows and cares, wherewith life is hourly beset; and that by song, as by letters, the memory of doctrine and the benefits of God might be forever preserved (as we are taught by that song of Moses[2] and those divine psalms of the sweet singer of Israel, who with his psaltery[3] so loudly resounded the mysteries and innumerable benefits of the Almighty Creator) and the service of God advanced (as we may find in 2 Samuel vi:5, Psalm 33, 21, 43, and 4, 108, 3,[4] and in sundry other places of scripture which for brevity I omit).

But, say our sectaries, the service of God is nothing advanced by singing and instruments as we use it in our cathedral churches, that is, by "antiphony,[5] rests, repetitions, variety of moods and proportions, with the like."

For the first, that it is not contrary but consonant to the word of God so in singing to answer either, the practice of Miriam, the prophetess and sister of Moses, when she answered the men in her song,[6] will approve; for repetition, nothing was more usual in the singing of the Levites, and among the psalms of David the 136th is wholly compounded of those two most graceful and sweet figures of repetition, symploce and anaphora. For resting and proportions, the nature of the Hebrew verse, as the meanest Hebrician knoweth, consisting many times of uneven feet, going sometime in this number, sometimes in that (one while, as St. Jerome saith,[7] in the numbers of Sappho, another while, of Alcaeus), doth of necessity require it. And wherein doth our practice of singing and playing with instruments in his Majesty's chapel and our cathedral churches differ from the practice of David, the priests, and Levites?[8] Do we not make one sign in praising and thanking God with voices and instruments of all sorts? "Donec," as St. Jerome saith,[9] "reboet laquear templi"; the roof of the church echoeth again, and which, lest they should cavil at as a Jewish cere-

---

1. Pythian Odes 1.13–14.
2. Deuteronomy 32. [Au.]
3. It was an instrument three square, of 72 strings, of incomparable sweetness. [Au.]
4. Peacham's reference is not clear.
5. Answering one another in the choir. [Au.]
6. Exodus 15:20–21.
7. *Epistola* 53.8.
8. 2 Chronicles 5:12–13. [Au.]
9. Compare *Epistola* 77.11: *Et aurata Templorum tecta reboans.*

mony, we know to have been practiced in the ancient purity of the church. But we return where we left.

The physicians will tell you that the exercise of music is a great lengthener of the life by stirring and reviving of the spirits, holding a secret sympathy with them; besides, the exercise of singing openeth the breast and pipes. It is an enemy to melancholy and dejection of the mind, which St. Chrysostom truly calleth the Devil's bath;[10] yea, a curer of some diseases—in Apulia in Italy and thereabouts it is most certain that those who are stung with the tarantula are cured only by music.[11] Beside the aforesaid benefit of singing, it is a most ready help for a bad pronunciation and distinct speaking which I have heard confirmed by many great divines; yea, I myself have known many children to have been holpen of their stammering in speech only by it.

Plato calleth it "a divine and heavenly practice,"[12] profitable for the seeking out of that which is good and honest.

Homer saith musicians are "worthy of honor and regard of the whole world,"[13] and we know, albeit Lycurgus imposed most straight and sharp laws upon the Lacedaemonians, yet he ever allowed them the exercise of music.[14]

Aristotle averreth music to be the only disposer of the mind to virtue and goodness, wherefore he reckoneth it among those four principal exercises wherein he would have children instructed.[15]

Tully saith there consisteth in the practice of singing and playing upon instruments great knowledge and the most excellent instruction of the mind, and for the effect it worketh in the mind he termeth it "Stabilem thesaurum, qui mores instuit, componitque, ac mollit irarum ardores, &c."; a lasting treasure which rectifieth and ordereth our manners and allayeth the heat and fury of our anger, &c.[16]

I might run into an infinite sea of the praise and use of so excellent an art, but I only show it you with the finger, because I desire not that any noble or gentleman should (save at his private recreation and leisurable hours) prove a master in the same or neglect his more weighty employments, though I avouch it a skill worthy the knowledge and exercise of the greatest prince.

King Henry the Eighth could not only sing his part sure, but of himself composed a service of four, five, and six parts, as Erasmus in a certain epistle testifieth of his own knowledge.[17]

The Duke of Venosa, an Italian prince,[18] in like manner of late years hath

---

10. In *Liber de angore animi*. [Au.]
11. Compare no. 2 above (Zarlino) p. 20, and no. 29 below (Ficino) p. 111.
12. Δαιμόνιον πραγμα [*Republic* 531c]. [Au.]
13. τιμῆς ἔμμοροί εἰσι καὶ αἰδοῦς [*Odyssey* 8.480]. [Au.]
14. See no. 2 above (Zarlino) p. 21, n. 33.
15. *Politics* 1337b. [Au.]
16. Cicero, *Tusculan Disputations* 1. [Au.] Peacham evidently has in mind 1.2, though his quotation is not found there.
17. In *Farragine epistola* [i.e., *Farrago nova epistolarum* (Basel, 1519)]. [Au.]
18. Carlo Gesualdo, Prince of Venosa.

given excellent proof of his knowledge and love to music, having himself composed many rare songs which I have seen.

・ ・ ・ ・ ・

To deliver you my opinion, whom among other authors you should imitate and allow for the best, there being so many equally good, is somewhat difficult; yet as in the rest herein you shall have my opinion.

For motets and music of piety and devotion, as well for the honor of our nation as the merit of the man, I prefer above all others our phoenix, Mr. William Byrd, whom in that kind I know not whether any may equal, I am sure none excel, even by the judgment of France and Italy, who are very sparing in the commendation of strangers in regard of that conceit they hold of themselves. His *Cantiones sacrae*, as also his *Gradualia*, are mere angelical and divine, and being of himself naturally disposed to gravity and piety his vein is not so much for light madrigals or canzonets, yet his "Virginelle" and some others in his First Set cannot be mended by the best Italian of them all.

For composition I prefer next Ludovico de Victoria, a most judicious and a sweet composer; after him Orlando di Lasso, a very rare and excellent author who lived some forty years since in the court of the Duke of Bavaria. He hath published as well in Latin as French many sets; his vein is grave and sweet; among his Latin songs his *Seven Penitential Psalms* are the best, and that French set of his wherein is "Susanna un jour," upon which ditty many others have since exercised their invention.[19]

For delicious air and sweet invention in madrigals, Luca Marenzio excelleth all other whosoever, having published more sets than any author else whosoever, and to say truth hath not an ill song, though sometime an oversight (which might be the printer's fault) of two eights or fifths escaped him, as between the tenor and bass in the last close of "I must depart all hapless," ending according to the nature of the ditty most artificially with a minim rest. His first, second, and third parts of "Tirsi," "Veggo dolce mio bene," "Che fa hogg'il mio sole," "Cantava," or "Sweet singing Amaryllis," are songs the muses themselves might not have been ashamed to have had composed.[20] Of stature and complexion he was a little and black man; he was organist in the Pope's chapel at Rome a good while; afterward he went into Poland, being in displeasure with the Pope for overmuch familiarity with a kinswoman of his (whom the Queen of Poland sent for by Luca Marenzio afterward, she being one of the rarest women in

19. For Lasso's work see *Sämtliche Werke,* ed. Franz Haberl and Adolf Sandberger (21 vols., Leipzig: Breitkopf & Härtel, 1894–1926), vol. 14, pp. 29–33. For other works based on it see Ferabosco (*The Old English Edition,* vol. 11, no. 1), Byrd (*The English Madrigal School,* vol. 14, no. 29 and vol. 15, no. 8), Sweelinck (*Works,* vol. 7, no. 8), and Farnaby (*The English Madrigal School,* vol. 20, no. 12).
20. "Io partirò" ("I must depart all hapless"), "Tirsi," and "Che fa hogg'il mio sole" appeared with English text in Yonge's *Musica transalpina* (1588); "Cantava" and "Veggo dolce mio bene" appeared in Watson's *Italian Madrigals Englished* (1590). The parallel fifths at the end of "Io partirò" occur in Yonge's reprint but not in the original composition.

Europe for her voice and the lute). But returning, he found the affection of the Pope so estranged from him that hereupon he took a conceit and died.

Alphonso Ferabosco the father, while he lived, for judgment and depth of skill (as also his son yet living) was inferior unto none; what he did was most elaborate and profound and pleasing enough in air, though Master Thomas Morley censureth him otherwise.[21] That of his, "I saw my lady weeping," and the "Nightingale" (upon which ditty Master Byrd and he in a friendly emulation exercised their invention),[22] cannot be bettered for sweetness of air or depth of judgment.

I bring you now mine own master, Horatio Vecchi of Modena, beside goodness of air most pleasing of all other for his conceit and variety, wherewith all his works are singularly beautified, as well his madrigals of five and six as those his canzonets, printed at Nuremberg, wherein for trial sing his "Vivo in fuoco amoroso, Lucretia mia," where upon "Io catenato moro" with excellent judgment he driveth a crotchet through many minims, causing it to resemble a chain with the links. Again, in "S'io potessi raccor'i mei sospiri," the breaking of the word "sospiri" with crotchet and crotchet rest into sighs, and that "Fa mi un canzone, &c.," to make one sleep at noon, with sundry other of like conceit and pleasant invention.

Then that great master, and master not long since of St. Mark's chapel in Venice,[23] second to none for a full, lofty, and sprightly vein, following none save his own humor, who while he lived was one of the most free and brave companions of the world. His *Penitential Psalms* are excellently composed and for piety are his best.

Nor must I here forget our rare countryman Peter Philips, organist to their Altezzas at Brussels, now one of the greatest masters of music in Europe. He hath sent us over many excellent songs, as well motets as madrigals; he affecteth altogether the Italian vein.

There are many other authors very excellent, as Boschetto[24] and Claudio de Monteverdi, equal to any before named, Giovanni Ferretti, Stephano Felis, Giulio Rinaldi, Philippe de Monte, Andrea Gabrieli, Cipriano de Rore, Pallavicino, Geminiano, with others yet living, whose several works for me here to examine would be over tedious and needless; and for me, please your own ear and fancy. Those whom I have before mentioned have been ever (within these thirty or forty years) held for the best.

I willingly, to avoid tediousness, forbear to speak of the worth and excellency of the rest of our English composers, Master Doctor Dowland, Thomas Morley, Mr. Alphonso, Mr. Wilbye, Mr. Kirbye, Mr. Weelkes, Michael East, Mr.

---

21. See no. 40 below (Morley), p. 201.
22. Ferabosco's setting is reprinted in *The Old English Edition*, vol. 11, no. 9, Byrd's in *The English Madrigal School*, vol. 15, no. 9; both were prompted by Lasso's chanson "Le rossignol" (*Sämtliche Werke* 14.82), printed with English text in Yonge's *Musica transalpina*.
23. Giovanni Croce. [Au.]
24. Boschetto, his motets of 8 parts printed in Rome, 1594. [Au.]

Bateson, Mr. Deering, with sundry others, inferior to none in the world (however much soever the Italian attributes to himself) for depth of skill and richness of conceit.

Infinite is the sweet variety that the theorique of music exerciseth the mind withal, as the contemplation of proportion, of concords and discords, diversity of moods and tones, infiniteness of invention, &c. But I dare affirm there is no one science in the world that so affecteth the free and generous spirit with a more delightful and inoffensive recreation or better disposeth the mind to what is commendable and virtuous.

The commonwealth of the Cynethenses in Arcadia, falling from the delight they formerly had in music, grew into seditious humors and civil wars, which Polybius took especially note of,[25] and I suppose hereupon it was ordained in Arcadia that everyone should practise music by the space of thirty years.

The ancient Gauls in like manner (whom Julian[26] termed barbarous) became most courteous and tractable by the practise of music.

Yea, in my opinion no rhetoric more persuadeth or hath greater power over the mind; nay, hath not music her figures, the same which rhetoric? What is a revert but her antistrophe? her reports, but sweet anaphoras? her counterchange of points, antimetaboles? her passionate airs, but prosopopoeias? with infinite other of the same nature.[27]

How doth music amaze us when of sound discords she maketh the sweetest harmony? And who can show us the reason why two basins, bowls, brass pots, or the like, of the same bigness, the one being full, the other empty, shall stricken be a just diapason in sound one to the other; or that there should be such sympathy in sounds that two lutes of equal size being laid upon a table and tuned unison, or alike in the Gamma, G *sol re ut,* or any other string, the one stricken, the other untouched shall answer it?

But to conclude, if all arts hold their esteem and value according to their effects, account this goodly science not among the number of those which Lucian placeth without the gates of hell as vain and unprofitable, but of such which are πηγαὶ τῶν καλῶν, the fountains of our lives' good and happiness.[28] Since it is a principal means of glorifying our merciful Creator, it heightens our devotion, it gives delight and ease to our travails, it expelleth sadness and heaviness of spirit, preserveth people in concord and amity, allayeth fierceness and anger, and lastly, is the best physic for many melancholy diseases.

---

25. *Histories* 4.20. [Au.]
26. *Epistola* 71. [Au.]
27. For rhetorical thinking along similar (if more technical) lines, see no. 38 below (Burmeister), pp. 189–93.
28. The Greek is not from Lucian, but seems instead to recall Xenophon, *Cyropaedia* 7.2.13, where Croesus calls the τεχναι "πηγάς . . . τῶν καλῶν" (information from Joseph Farrell). This passage reads "arts and sciences, which be fountains of all good things" in William Barker's 1567 translation of the *Cyropaedia* (ed. James Tatum, New York: Garland, 1987, p. 169). I have not located the Lucianic passage alluded to by Peacham.

19 Vincenzo Giustiniani

Vincenzo Giustiniani was born of ancient Venetian stock on Chios, an island in the Aegean Sea, in 1564, and moved with his family to Rome when the Turks seized the island two years later. There he grew up amid the privileges of his high social status, circulating in the milieu of popes and cardinals and amassing a large art collection, a catalogue of which he published in 1631. He died in 1637.

Giustiniani's *Discourse on the Music of His Times (Discorso sopra la musica de' suoi tempi)* is the report of an informed amateur on Italian musical developments from the 1570s to the 1620s. It provides detailed observations on a new style of singing and composing inaugurated in the years after 1575. It is revealing that from his contemporary vantage point Giustiniani sees no such dramatic shift in musical style in the years around 1600. Rather he takes for granted the coexistence of solo song and polyphonic genres throughout the period he describes. And he incorporates into this varied musical landscape the recent "recitative style," by which he means not only dramatic recitative per se but also other manners of more or less declamatory song for one, two, or three voices with basso continuo.

FROM *Discourse on the Music of His Times*
(1628)

1. In my youth my father (of blessed memory) sent me to a school of music, and I observed that the compositions of Arcadelt, Orlando di Lasso, Striggio, Cipriano de Rore, and Filippo di Monte were in use and esteemed to be the best of those days, as in effect they were. In solo singing with instrumental accompaniment the fashion of *villanelle napolitane* was preferred, in imitation of which many were composed even in Rome, especially by a certain Pitio,[1] a great musician and eminent comedian.

TEXT: *Discorso sopra la musica de' suoi tempi*, in Angelo Solerti, ed., *Le origini del melodramma: testimonianze dei contemporanei* (Turin: Bocca, 1903), pp. 103–28. Translation by Gary Tomlinson. Where I have been able, I have identified the musicians mentioned who are not clearly named or included in standard reference works.

1. A bass singer especially known for his solo songs with lute accompaniment. See Anthony Newcomb, *The Madrigal at Ferrara 1579–97* (2 vols., Princeton: Princeton University Press, 1980), vol. 1, p. 47.

2. In a short time the taste in music changed and the compositions of Luca Marenzio and Ruggero Giovanelli appeared. Both those to be sung by many voices and those for solo voice and instrument were filled with inventions of delightful novelty. The excellence of this style consisted in a new sort of air, pleasing to the ears, with some easy runs and without extraordinary artifice. At the same time Palestrina, Soriano, and Giovanni Maria Nanino composed pieces to be sung in church. These were made effortlessly with a good, solid counterpoint, with a good air, and with suitable decorum, as is manifest in the fact that even today they are sung among the works of more modern composers (who have all learned from their elders their discipline, which they have sought to vary more often with pretty ornaments than with fundamental and substantial workmanship).

3. In the year or our Lord 1575 or a little after and for the following few years a new kind of singing appeared, very different from earlier kinds. It was especially apparent in solo song with instrumental accompaniment and in the examples of the Neapolitan Giovanni Andrea, Sig. Giulio Cesare Brancaccio, and the Roman Alessandro Merlo, who all sang bass with a range of three octaves and with a variety of runs new and pleasing to the ears of everyone.[2] These singers stimulated composers to write works, whether for many voices or for one over an instrument, imitating both their style and that of a certain woman named Femia,[3] but with greater invention and artifice. There resulted a style of mixed villanelle, halfway between florid madrigals and villanelle, which is seen today in many books of the above-named composers and of Orazio Vecchi and others. But just as these villanelle acquired greater perfection through this more skilled composition, so each composer sought to advance himself in writing for several voices so that his compositions would succeed in the general fashion. This was particularly true of Giaches de Wert in Mantua and Luzzasco in Ferrara, who were in charge of all the music of the dukes of those cities.[4] These dukes took the greatest delight in such music, especially in gathering many important gentlewomen and gentlemen to play and sing excellently. So great was their delight that they lingered sometimes for whole days in some little chambers they had ornately outfitted with pictures and tapestries for this sole purpose. There was a great rivalry between the women of Mantua and Ferrara, a competition not only in the timbre and disposition of their voices but also in ornamentation with exquisite runs joined opportunely and not excessively (from which excess Giovanni Luca, a falsettist from Rome who also served in Ferrara, often suffered).[5] There was competition

---

2. On Brancaccio, another renowned bass and a published military strategist, see Newcomb, *The Madrigal,* vol. 1, pp. 12–14 and 185–86; Merlo was a well-published composer as well as singer.

3. Probably Eufemia Jozola; see Newcomb, *The Madrigal,* vol. 1, p. 17, n. 50.

4. A selection of Luzzasco Luzzaschi's works of this type was later published as *Madrigali . . . per cantare, et sonare a uno, e doi, e tre soprani* (Rome, 1601).

5. That is, Giovanni Luca Conforto; see Vincenzo Giustiniani, *Discorso sopra la musica,* trans. Carol MacClintock (American Institute of Musicology, 1962), p. 69, and Newcomb, *The Madrigal,* vol. 1, p. 170.

even more in moderating or enlarging the voice, loud or soft, attenuating it or fattening it as was called for, now drawing it out, now breaking it off with the accompaniment of a sweet interrupted sigh, now giving out long runs, distinct and well followed, now turns, now leaps, now long trills, now short ones, now sweet runs sung quietly, to which sometimes one suddenly heard an echo respond; and more still in the participation of the face, and of the looks and gestures that accompanied appropriately the music and conceits of the poetry; and above all, without any indecorous motions of body, mouth, or hands that might have diminished the effect of their songs, in enunciating the words so well that each one could be heard down to the last syllable and was not interrupted or overwhelmed by the runs and other ornaments. And many other particular artifices could be observed in these singers and recorded by one more expert than I. And in such noble situations these excellent singers strove with all their might to win grace from their masters, the princes, and also fame for them—wherein lay their usefulness.

4. Following the example of these courts and of the two Neapolitan basses mentioned above, Roman composers began to vary their mode of composing both figured partsongs for several voices and songs for one or at most two voices with instrumental accompaniment. Prince Gesualdo of Venosa, who played excellently the lute and Neapolitan guitar, began to compose madrigals full of great artifice and exquisite counterpoint, with difficult and charming melodies in each part interwoven with such proportion that there was not in them a single superfluous note not contained in the initial melody, which itself was later sung in reverse. And because such exquisite discipline usually renders a work harsh and rough, Gesualdo tried with all his power and industry to choose melodies that were fluid, sweet, and smoothly shaped, even if they were the more difficult to compose. Indeed in singing them his melodies appeared to everyone easy to compose, but in the event they were found to be difficult and not for just any composer. In this style the Neapolitans Stella, Nenna, and Scipione de Ritici composed, following the abovementioned Prince of Venosa and also Count Alfonso Fontanelli.

5. At the same time Cardinal Ferdinando de' Medici, later Duke of Florence, stimulated by his own taste and by the examples of the princes mentioned above, excelled in finding excellent musicians. Among them above all was the famous Vittoria,[6] who almost originated the true female style of singing and was the wife of Antonio di Santa Fiore, named thus because he had been since childhood the excellent musician of the Cardinal of Santa Fiore. Following her example many others in Rome attempted her style of singing, so much so that they excelled all the other musicians of the places and princes mentioned above. Thus emerged Giulio Romano, Giuseppino, Giovanni Domenico and

6. That is, the singer Vittoria Concarini Archilei.

Rasi, who studied in Florence with Giulio Romano.[7] They all sang bass or tenor with a very wide range, with exquisite turns of phrase and runs, and with extraordinary feeling and a special talent for making the words audible. Beyond these, there were many sopranos, such as Giovanni Luca, Ottavio Durante, Simoncino, and Ludovico, who all sang falsetto, and many castrati of the Sistine Chapel, and others like Onofrio from Pistoia, a certain Mathias from Spain, Giovanni Gironimo from Perugia and many others whom I omit for the sake of brevity. Cardinal Montalto succeeded Cardinal Ferdinando de' Medici. He delighted in music no less than his predecessor, playing the cembalo excellently and singing in a sweet and affecting manner. In his household he kept many musicians who exceeded mediocrity, for example the Cavaliere del Leuto and Scipione Dentice del Cembalo, both excellent players and composers, and then Orazio, a virtuoso on the double harp. His singers included the castrato Onofrio Gualfreducci, Ippolita from Naples, the bass Melchior,[8] and many others to whom he gave generous provisions. With the example of these and all the others mentioned already music was revived, so that many papal relatives and other cardinals and princes could delight in it. Above all the chapelmasters undertook to train various castrati and other boys to sing with new and affecting runs and turns of phrase. Giovanni Bernardino Nanino, chapelmaster in San Luigi, and Ruggero Giovanelli had great success with their students who, because they are alive and many in number, I omit to name for now.

6. Just before the present time many composers, like Claudio Monteverdi, Giovanni Bernardino Nanino, Felice Anerio and others, without leaving behind the manner of Gesualdo, tried to sweeten and make more accessible the styles of composition. They composed especially works for church in various manners and scorings for as many as twelve choirs. This style is still in use today, and works are composed in it for large numbers of skilled singers. Indeed I might say that in our time music has been ennobled and made more illustrious than ever before, inasmuch as King Philip IV of Spain and both his brothers delight in it and often sing partsongs or play music for viols together (with the help of a few other musicians to fill out the consort, among whom Filippo Piccinini from Bologna, an excellent player of lute and pandora, stands

---

7. That is, Giulio Caccini; the Roman singer-composers Giovanni Domenico Puliaschi and, probably, Giuseppe Giamberti; and Francesco Rasi. All published books of song in the early seventeenth century.

8. On Onofrio Gualfreducci, singer at the Sistine Chapel, see Warren Kirkendale, *The Court Musicians in Florence during the Principate of the Medici* (Florence: Leo S. Olschki Editore, 1993), pp. 246–50. Ippolita is Hippolita Marotta Recupito; see *The Letters of Claudio Monteverdi*, ed. Denis Stevens (Cambridge: Cambridge University Press, 1980), pp. 75–77. Melchior is Melchior Palentrotti, famous for his roles in two Caccini music dramas of 1600, *Il rapimento di Cefalo* and *L'Euridice*. The double harpist is Orazio Michi; see Alberto Cametti, "Orazio Michi 'dell'Arpa,' virtuoso e compositore di musica della prima metà del seicento," *Rivista musicale italiana* 21 (1914): 203–7.

out).[9] Moreover the same king and his brothers compose works not only for their own delight but also for singing in the court chapel and other churches during the Office services. And this musical aptitude and taste of His Majesty will cause many noblemen to delight in music and many others to apply themselves to it, as the verse says: "The whole world is made in the image of the king."[10]

7. All these things confirm what I said before, that is, that the fashion and manner of singing changes from time to time according to the tastes of the noblemen and princes who delight in it, just as happens in styles of dress, whose fashions are always changing according to things introduced at important courts. . . .

8. . . . At the present time music is not much in use, not being practiced by gentlemen in Rome; neither do we hear the singing of partsongs as often as we used to, notwithstanding the fact that there are many opportunities to do so. It is true that music has been brought to an extraordinary and novel perfection through the practice of a great number of good musicians who, taught by the good masters mentioned before, offer much delight in their sweet and skilful song. Having left behind the older style, which was somewhat rough, and in particular the excessive runs with which it was ornamented, they mostly adhere now to a recitative style endowed with grace and ornaments appropriate to the words, with an occasional run sung clearly and with good judgment, and with just and varied consonances marking the end of each period—periods that in the works of today's composers bring such frequent cadences as to become tiresome. Above all in this recitative style the singer makes the words easily understood, applying to each syllable one note—quiet or loud, slow or fast— and displaying the thought that is sung by means of moderate and not excessive gestures and facial expressions. The songs are for one to three voices with the accompaniment of instruments appropriate to the circumstance: theorbo, guitar, harpsichord, or organ. Most often these songs are sung, with novel invention in their tunes and their ornaments, in the Spanish or Italian manner, the latter being similar to the former but with greater artifice and ornament. This is true whether they are sung in Rome, in Naples, or in Genoa, where the most prominent composers of them are il Todesco della Tiorba named Giovanni Geronimo[11] (in Rome), Gutierrez and later his son Pietro and Gallo and others (in Naples), and (in Genoa) a certain Cicco, who composes and sings and offers great delight to gentlemen in their academies and soirées, which are more popular there than elsewhere.

This recitative style was once customary in plays sung by ladies in Rome, and is still thus heard. But in these plays it is so crude and unvaried in conso-

9. Filippo Piccinini had earlier served with his father and brothers at the court of Ferrara. See Newcomb, *The Madrigal*, vol. 1, p. 179.

10. *Regis ad exemplum totus componitur orbis;* Claudianus, *De IV consolatu honorii* vol. 1, p. 299 (see Giustiniani, *Discorso,* trans. MacClintock, p. 72).

11. That is, Johann Hieronymus Kapsberger.

nance and ornament that if the boredom of listening was not moderated by the presence of the actors the audience would leave the seats and the room would be left empty.

Giulio Romano and Giuseppino were the ones who invented this style, as I said before, or at least who first shaped it well. After them it has grown more perfect from singer to singer to the point where it seems that little can be added to it in the future. And it has been introduced also for the singing of Latin verses, hymns, and odes full of holiness and devotion, in a sweet, decorous manner that clearly puts across the thoughts and words.

MUSIC AND RELIGIOUS REFORM

20 Martin Luther

Martin Luther, the famous German theologian and initiator of the Reformation, was born at Eisleben in 1483 and died there in 1546. From 1522 on he directed much of his attention toward recasting the services of the Roman Church so that the congregation would participate in them more fully. This plan did not at first involve a wholesale translation of the Latin Mass into German, but rather called for incorporating vernacular spiritual songs here and there in a reorganized Latin framework. In 1524, however, Luther worked out a fully German Mass, intended at first for smaller congregations with clergy not tutored in Latin, which substituted German devotional songs for the Latin Ordinary; it was published in 1526. In 1523–24 he began to write, translate, and arrange texts for songs that might be used in either service. Many of these were published, along with texts by others all set to music for four voices, in the *Wittemberg Gesangbuch* of 1524. Luther's precise role in the composition of the settings has remained obscure, although his extensive musical aptitude and training make him a plausible candidate for the task. Already by the end of the sixteenth century this sort of spiritual song was referred to as a chorale, the term we still use for it today.

Wittemberg Gesangbuch
(1524)

FOREWORD

That the singing of spiritual songs is a good thing and one pleasing to God is, I believe, not hidden from any Christian, for not only the example of the prophets and kings in the Old Testament (who praised God with singing and playing, with hymns and the sound of all manner of stringed instruments), but also the special custom of singing psalms, have been known to everyone and to universal Christianity from the beginning. Nay, St. Paul establishes this also, 1 Corinthians 14, and orders the Colossians to sing psalms and spiritual songs to the Lord in their hearts, in order that God's word and Christ's teaching may be thus spread abroad and practised in every way.

Accordingly, as a good beginning and to encourage those who can do better, I and several others have brought together certain spiritual songs with a view to spreading abroad and setting in motion the holy Gospel which now, by the grace of God, has again emerged, so that we too may pride ourselves, as Moses does in his song, Exodus 15, that Christ is our strength and song and may not know anything to sing or to say, save Jesus Christ our Savior, as Paul says, 1 Corinthians 2.

TEXT: Johann Walther, *Wittembergisch geistlich Gesangbuch von 1524*, ed. Otto Kade (Publikationen älterer praktischer und theoretischer Musikwerke 7 [Berlin, 1878]), preceding p. 1 of score. Translation by Oliver Strunk.

These, further, are set for four voices for no other reason than that I wished that the young (who, apart from this, should and must be trained in music and in other proper arts) might have something to rid them of their love ditties and wanton songs and might, instead of these, learn wholesome things and thus yield willingly, as becomes them, to the good; also, because I am not of the opinion that all the arts shall be crushed to earth and perish through the Gospel, as some bigoted persons pretend, but would willingly see them all, and especially music, servants of him who gave and created them. So I pray that every pious Christian may bear with this and, should God grant him an equal or a greater talent, help to further it. Besides, unfortunately, the world is so lax and so forgetful in training and teaching its neglected young people that one might well encourage this first of all. God grant us his grace. Amen.

21 Desiderius Erasmus

Irenics, the branch of Christian theology concerned with reconciliation among churches, found its greatest Renaissance advocate in the figure of Desiderius Erasmus of Rotterdam (ca. 1469–1536). Amid the firestorm of debate that sprang up in the wake of Luther's ninety-five theses, Erasmus maintained a stance of pragmatic moderation and compromise. This posture was not, in its day, wholly effective, earning him the enmity of both extremes: Roman prelates saw his writings as leaning toward Lutheranism while the reformers resented his clashes with Luther on the question of free will and other issues.

Erasmus's religious convictions urged him toward the personal piety and evangelicalism of the *Devotio moderna* rather than the theological disputation of the University of Paris (where he studied in the 1490s). His intellectual preference was for the careful philology and persuasive rhetoric of the humanists rather than the labyrinthine logic of the scholastics. These two facets, spiritual and scholarly, joined in his pathbreaking edition of the Greek New Testament (1516) and in his commentaries and treatises on religious issues, while his immense capacity for sardonic rhetorical wit came to the fore in the famous *Praise of Folly* (1511).

Erasmus's general stance is captured well in the following remarks on the Mass and its music. They come from a late work, *On Restoring the Harmony of the Church (Liber de sarcienda ecclesiae concordia,* 1533); it is an eloquent plea for Roman stalwarts and radical reformers to confine their doctrinal differences to synods and ecclesiastical councils and reunite their churches in a single devotion to Christ and the Gospels.

FROM *On Restoring the Harmony of the Church*

(1533)

If some superstition or impropriety has crept into the Mass, it is well to correct it. But I do not see why we should condemn the Mass through and through. It consists of psalmody (called the Introit), the Doxology, prayer, sacred songs, the recitation of the words of the prophets and apostles (called the Epistle), the recitation of the Gospel, the profession of Catholic faith, the giving of thanks (called the Eucharist), and the religious commemoration of the Lord's death; then more prayers, among them the Lord's Prayer; then follow the symbol of Christian peace, Communion, another sacred song, and prayer. Finally the priest commends to God the whole congregation, as a group under his guardianship, and enjoins it to go forth in a spirit of piety and charity. What is there in this that is not pious and worthy of veneration? Whoever is offended by the mean crowd of hired priests should expel the unworthy ones and keep the worthy. Whoever dislikes the sequences, especially the inept ones, may omit them; the Roman Church does not recognize any sequences.[1] Likewise the songs they sing these days in many churches after the consecration of the body and blood of the Lord—songs for peace or against pestilence or for a successful crop—may be omitted without any detriment to religion.[2] All this has been added onto the ancient usages.

•　　•　　•　　•　　•

If modulated music[3] and song with musical instruments do not please you in church, they may be omitted with no prejudice to piety; if they do please you, you must take care that such music is worthy of a church of God. But what happens presently in some churches, where they omit or shorten important parts of the service for the sake of music of voices and instruments,

---

TEXT: *Liber de sarcienda ecclesiae concordia*, ed. R. Stupperich, in Desiderius Erasmus of Rotterdam, *Opera omnia*, ed. Conseil International pour l'Édition des Oeuvres Complètes d'Érasme, ordo 3, vol. 5 (Amsterdam: North-Holland Publishing Co., 1986), pp. 245–313; see pp. 307–8. Translation by Gary Tomlinson. For a translation of the complete *Liber*, see John P. Dolan, ed., *The Essential Erasmus* (New York: New American Library, 1964), pp. 327–88.

1. Erasmus reiterated this concern with the abuse of sequences elsewhere in his writings; see Clement A. Miller, "Erasmus on Music," *The Musical Quarterly* 51 (1966): 332–49; esp. pp. 336–37. In the decades after his death the use of sequences in the Mass would be sharply restricted at the Council of Trent.
2. Erasmus refers here to extraliturgical songs of various kinds, probably including polyphonic settings of votive antiphon texts and the like. On such music in the British Isles during this period see Frank Ll. Harrison, *Music in Medieval Britain* (London: Routledge and Paul, 1958), chaps. 6–7.
3. That is, polyphony.

is not right. Nearly an hour is spent on the sequence, while the Creed is short-ened and the Lord's Prayer omitted. And they consume almost as much time in those melismas sung at length on a single verse. It would be better not to extend the solemn rite into tediousness with such gratuitous additions.

22 Jean Calvin

Jean Calvin (or Cauvin), the leading Franco-Swiss religious reformer, was born at Noyon, France, in 1509 and died at Geneva in 1564. He lived first in Paris but was forced to leave because of his leanings toward the cause of reformation. He fled to Basle in 1534 and published there his great programmatic work of religious reform, the *Christianae religionis institutio* (1536). Subsequently, Calvin settled and taught in Geneva, where he spent the rest of his life building up a church community in accordance with his religious convictions. In regard to music, these were more restrictive than Luther's or Erasmus's. They required that polyphony be banned from church, since only monophonic singing by the congregation assured the proper attentiveness to liturgical words. Marot and Calvin's French translation of the Psalter, which in later, expanded editions was to assume great importance for the service of the Calvinist Church, was pub-lished in Geneva in 1542.

The Geneva Psalter

(1542)

EPISTLE TO THE READER

Jean Calvin to all Christians and lovers of God's Word, Salutation:

As it is a thing indeed demanded by Christianity, and one of the most neces-sary, that each of the faithful observe and maintain the communion of the Church in his neighborhood, attending the assemblies which are held both on the Lord's day and on other days to honor and serve God, so it is also expedient and reasonable that all should know and hear what is said and done in the temple, to receive fruit and edification therefrom. For our Lord did not insti-tute the order which we must observe when we gather together in his name merely that the world might be amused by seeing and looking upon it, but

TEXT: *Oeuvres choisies. Publiées par la Compagnie des pasteurs de Genève* (Geneva, 1909), pp. 169–70, 173–76. Translation by Oliver Strunk.

wished rather that therefrom should come profit to all his people. Thus witnesseth Saint Paul,[1] commanding that all which is done in the Church be directed unto the common edifying of all, a thing the servant would not have commanded, had it not been the intention of the Master. For to say that we can have devotion, either at prayers or at ceremonies, without understanding anything of them, is a great mockery, however much it be commonly said. A good affection toward God is not a thing dead and brutish, but a lively movement, proceeding from the Holy Spirit when the heart is rightly touched and the understanding enlightened. And indeed, if one could be edified by the things which one sees without knowing what they mean, Saint Paul would not so rigorously forbid speaking in an unknown tongue and would not use the argument that where there is no doctrine, there is no edification.[2] Yet if we wish to honor well the holy decrees of our Lord, as used in the Church, the main thing is to know what they contain, what they mean, and to what end they tend, in order that their observance may be useful and salutary and in consequence rightly ruled.

Now there are in brief three things that our Lord has commanded us to observe in our spiritual assemblies, namely, the preaching of his Word, the public and solemn prayers, and the administration of his sacraments. I abstain at this time from speaking of preaching, seeing that there is no question thereof. . . . Of the sacraments I shall speak later.

As to the public prayers, these are of two kinds: some are offered by means of words alone, the others with song. And this is not a thing invented a little time ago, for it has existed since the first origin of the Church; this appears from the histories, and even Saint Paul speaks not only of praying by word of mouth, but also of singing.[3] And in truth we know by experience that song has great force and vigor to move and inflame the hearts of men to invoke and praise God with a more vehement and ardent zeal. It must always be looked to that the song be not light and frivolous but have weight and majesty, as Saint Augustine says,[4] and there is likewise a great difference between the music one makes to entertain men at table and in their homes, and the psalms which are sung in the Church in the presence of God and his angels.

Therefore, when anyone wishes to judge rightly of the form that is here presented, we hope that he will find it holy and pure, for it is entirely directed toward that edification of which we have spoken, however more widely the practice of singing may extend. For even in our homes and in the fields it should be an incentive, and as it were an organ for praising God and lifting up our hearts to him, to console us by meditating upon his virtue, goodness, wisdom, and justice, a thing more necessary than one can say. In the first place, it is not without reason that the Holy Spirit exhorts us so carefully by means of

1. 1 Corinthians 14:26.
2. 1 Corinthians 14:19.
3. 1 Corinthians 14:15.
4. *Epistola* 55.18.34.

the holy scripture to rejoice in God and that all our joy is there reduced to its true end, for he knows how much we are inclined to delight in vanity. Just as our nature, then, draws us and induces us to seek all means of foolish and vicious rejoicing, so, to the contrary, our Lord, to distract us and withdraw us from the enticements of the flesh and the world, presents to us all possible means in order to occupy us in that spiritual joy which he so much recommends to us.[5] Now among the other things proper to recreate man and give him pleasure, music is either the first or one of the principal, and we must think that it is a gift of God deputed to that purpose. For which reason we must be the more careful not to abuse it, for fear of soiling and contaminating it, converting it to our condemnation when it has been dedicated to our profit and welfare. Were there no other consideration than this alone, it might well move us to moderate the use of music to make it serve all that is of good repute and that it should not be the occasion of our giving free rein to dissoluteness or of our making ourselves effeminate with disordered pleasures and that it should not become the instrument of lasciviousness or of any shamelessness. But there is still more, for there is hardly anything in the world with more power to turn or bend, this way and that, the morals of men, as Plato has prudently considered.[6] And in fact we find by experience that it has a secret and almost incredible power to move our hearts in one way or another.

Wherefore we must be the more diligent in ruling it in such a manner that it may be useful to us and in no way pernicious. For this reason the early doctors of the Church often complain that the people of their times are addicted to dishonest and shameless songs, which not without reason they call mortal and Satanic poison for the corruption of the world. Now in speaking of music I understand two parts, namely, the letter, or subject and matter, and the song, or melody. It is true that, as Saint Paul says, every evil word corrupts good manners,[7] but when it has the melody with it, it pierces the heart much more strongly and enters within; as wine is poured into the cask with a funnel, so venom and corruption are distilled to the very depths of the heart by melody. Now what is there to do? It is to have songs not merely honest but also holy, which will be like spurs to incite us to pray to God and praise him, and to meditate upon his works in order to love, fear, honor, and glorify him. Now what Saint Augustine says is true—that no one can sing things worthy of God save what he has received from him.[8] Wherefore, although we look far and wide and search on every hand, we shall not find better songs nor songs better suited to that end than the Psalms of David which the Holy Spirit made and uttered through him. And for this reason, when we sing them we may be cer-

---

5. Here ends the preface in the first edition (1542). What follows is found only in the 1545 edition and in editions of the Psalter.
6. *Republic* 401d.
7. Ephesians 4:29.
8. *In Psalmum XXXIV enarratio* 1.1.

tain that God puts the words in our mouths as if himself sang in us to exalt his glory. Wherefore Chrysostom exhorts men as well as women and little children to accustom themselves to sing them, in order that this may be like a meditation to associate them with the company of angels.[9] Then we must remember what Saint Paul says—that spiritual songs cannot be well sung save with the heart.[10] Now the heart requires the intelligence, and therein, says Saint Augustine, lies the difference between the singing of men and of birds.[11] For a linnet, a nightingale, a parrot will sing well, but it will be without understanding. Now the peculiar gift of man is to sing knowing what he is saying. After the intelligence must follow the heart and the affection, which cannot be unless we have the hymn imprinted on our memory in order never to cease singing.

For these reasons the present book, even for this cause, besides the rest which has been said, should be in singular favor with everyone who desires to enjoy himself honestly and in God's way, that is, for his welfare and to the profit of his neighbors, and thus it has no need to be much recommended by me, seeing that it carries its value and its praise. But may the world be so well advised that instead of the songs that it has previously used, in part vain and frivolous, in part stupid and dull, in part foul and vile and consequently evil and harmful, it may accustom itself hereafter to sing these divine and celestial hymns with the good King David. Touching the melody, it has seemed best that it be moderated in the way that we have adopted in order that it may have the weight and majesty proper to the subject and may even be suitable for singing in church, according to what has been said.

Geneva, June 10, 1543.

9. *Exposition of Psalm XLI.*
10. Ephesians 5:19.
11. *In Psalmum XVIII enarratio 2.1.*

23 Claude Goudimel

Born at Besançon around 1515, the composer of chansons and sacred works Claude Goudimel was killed in 1572 in the St. Bartholomew's Day massacres at Lyon. His first compositions are found in the extensive collections of French chansons published in 1549 by Nicolas du Chemin in Paris. In 1557 and 1558 Goudimel published a Magnificat and four masses—his last music for the services of the Roman Church. In all, Goudimel published three distinct settings of the tunes in the Huguenot Psalters, one in contrapuntal style between 1551 and 1566 and two for four voices, simply harmonized, in 1564 and 1565.

The Geneva Psalter

(1565)

FOREWORD

To our readers:

To the melody of the psalms we have, in this little volume, adapted three parts, not to induce you to sing them in church, but that you may rejoice in God, particularly in your homes. This should not be found an ill thing, the more so since the melody used in church is left in its entirety, just as though it were alone.

TEXT: The facsimile of the original edition (Geneva, 1565) ed. Pierre Pidoux and Konrad Ameln (Kassel: Bärenreiter, 1935). Translation by Oliver Strunk.

24 Bernardino Cirillo

From humble beginnings in Aquila, where he was born in 1500, Bernardino Cirillo rose to become a prominent churchman in mid-sixteenth-century Rome. He was rector of Santa Casa of Loreto from 1535 to 1553, served as vicar of Fermo for the next two years, and reached Rome in late 1555 or early 1556. There he remained until his death in 1575, occupying various ecclesiastical posts and involving himself cautiously in the currents of reform swirling around the Roman Church in the years of the Council of Trent (1545–63). His surviving works include ecclesiastical and civil histories and many volumes of manuscript correspondence. Here, in a letter published during his lifetime, he attacks the expressive license he found in much church polyphony of his time from the somewhat incongruous perspective of ancient doctrines of modal ethos.

Letter to Ugolino Gualteruzzi[1]
(1549)

For many years my mind has been burdened with an idea that, for lack of ability to express it, has almost stopped the flow of my thoughts. Now I am determined to bear it no longer on my brain, and, as best I can, I propose to portray it for you in this letter with the aim and hope that you will read in it much more than I shall write to you, and that, thanks to your fine understanding, you will formulate my idea in your mind—for I cannot give a complete exposition of it, but can only sketch it out.

Now the subject is this—that music among the ancients was the most splendid of all the fine arts. With it they created powerful effects that we nowadays cannot produce either with rhetoric or with oratory in moving the passions and affections of the soul. With the power of song it was easy for them to drive a wise mind from the use of reason and bring it to a state of madness and willfulness. By this means it is said that the Lacedaemonians were incited to take up arms against the Cretans; that Timotheus was roused against Alexander; that a young man of Taormina was induced to set fire to the house in which his beloved was concealed; that in the sacrifices of Bacchus people were roused to frenzy; and similar effects.[2] And the mode or species that incited this state of mind was called Phrygian.

To this species there was opposed another, called Lydian, with which men could be easily withdrawn from the condition of frenzy and madness into which they had been plunged by the first kind of music.

The third was called Dorian, which attracted and moved the affections of the soul to gravity and modesty, and with so much strength and force that it was not only difficult, but almost impossible for anyone hearing it to bend his spirit toward a vicious or ignoble action. They say that Agamemnon, on going to the Trojan Wars, left a Dorian musician with his wife Clytemnestra, whose task it was, by means of his music, to charm her away from infidelity; and

TEXT: Aldo Manuzio, *Lettere volgari di diversi nobilissimi huomini . . . libro terzo* (Venice, 1564), pp. 114–18. Reprinted from Giovanni Pierluigi da Palestrina, *Pope Marcellus Mass,* A Norton Critical Score, ed. Lewis Lockwood (New York, 1975), by permission of W. W. Norton & Company, Inc. Translation by Lewis Lockwood.

1. In Cirillo's manuscript correspondence the recipient of the letter is identified instead as Cavaliere Ugolino Guastanezzo (see Pietro de Angelis, *Musica e musicisti nell'Arcispedale di Santo Spirito in Saxia* [Rome: Collana di studi storici in Saxia, 1950], p. 39).
2. For the Lacedaemonians (i.e., Spartans) and for Timotheus, see no. 2 above (Zarlino), p. 20, n. 27 and p. 21, no. 33. Cirillo has garbled the story of Timotheus, who was not roused against Alexander but instead with his music incited Alexander to take up arms; see no. 10 above (Castiglione), n. 2. For the Taorminian youth and Bacchic frenzies, Quintilian, *Institutio oratoria* 1.10.32.

Aegisthus could not corrupt her until he had the musician murdered.[3] This kind of music was always highly valued and esteemed.

Then we have the fourth species, called Mixolydian, by which anyone hearing it was immediately moved to tears, cries, and lamentation; this was used for sad and mournful occasions.

See, my Lord, what a splendid thing this is! By means of the power of song a slow and lazy man becomes lively and active; an angry man is calmed; a dissolute man becomes temperate; an afflicted man is consoled; a miserable man becomes happy; and thus music governs human affections and has the power to alter them as need be. Now, where has this led?

I see and hear the music of our time, which some say has been brought to a degree of refinement and perfection that never was nor could be known before. And yet I neither see nor hear any of the aforesaid ancient modes, and testimony to this is given by the movements of the soul that arise from it (perhaps you will say to me, "Shoemaker, stick to your last"). This much is clear—that the music of today is not the product of theory, but is merely an application of practice. *Kyrie eleison* means "Lord, have mercy upon us." The ancient musician would have expressed this affection of asking the Lord's pardon by using the Mixolydian mode, which would have evoked a feeling of contrition in the heart and soul. And if it had not moved the listener to tears, at least it would have swayed each hardened mind to piety. Thus he would have used similar modes in accordance with the words, and would have made a contrast between Kyrie and Agnus Dei, between Gloria and Credo, Sanctus and Pleni, psalm and motet. Nowadays they sing these things in any way at all, mixing them in an indifferent and uncertain manner. And then, you see what they invariably do. They say, "Oh, what a fine mass was sung in chapel!" And what is it, if you please? It is *L'homme armé*, or *Hercules Dux Ferrariae* or *Philomena*.[4] What the devil has the Mass to do with the armed man, or with Philomena, or with the duke of Ferrara? What numbers, what intervals, what sounds, what motions of the spirit, of devotion, or piety can be gathered from them, and how can music agree with such subjects as the armed man or the duke of Ferrara? Now, my dear Lord, read what little I have said and draw your own conclusions, for what I say of the music of the church I say of all other music as well. When I reflect upon ancient music in comparison with music of today, I see nothing of value but the pavane and the galliard, at the sound of which those good ladies of San Rocco and of Piazza Lombarda begin their movements, and it almost seems that they are listening to the Dionysiac dithyramb.

3. See no. 3 above (Ronsard), p. 23, n. 3.
4. Cirillo's complaint concerns polyphonic Mass cycles incorporating nonliturgical material, whether the famous *L'homme armé* melody, employed by Du Fay, Josquin, Palestrina, and many others, the solmization tune Josquin derived from the name and title of his supporter "Hercules Dux Ferrariae," or the polyphony of Jean Richafort's motet *Philomena praevia*. See Lockwood, ed., *Pope Marcellus Mass*, p. 12 n. 4.

I consider the painting and sculpture of Michelangelo Buonarroti to be a miracle of nature; but when he decided to depict the scene of *Posteriora mea videbis* [roughly: see my behind] on the ceiling of the Sistine Chapel to show his ability in painting—and also so many nude figures, which he made in order to show off his skill—he might have done much better to paint them in the loggia of some garden, where it would have been more appropriate.[5] The quartered cloak was suitable attire for Captain Todeschino of the lancers when he was jousting, but when worn by our friend it is abominable; and nevertheless the cloak by itself is admirable. "The shoes are excellent, but they do not fit Socrates."

I should like, in short, when a mass is to be sung in church, the music to be framed to the fundamental meaning of the words, in certain intervals and numbers apt to move our affections to religion and piety, and likewise in psalms, hymns, and other praises that are offered to the Lord. And in the pavane and galliard, if the numbers and cadences they have are not sufficient, then let others be added to them so that they may be made to dance up to the very walls of the houses. Each mode should be adapted to its subject, and when one has a lullaby to sing, or a plaintive song, one should do likewise. Thus the musicians of today should endeavor in their profession to do what the sculptors, painters, and architects of our time have done, who have recovered the art of the ancients; and the writers, who have reclaimed literature from the hell to which it was banished by corrupt ages; and as the sciences have been explained and given in their purity to our times. Thus the musicians should seek to recover the styles and modes, and the power of the Phrygian, Lydian, Dorian, and Mixolydian compositions, with which they would be able to do what they wish. I do not say that they should try to recover the enharmonic, diatonic, and chromatic genera, for these were dismissed by the ancients themselves;[6] but that they should approximate as much as possible the four above-mentioned modes, and that they should lend beauty and individuality to sacred music. In our times they have put all their industry and effort into the writing of imitative passages, so that while one voice says "Sanctus," another says "Sabaoth," still another says "Gloria tua," with howling, bellowing, and stammering, so that they seem at times like cats in January or bulls in May. I hope that you will bear with me.

Now to conclude, for it is time. Again, where has this led? You, my Lord, are in Rome (Who knows? Sometimes things are first thought, then they are uttered, and at last at times they are even done), where it is imagined that

5. On the criticism by Cirillo and others of the nudity in Michelangelo's frescoes for the Sistine Chapel, see John Shearman, *Mannerism* (London: Penguin, 1967), pp. 167–69 (cited in Lockwood, *Pope Marcellus Mass*, p. 13).

6. Perhaps Cirillo refers loosely to pseudo-Plutarch, *De musica* 1137e–f and 1143e–f, or to various passages in Ptolemy, *Harmonics* 1.13–16 (a less likely source than pseudo-Plutarch for Cirillo to have known); but neither of these works simply "dismisses" the genera.

there are men gifted with all wisdom. See if you can find there some good, genial, and willing musician who is accustomed to reasoned discourse, and discuss this letter a bit with him. Impress upon him the idea of what the ancients achieved, and that today no such effects are known, for today everything follows a single mold, always in the same way. Thus let us see if certain corrupt practices could be banished from the church, and if some music could be introduced that would move men to religion, piety, and devotion. And if they should say that they are only guided by plainsong, I would not be concerned (be it said with sincerity and reverence) if they should depart from that kind of music, in which one recognizes less of that power but can add a great deal more if only one would apply himself to recovering the ancient art. I believe so strongly in the ingenuity of our men of today that it seems to me that they can penetrate wherever they will. And if anyone should say to me, "Your idea is not new, it has been said before by others and attempted by musicians," I would reply that I observe the world to be dedicated to that which it does, and not what it ought to do, and I believe that musicians follow the same path.

•   •   •   •   •

If this discourse seems to you reasonable, say a word on its behalf to Signor Beccadelli.[7] He, who has labored so much over his *Cosmography* for the benefit of the public, may labor too on this matter, to see to it that the praises of the Lord are sung well and in a manner different from those of secular texts. For this is all that stirs me: let them make their motets, chansons, madrigals, and ballate in their own way, as long as our church bends its own efforts to move men to religion and piety.

•   •   •   •   •

From Loreto
February 16, 1549

---

7. Both possible recipients of Cirillo's letter (see n. 1 above) seem to have been in the employ of the cleric Lodovico Beccadelli; see de Angelis, *Musica e musicisti*, p. 37, and Lockwood, ed., *Pope Marcellus Mass*, p. 10.

25 Giovanni Pierluigi da Palestrina

Giovanni Pierluigi da Palestrina was born in 1525 or early 1526 at Palestrina, not far from Rome. He received his early musical training in Rome and, after leaving to serve for seven years (ca. 1544–51) as organist and choirmaster of San Agapito in Palestrina, returned and spent the remainder of his career there. In 1551 he was appointed *maestro* of the Cappella Giulia and in 1555 member of the Cappella Sistina. He was dismissed from that position some months later with a change of popes, because his married status violated the chapel's statutes. For the next sixteen years he occupied various positions, including chapelmaster at San Giovanni in Laterano and Santa Maria Maggiore. In 1571 he returned to the Cappella Giulia, where he remained until his death in 1594.

Palestrina's huge output includes over one hundred masses, close to four hundred motets, and many other works. Probably the most famous of all these works is the *Pope Marcellus Mass,* published in 1567 in his Second Book of Masses. Since the early nineteenth century, scholars have debated, with equivocal results, whether this work was written in order to convince a commission of cardinals associated with the Council of Trent of the propriety of polyphonic Mass settings; the story that Palestrina's work "saved" polyphony for the Roman Church reaches back much further, at least to 1607. What seems undeniable is that the *Pope Marcellus Mass* reflects, in its emphasis on chordal texture and the resulting increase in the intelligibility of the words, the "new manner" of setting the Mass that Palestrina mentions in his dedication of the Second Book. In this it comes close to at least one of the ideals for church polyphony advocated by Bernardino Cirillo (see no. 24 above, p. 93).

Second Book of Masses
(1567)

DEDICATION

To Philip of Austria, Catholic and Invincible King:

Since the utility and pleasure afforded by the art of music is a gift of heaven greater than all human teachings, and since it is particularly valued and approved by the ancient and authoritative writings of holy scripture, so it

TEXT: *Joannis Petri Aloysi Praenestini Missarum liber secundus,* Rome, 1567. Reprinted from Giovanni Pierluigi da Palestrina, *Pope Marcellus Mass,* A Norton Critical Score, ed. Lewis Lockwood (New York, 1975), by permission of W. W. Norton & Company, Inc. Translation by Lewis Lockwood.

appears that this art can be properly exercised upon holy and divine subjects. I, therefore, who have been engaged in this art for many years, not wholly unsuccessfully (if I may rely on the judgment of others more than on my own), have considered it my task, in accordance with the views of most serious and most religious-minded men, to bend all my knowledge, effort, and industry toward that which is the holiest and most divine of all things in the Christian religion—that is, to adorn the holy sacrifice of the Mass in a new manner. I have, therefore, worked out these masses with the greatest possible care, to do honor to the worship of almighty God, to which this gift, as small as it may be, is offered and accommodated. And these products of my spirit—not the first, but, as I hope, the more successful—I decided to dedicate to your Majesty, who have taken your own name from the tradition of the Catholic faith, and who also guard the purity of the orthodox religion most ardently, and who honor and adorn the sacred services through the works and ministrations of most excellent musicians. Accept, then, most mighty and God-fearing king, these my labors as testimony of my perpetual loyalty toward your Majesty— and accept them with that kingly greatness of spirit with which you are wont to receive such gifts. If these labors should please you, then I would consider it their greatest success if they should satisfy your judgment. If they should not please you, then nonetheless my loyal affection will not waver toward the magnanimous and noble king whom may God, the bestower of kingdoms and giver of all good things, keep for Christendom in health and well-being as long as may be possible, and grant all good wishes of honorable men. Farewell, ornament and bulwark of all who bear the name of Christians.

Giovanni Petroaloysio Palestrina

26 Pope Gregory XIII

The brief of Gregory XIII, entrusting Palestrina and his colleague Annibale Zoilo with the revision of the music of the Roman Gradual and Antiphoner, was a natural outgrowth of the publication, in 1568 and 1570, of the reformed Breviary and Missal ordered by the Council of Trent and approved by Gregory's predecessor, Paul V. The aim of this proposed revision was twofold. On the one hand, it was to bring the choir books into agreement with the liturgical revisions already made official. On the other, it was to rid the plainsong melodies of what were deemed to be superabundant melismas, incorrect Latin accentuation, awkward melodic intervals, etc. (the "barbarisms, obscurities, contrarieties, and superfluities" Gregory alludes to). During the year 1578, as his correspondence shows, Palestrina was deeply preoccupied with this work of revision; later on, however, he seems to have set it aside, never to take it up again. In 1611, some years after his death, other hands were charged with the responsibility, and although it seems clear that the so-called Editio Medicaea, published in 1614, is not very different from the revised version that Palestrina must have had in mind, it is unlikely that it includes any work of his.

Pope from 1572 to 1585, Gregory XIII (Ugo Buoncompagno) inaugurated important changes in the musical arrangements at St. Peter's. His revision of the calendar once made his name a household word. To him Palestrina dedicated his Fourth Book of Masses (1582) and his motets on the Song of Solomon (Book V, 1584).

Brief on the Reform of the Chant
(1577)

TO PALESTRINA AND ZOILO

Beloved sons:

Greetings and apostolic benediction!

Inasmuch as it has come to our attention that the Antiphoners, Graduals, and Psalters that have been provided with music for the celebration of the divine praises and offices in plainsong (as it is called) since the publication of the Breviary and Missal ordered by the Council of Trent have been filled to overflowing with barbarisms, obscurities, contrarieties, and superfluities as a result of the clumsiness or negligence or even wickedness of the composers, scribes, and printers:[1] in order that these books may agree with the aforesaid Breviary and Missal, as is appropriate and fitting, and may at the same time be so ordered, their superfluities having been shorn away and their barbarisms and obscurities removed, that through their agency God's name may be reverently, distinctly, and devoutly praised; desiring to provide for this in so far as with God's help we may, we have decided to turn to you, whose skill in the art of music and in singing, whose faithfulness and diligence, and whose piety toward God have been fully tested, and to assign to you this all-important task, trusting confidently that you will amply satisfy this desire of ours. And thus we charge you with the business of revising and (so far as shall seem expedient to you) of purging, correcting, and reforming these Antiphoners, Graduals, and Psalters, together with such other chants as are used in our churches according to the rite of Holy Roman Church, whether at the Canonical Hours or at Mass or at other divine services, and over all of these things we entrust you for the present with full and unrestricted jurisdiction and power by virtue of our apostolic authority, and in order that you may pursue the aforesaid more quickly and diligently you have our permission to admit other skilled musicians as assis-

---

TEXT: Raphael Molitor, *Die nach-Tridentinische Choral-Reform zu Rom* (Leipzig: F. E. C. Leuckart, 1901–2), vol. 1, pp. 297–98. Translation by Oliver Strunk.

1. For Zarlino's view of barbarous misaccentuation in plainchant see no. 36 below, pp. 181–82.

tants if you so desire. The Apostolic Constitutions and any other regulations that may be to the contrary notwithstanding. Given at St. Peter's in Rome under Peter's seal this twenty-fifth day of October, 1577, in the sixth year of our pontificate.

To our beloved sons Giovanni Pierluigi da Palestrina and Annibale Zoilo Romano, musicians of our private chapel.

27 Thomas East

An important typographer and publisher, Thomas East (also Easte, Este) is remembered as the printer of much Elizabethan and Jacobean music. Starting with William Byrd's *Psalmes, Sonets, & Songs of Sadnes and Pietie* of 1588 (see no. 4 above, pp. 25–26), he printed a long series of works by Byrd, Nicholas Yonge, Thomas Watson, Thomas Morley, George Kirbye, John Wilbye, John Dowland, Robert Jones, and other composers. And he published three of the most famous Elizabethan music anthologies: the two volumes of *Musica transalpina* (1588 and 1597) and *The Triumphes of Oriana* (1601).

In 1592, East collected tunes for the English metrical Psalter, engaged a number of composers to harmonize them in four parts (including Kirbye, Dowland, John Farmer, and Giles Farnaby), and published the result as *The Whole Booke of Psalmes: with their Wonted Tunes, as they are song in Churches.* Unlike earlier English collections of harmonized psalms, East's book includes the full texts of the complete Psalter and presents the four musical lines of each setting on a single page opening instead of in separate partbooks. East's *Whole Booke* saw four editions, the last of them in 1611.

The Whole Booke of Psalmes
(1592)

DEDICATION

To the Right Honorable Sir John Puckering, Knight, Lord Keeper of the Great Seal of England:

The word of God, Right Honorable, delighteth those which are spiritually minded; the art of music recreateth such as are not sensually affected; where

Text: The original edition (London, 1592). A reprint, ed. E. F. Rimbault, was published in 1844 as vol. 11 of the series brought out by the Musical Antiquarian Society.

zeal in the one and skill in the other do meet, the whole man is revived. The mercies of God are great provoking unto thankfulness; the necessities of man are great, enforcing unto prayer; the state of us all is such that the publishing of God's glory for the edifying one of another cannot be overslipped; in all these the heart must be the workmaster, the tongue the instrument, and a sanctified knowledge as the hand to polish the work. The Psalms of David are a paraphrasis of the Scriptures; they teach us thankfulness, prayer, and all the duties of a Christian whatsoever; they have such comfort in them that such as will be conversant in the same cannot possibly lose their labor. Blessed is that man which delighteth therein and meditateth in the same continually. He that is heavy hath the Psalms to help his prayer; he that is merry hath the Psalms to guide his affections; and he that hath a desire to be seriously employed in either of these duties hath this excellent gift of God, the knowledge of music, offered him for his further help; that the heart rejoicing in the word and the ears delighting in the notes and tunes, both these might join together unto the praise of God. Some have pleased themselves with pastorals, others with madrigals, but such as are endued with David's heart desire with David to sing unto God psalms and hymns and spiritual songs. For whose sake I have set forth this work that they busy themselves in the psalms of this holy man, being by men of skill put into four parts that each man may sing that part which best may serve his voice.

In this book the church tunes are carefully corrected and other short tunes added which are sung in London and other places of this realm. And regarding chiefly to help the simple, curiosity is shunned. The profit is theirs that will use this book; the pains theirs that have compiled it; the charges his who, setting it forth, respecteth a public benefit, not his private gain. Now having finished it, in most humble manner I present it unto Your Honor as to a maintainer of godliness, a friend to virtue, and a lover of music, hoping of Your Lordship's favorable acceptance, craving your honorable patronage and countenance, and praying unto God long to continue Your Lordship a protector of the just and the same God to be a protector of Your Lordship's welfare forever.

Your good Lordship's most humbly at command
Thomas East.

PREFACE

Although I might have used the skill of some one learned musician in the setting of these psalms in four parts, yet for variety's sake I have entreated the help of many, being such as I know to be expert in the art and sufficient to answer such curious carping musicians whose skill hath not been employed to the furthering of this work.[1] And I have not only set down in this book all the

---

1. East's contributors were John Farmer, George Kirbye, Richard Allison, Giles Farnaby, Edward Blancks, John Dowland, William Cobbold, Edmund Hooper, Edward Johnson, and Michael Cavendish.

tunes usually printed heretofore with as much truth as I could possibly gather among divers of our ordinary psalm books, but also have added those which are commonly sung nowadays and not printed in our common psalm books with the rest. And all this have I so orderly cast that the four parts lie always together in open sight. The which my travail, as it hath been to the furtherance of music in all Godly sort and to the comfort of all good Christians, so I pray thee to take it in good part and use it to the glory of God.

 T. E.

28 William Byrd

Gradualia
(1605–7)

DEDICATIONS AND FOREWORD

To that Most Illustrious and Distinguished Man, and his
Right Honorable Lord, Henry Howard, Earl of North-
ampton, Warden of the Cinque Ports, and one of
the Privy Council of His Most Serene Majesty, James, King of Great Britain

 The swan, they say, when his death is near, sings more sweetly. However little I may be able to attain to the sweetness of that bird in these songs which I have judged should be dedicated to you, most illustrious Henry, I have had two defences or incentives of no common rate for emulating that sweetness in some sort at least. The one was the sweetness of the words themselves, the other your worthiness. For even as among artisans it is shameful in a craftsman to make a rude piece of work from some precious material, so indeed to sacred words in which the praises of God and of the Heavenly host are sung, none but some celestial harmony (so far as our powers avail) will be proper. Moreover in these words, as I have learned by trial, there is such a concealed and hidden power that to one thinking upon things divine and diligently and earnestly pondering them, all the fittest numbers occur as if of themselves and freely offer themselves to the mind which is not indolent or inert. Truly your worthi-

TEXT: *Tudor Church Music* 7 (Oxford: Oxford University Press, 1927), facs. before pp. 3 and 209. Translation by Oliver Strunk.

ness is as great as that of your most ancient family, which, long beaten by bitter storms and stricken, as it were, by the frost of adverse fortune, now in part flourishes again in your own person, and in part, encouraged by the King's Most Serene Majesty, sends out, by your labor and merits, rays of its ancient splendor to the eager eyes of all Englishmen. Since you are also of the King's Privy Council, you always suggest, always further, those things which tend to the greater glory of God, to the greatness of this entire realm, now happily united under one sovereign, James, and most particularly to the honorable tranquillity and peace of all honest private men. In these things the praise due to you is the greater for that in their accomplishment you direct and aim all your efforts, not at popular favor, which you deem vain, nor at the desire of gain, which you consider base, but to the honor only of God, who sees in dark places. And these matters are indeed public, and truly honorable, such as not merely by any songs of mine, but by the mouth and pen of all, will be transmitted to our posterity and to foreign nations, among whom your name is renowned.

But private reasons also impelled me to use my utmost industry in this matter. I have had and still have you, if I err not, as a most benevolent patron in the distressed affairs of my family. You have often listened with pleasure to my melodies, which from men like yourself is a reward to musicians and, so to speak, their highest honorarium. At your plea and request, the Most Serene King has augmented me and my fellows who serve His Majesty's person in music with new benefits and with increases of stipend. For this reason I have resolved that this work of mine (if by chance it shall be of such desert) shall stand as an everlasting testimony of the gratitude of all our hearts to His Majesty and to yourself, distinguished patron, and of my affectionate wishes for those eminent men, whom I love and honor as I perform this office for them. You see, Right Honorable Earl, with what defenders I am provided and by what incentives I am prompted in wishing (if only I could) to imitate the swan.

With truly excellent judgment Alexander forbade any but Apelles or Lysippus to paint him or to sculpture him in bronze.[1] Nor has it been in any way granted to me to satisfy my task, save only that I have tried to ornament things divine with the highest art at my command and to offer nothing not wrought with care to so distinguished a man as yourself. If I have accomplished this, I shall declare these lucubrations of mine (for so without falsehood I may call the products of nightly toil) my swan songs. This they will surely be, if not for their sweetness, at least as proceeding from such age. While I indeed decided at the request of friends to work upon them and to spread them abroad, it was you alone that I set before me in my mind as shining above me like a star guiding me on a course beset with rocks. If in your judgment I have brought back wares not wholly without use, it will be the unique consolation of my old

---

1. The story is told in a number of ancient biographies of Alexander and in Pliny, *Natural History* 7.37.125 (Byrd's most likely source).

age to have brought into the light a work not unmeet for our Most Serene King, whose honor I have wished to augment in my epistle, nor for you, most generous Lord, skilled in the knowledge of human and divine letters, nor unworthy of my years, which I have all consumed in music. Farewell.

To your most Worshipful Honor,
William Byrd.

•   •   •

The Author
To the True Lovers of Music

For you, most high-minded and righteous, who delight at times to sing to God in hymns and spiritual songs, are here set forth for your exercising the Offices for the whole year which are proper to the chief Feasts of the Blessed Virgin Mary and of All Saints; moreover others in five voices with their words drawn from the fountain of Holy Writ; also the Office at the Feast of Corpus Christi, with the more customary antiphons of the same Blessed Virgin and other songs in four voices of the same kind; also all the hymns composed in honor of the Virgin; finally, various songs in three voices sung at the Feast of Easter. Further, to the end that they may be ordered each in its own place in the various parts of the service, I have added a special index at the end of the book; here all that are proper to the same feasts may easily be found grouped together, though differing in the number of voices.

If to these pious words I have set notes not unfitting (as I have wished and as they require), may the honor, as is just, be to God and the pleasure be yours. Howsoever this may be, give them fair and friendly judgment, and commend me to God in your prayers. Farewell.

To the Right Illustrious and Honorable
John Lord Petre of Writtle, his
most clement Maecenas,
Salutation

Since I have attained to such length of years, relying upon the divine mercy, that I have seen many of my pupils in music, men indeed peculiarly skillful in that art, finish their allotted time while I survived, and since also in my own house I consider that the benefits of the divine bounty have been directed toward me, indeed have been showered upon me, my mind is eager, remembering my faith, duty, and piety to God, to leave to posterity a public testimony, at least in some sort, of a heart grateful and referring all things, if this be counted a merit, to my Creator. Having attained to this age, I have attempted, out of devotion to the divine worship, myself unworthy and unequal, to affix notes, to serve as a garland, to certain pious and honeyed praises of the Christian rite to be sung by four, five, or six voices. These are adapted to the glorious

Nativity of Christ our Savior, the Epiphany, the Resurrection, and finally to the Feast of Saints Peter and Paul.

These songs, most Christian Sir, long since completed by me and committed to the press, should in my judgment be dedicated to you above all others, for you are held renowned for the harmony of virtues and letters and distinguished by your love for all the daughters of the Muses and of science. Inasmuch as these musical lucubrations, like fruits sprung from a fertile soil, have mostly proceeded from your house (truly most friendly to me and mine), and from that tempering of the sky have brought forth more grateful and abundant fruits, receive, then, Right Honorable Lord, these little flowers, plucked as it were from your gardens and most rightfully due to you as tithes, and may it be no burden to you to protect these my last labors, to the end that they may go forth to the public under the auspices of your most renowned name, to the glory of God the Greatest and Best, to the greatness of your honor, and finally for the pleasure of all who properly cultivate the Muses. Meanwhile I pray from my soul that all present things may be of good omen to you and all future things happy. Farewell.

The third day of April in the year of man's salvation restored 1607.

Your Honor's most dutiful
William Byrde.

IV

MUSIC, MAGIC, GNOSIS

29 Marsilio Ficino

Marsilio Ficino (1433–99), physician, musician, magician, scholar, translator, Neoplatonic philosopher, and semi-official cultural leader in Florence through much of the late fifteenth century, is a figure also of broader and enduring cultural resonance. His central life's work consisted in translating into Latin and interpreting a huge body of ancient Greek writings previously inaccessible to western Europeans. He provided the first complete Latin version of the Platonic corpus and the first translations of many Neoplatonists of Late Antiquity: Plotinus, Porphyry, Proclus, Iamblichus, the so-called Hermes Trismegistus, and others. To these translations Ficino appended more or less extensive interpretive glosses. *De amore* (1468–1469), his lengthy commentary on Plato's *Symposium,* singlehandedly set the course of a large sixteenth-century literature on the psychology of love and stands behind both Pietro Bembo's and Baldassare Castiglione's conceptions of the subject. Ficino's translations and commentaries served as the bases for study and further translation for centuries after his death, and some of them continued to be republished well into the 1800s.

Three Books on Life (De vita libri tres) was first printed in 1489 and reappeared in almost thirty editions and translations over the next century and a half. It is in essence a work of therapeutic magic. Its third and largest book, titled *De vita coelitus comparanda (On Obtaining Life from the Heavens),* started as a commentary on passages in Plotinus's *Enneads* and turns the medico-magical practices of the first two books in an astrological direction. Here in Chapter 21 Ficino discusses subjects always close to his heart: the heavenly sources of the powers of song, music's intimate relation to the human spirit (for Ficino a subtle intermediary between body and soul), and the ways to perform astrologically effective song.

FROM *Three Books on Life*

(1489)

BOOK 3

CHAPTER 21: ON THE POWER OF WORDS AND SONGS FOR CAPTURING CELESTIAL BENEFITS AND ON THE SEVEN STEPS THAT LEAD TO CELESTIAL THINGS

• • • • •

That a specific and great power exists in specific words is the claim of Origen in *Contra Celsum,* of Synesius and Al-Kindi where they argue about magic,

TEXT: *Marsilio Ficino: Three Books on Life,* ed. Carol V. Kaske and John R. Clark, Medieval & Renaissance Texts & Studies, vol. 57 (Binghamton, N.Y., 1989), pp. 354–63. Copyright by the Center for Medieval and Early Renaissance Studies, SUNY Binghamton. Translation by Carol V. Kaske. I have adapted and sometimes shortened Kaske's annotations.

and likewise of Zoroaster where he forbids the alteration of barbarian words, and also of Iamblichus in the course of the same argument.[1] The Pythagoreans also make this claim, who used to perform wonders by words, songs, and sounds in the Phoebean and Orphic manner.[2] The Hebrew doctors of old practiced this more than anyone else; and all poets sing of the wondrous things that are brought about by songs[3] And even the famous and venerable Cato in his *De re rustica* sometimes uses barbarous incantations to cure the diseases of his farm animals.[4] But it is better to skip incantations. Nevertheless, that singing through which the young David used to relieve Saul's insanity—unless the sacred text demands that it be attributed to divine agency—one might attribute to nature.[5]

Now since the planets are seven in number, there are also seven steps through which something from on high can be attracted to the lower things. Sounds occupy the middle position and are dedicated to Apollo. Harder materials, stones and metals, hold the lowest rank and thus seem to resemble the Moon. Second in ascending order are things composed of plants, fruits of trees, their gums, and the members of animals, and all these correspond to Mercury—if we follow in the heavens the order of the Chaldeans.[6] Third are very fine powders and their vapors selected from among the materials I have already mentioned and the odors of plants and flowers used as simples, and of ointments; they pertain to Venus. Fourth are words, song, and sounds, all of which are rightly dedicated to Apollo whose greatest invention is music. Fifth are the strong concepts of the imagination—forms, motions, passions—which suggest the force of Mars. Sixth are the sequential arguments and deliberations of the human reason which pertain designedly to Jupiter. Seventh are the more remote and simple operations of the understanding, almost now disjoined from motion and conjoined to the divine; they are meant for Saturn, whom deservedly the Hebrews call "Sabbath" from the word for "rest."

Why all of this? To teach you that even as a certain compound of plants and

---

1. Origen, *Contra Celsum* 1.25; also 5.45 and 8.37; Synesius *De insomniis* 132c (section 3 in Ficino's translation; see the facsimile of the Basle, 1576 *Opera omnia*, ed. M. Sancipriano and Paul Oskar Kristeller [4 vols., Turin: Bottega d'Erasmo, 1959], p. 1969); Al-Kindi, *De radiis*, ed. M.-T. d'Alverny and F. Hudry in *Archives d'histoire doctrinale et littéraire du moyen âge* 41 (1974), chap. 6; Zoroaster, fragment no. 150 of *Oracles chaldaïques*, ed. Édouard des Places (Paris: Société d'edition "Les Belles Lettres," 1971), p. 103; Iamblichus, *De mysteriis* 7.4–5 (see Ficino, *Opera Omnia*, p. 1902). [Tr.]
2. See Iamblichus, *De vita pythagorica* 15.64–67 and 25.110–14, and Philostratus, *Vita Apollonii* 3.15. [Tr.]
3. For example, Virgil, *Aeneid* 4.487–91; Horace, *Epodes* 5.45–46. [Tr.]
4. Cato, *De agricultura* 160. [Tr.]
5. 1 Samuel 16:14–23. [Tr.] See also no. 2 above (Zarlino), p. 20.
6. For a diagram of Ficino's geocentric "Chaldaean" ordering of the heavens, also sometimes called "Ptolemaic," see the woodcut in no. 30 below (Gafori), p. 116. Note that throughout this chapter (and elsewhere) Ficino uses Apollo and Phoebus as synonyms for the middle "planet" in this order, the sun.

vapors made through both medical and astronomical science yields a common form of a medicine, like a harmony endowed with gifts from the stars; so tones first chosen by the rule of the stars and then combined according to the congruity of these stars with each other make a sort of common form, and in it a celestial power arises. It is indeed very difficult to judge exactly what kinds of tones are suitable for what sorts of stars, what combinations of tones especially accord with what sorts of constellations and aspects. But we can attain this, partly through our own efforts, partly by some divine destiny. . . .

We will apply three principal rules for this undertaking, provided you be warned beforehand not to think we are speaking here of worshipping the stars, but rather of imitating them and thereby trying to capture them. And do not believe that we are dealing with gifts which the stars are going to give by their own election but rather by a natural influence. We strive to adapt ourselves to this multifarious and occult influence by the same studied methods we use every day to make ourselves fit to receive in a healthy manner the perceivable light and heat of the Sun. But it is the wise man alone who adapts himself to the occult and wonderful gifts of this influence. Now, however, let us go on to the rules that are going to accommodate our songs to the stars. The first is to inquire diligently what powers in itself or what effects from itself a given star, constellation, or aspect has—what do they remove, what do they bring?—and to insert these into the meaning of our words, so as to detest what they remove and to approve what they bring. The second rule is to take note of what special star rules what place or person and then to observe what sorts of tones and songs these regions and persons generally use, so that you may supply similar ones, together with the meanings I have just mentioned, to the words which you are trying to expose to the same stars. Thirdly, observe the daily positions and aspects of the stars and discover to what principal speeches, songs, motions, dances, moral behavior, and actions most people are usually incited by these, so that you may imitate such things as far as possible in your song, which aims to please the particular part of heaven that resembles them and to catch an influence that resembles them.

But remember that song is a most powerful imitator of all things. It imitates the intentions and passions of the soul as well as words; it represents also people's physical gestures, motions, and actions as well as their characters and imitates all these and acts them out so forcibly that it immediately provokes both the singer and the audience to imitate and act out the same things. By the same power, when it imitates the celestials, it also wonderfully arouses our spirit upwards to the celestial influence and the celestial influence downwards to our spirit. Now the very matter of song, indeed, is altogether purer and more similar to the heavens than is the matter of medicine. For this too is air, hot or warm, still breathing and somehow living; like an animal, it is composed of certain parts and limbs of its own and not only possesses motion and displays passion but even carries meaning like a mind, so that it can be said to be a kind of airy and rational animal. Song, therefore, which is full of spirit and meaning—if it corresponds to this or that constellation not only in the things it signifies, its parts, and the form that results from those parts, but also in the disposition of the imagination—has as much power as does any other combination of things and casts it into the singer and from him into the nearby listener. It has this power as long as it keeps the vigor and the spirit of the singer, especially if the singer himself be Phoebean by nature and have in his heart a powerful vital and animal spirit. For just as the natural power and spirit, when it is strongest, not only immediately softens and dissolves the hardest food and soon renders harsh food sweet but also generates offspring outside of itself by the emission of the seminal spirit, so the vital and animal power, when it is most efficacious, not only acts powerfully on its own body when its spirit undergoes a very intense conception and agitation through song but soon also moves a neighboring body by emanation. This power influences both its own and the other body by a certain stellar property which it drew both from its own form and from the election of a suitable astrological hour. For this reason in particular many dwellers in the East and South, especially Indians, are said to have an admirable power in their words, as these peoples are for the most part Solar. I say that they are the most powerful of all, not in their natural, but in their vital and animal forces; and the same goes for all persons in other areas who are especially Phoebean.

Now song which arises from this power, timeliness, and intention is undoubtedly nothing else but another spirit recently conceived in you in the power of your spirit—a spirit made Solar and acting both in you and in the bystander by the power of the Sun. For if a certain vapor and spirit directed outwards through the rays of the eyes or by other means can sometimes fascinate, infect, or otherwise influence a bystander, much more can a spirit do this, when it pours out from both the imagination and heart at the same time, more abundant, more fervent, and more apt to motion. Hence it is no wonder at all that by means of song certain diseases, both mental and physical, can sometimes be cured or brought on, especially since a musical spirit of this kind properly touches and acts on the spirit which is the mean between body and soul, and immediately affects both the one and the other with its influence. You will allow that there is a wondrous power in an aroused and singing spirit, if you allow to the Pythagoreans and Platonists that the heavens are a spirit and that they order all things through their motions and tones.

Remember that all music proceeds from Apollo; that Jupiter is musical to the extent that he is consonant with Apollo; and that Venus and Mercury claim music by their proximity to Apollo. Likewise remember that song pertains to only those four; the other three planets have voices but not songs. Now we attribute to Saturn voices that are slow, deep, harsh, and plaintive; to Mars, voices that are the opposite—quick, sharp, fierce, and menacing; the Moon has the voices in between. The music, however, of Jupiter is deep, earnest, sweet, and joyful with stability. To Venus, on the contrary, we ascribe songs voluptuous with wantonness and softness. The songs between these two extremes we ascribe to the Sun and Mercury: if with their grace and smoothness they are reverential, simple, and earnest, the songs are judged to be Apollo's; if they are somewhat more relaxed, along with their gaiety, but vigorous and complex, they are Mercury's. Accordingly, you will win over one of these four to yourself by using their songs, especially if you supply musical notes that fit their songs. When at the right astrological hour you declaim aloud by singing and playing in the manners we have specified for the four gods, they seem to be just about to answer you like an echo or like a string in a lute trembling to the vibration of another which has been similarly tuned. And this will happen to you from heaven as naturally, say Plotinus and Iamblichus,[7] as a tremor re-echoes from a lute or an echo arises from an opposite wall. Assuredly, whenever your spirit—by frequent use of Jovial, Mercurial, or Venereal harmony, a harmony performed while these planets are dignified—singing at the same time most intently and conforming itself to the harmony, becomes Jovial, Mercurial, or Venereal, it will meanwhile become Phoebean as well, since the power of Phoebus himself, the ruler of music, flourishes in every consonance. And conversely when you become Phoebean from Phoebean song and notes, you at the same time lay claim to the power of Jupiter, Venus, and Mercury. And again, from your spirit influenced within, you have a similar influence on your soul and body.

Remember, moreover, that a prayer, when it has been suitably and seasonably composed and is full of emotion and forceful, has a power similar to a song. There is no use in reporting what great power Damis and Philostratus tell us certain Indian priests have in their prayers, nor in mentioning the words they say that Apollonius employed to call up the shade of Achilles.[8] For we are not now speaking of worshipping divinities but of a natural power in speech, song, and words. That there is indeed in certain sounds a Phoebean and medical power is clear from the fact that in Puglia everyone who is stung by the phalangium[9] becomes stunned and lies half-dead until each hears a certain sound proper to him. For then he dances along with the sound, works up a sweat, and gets well. And if ten years later he hears a similar sound, he feels a sudden urge to dance. I gather from the evidence that this sound is Solar and Jovial.

7. Plotinus, *Enneads* 4.3.12, 4.4.41; Iamblichus, *De mysteriis* 3.9 (see Ficino, *Opera omnia,* p. 1885). [Tr.] The sympathetic vibration of similarly tuned lute strings was a favorite Renaissance example of the wondrous (or magical) powers of music. For another mention of it see no. 18 above (Peacham), p. 73.
8. Philostratus, *Vita Apollonii* 4.16. [Tr.]
9. That is, the southern Italian wolf spider, commonly referred to as a tarantula. For other references to this musical tarantism see no. 2 (Zarlino), p. 20, and no. 18 (Peacham), p. 70.

30 Franchino Gafori

The music theorist and composer Franchino Gafori was born at Lodi in 1451. During an early stay at Naples, he befriended Tinctoris. After returning to Lodi, where he taught from 1480 to 1484, he was appointed chapelmaster of the Milan Cathedral. He remained in Milan for the rest of his life and died there in 1522.

At Milan in the 1490s, Gafori completed his three most important treatises. The *Theorica musicae* was published in 1492 and the *Practica musicae* in 1496; *De harmonia musicorum instrumentorum opus (A Work on the Harmony of Musical Instruments)*, drafted by 1500, circulated in manuscript until its publication in 1518. All three treatises reveal Gafori's extensive knowledge of earlier music theorists, ancient and modern, and *De harmonia* in particular exploits Latin translations of Aristides Quintilianus and Ptolemy that Gafori himself commissioned. From these and other sources, and under the sway of Ficinian Platonism and Neoplatonism, Gafori indulged a tendency to speculate on musical cosmology stronger than that of most other Renaissance music theorists.

In Book 4, Chapter 12 of *De harmonia,* Gafori elaborates on correspondences between the modes and the planets advanced in the *Musica practica* of Bartolomé Ramis de Pareia (1.3). The author of the couplets here relating the Muses, modes, and planets is unknown; these verses reappeared some years later, no doubt culled from Gafori, in the magic treatise *De occulta philosophia* by Henry Cornelius Agrippa, the arch-magus of the Renaissance (for Agrippa see no. 5 above, pp. 26–30). The famous woodcut representing these correspondences first appeared, incongruously, as the frontispiece of *Practica musicae*. Perhaps it was prepared for a planned contemporaneous publication of *De harmonia* that was subsequently postponed.

FROM *De harmonia musicorum instrumentorum opus*

(1518)

BOOK FOUR

CHAPTER 12: THAT THE MUSES, STARS, MODES, AND STRINGS CORRESPOND TO ONE ANOTHER

There are those who believe that the Muses follow the order of the stars and the modes. Some count only three Muses, daughters of heaven and earth, while others have listed nine born of Jupiter and Mnemosyne. These nine Ovid calls

TEXT: facsimile of the edition of Milan, 1518 (New York: Broude Brothers, 1979), fols. 92–94. Translation by Gary Tomlinson. Gafori's postils add no new information to his account; I have omitted them.

the Mnemonides in Book 5 of the *Metamorphoses*, writing: "He said: 'O daughters of Mnemosyne'—for he knew us—'stay your steps.' "[1] And Diodorus Siculus in Book 5 famously interpreted them, almost describing the parts of the musical art associated with each one.[2] Homer also granted them extraordinary renown.[3] St. Augustine, moreover, named nine Muses in Book 2 of *De doctrina christiana*. He denied that they were daughters of Jupiter and Mnemosyne, accepting instead Varro's idea that three craftsmen made three statues each for the Temple of Apollo, which were then given names by Hesiod in his *Theogony*.[4] Just in this manner the ancients wished to give the Muses names to teach men good and useful things not known to the unlearned.

Some imagine the Muses to have sprung from Apollo's head, as this line from the poet expresses: "The power of Apollo's mind arouses Muses everywhere."[5] Others say they were taught by Apollo, on account of which they call Apollo himself a musician, as I described at length in Book 1 of my *Theorica musicae*.[6] Most agree that Apollo was depicted with a ten-stringed lyre, while others think it had seven, corresponding to the seven fundamental strings Virgil recounts with these lines from Book 6 of the *Aeneid*:

> There, too, the long-robed Thracian priest
> matches their measures with the seven clear notes.[7]

Moreover seven intervals come from these strings: the major third, minor third, fourth, fifth, major sixth, minor sixth, and octave. And the number seven is structured according to a certain perfection, since it is understood to make twenty-eight by the sum of itself and its individual parts, and twenty-eight is the only number between 10 and 100 that is the sum of its own aliquot parts.[8] They say that the Muse Clio invented history, Melpomene tragedy, Thalia comedy, Euterpe the music of pipes, Terpsichore the music of the psaltery, Erato geometry, Calliope writing, Urania astronomy, and Polyhymnia rhetoric. . . .

Callimichus, a poet of no mean authority among the Greeks, proclaimed the gifts of the Muses in this epigram:

> Calliope invented the wisdom of heroic song,
> Clio the sweet song of lovely dance and lyre,
> Euterpe the resounding voice of tragic chorus;

1. 5.280; trans. Frank Justus Miller, Ovid, *Metamorphoses* (2 vols., London: Heinemann, 1916), vol. 1, p. 257.
2. Gafori's reference to Book 5 is mistaken; see Diodorus Siculus, *Library of History* 4.7.2–4.
3. For example, *Iliad* 1.601–4, 11.218; *Odyssey* 8.487–88, 24.60–62.
4. See *De doctrina christiana* 2.17.27.
5. *Mentis Apollineae vis has movet undique musas*. The verse was thought in the Renaissance to be by Virgil, "the poet" Gafori refers to; it is now associated with Ausonius. See Edgar Wind, *Pagan Mysteries in the Renaissance* (New York: Norton, 1968), pp. 267–68.
6. See chap. 1, fol. aiir.
7. Ll. 645–46. Trans. H. Rushton Fairclough, *Virgil in Two Volumes* (London: Heinemann, 1922), vol. 1, p. 551. The priest of Thrace is, of course, Orpheus.
8. That is, 7 is numerologically significant because $7+6+5+4+3+2+1=28$; 28 in turn is important for numerologists because the sum of its factors (excluding 28 itself) = 28 (i.e., $1+2+4+7+14=28$). There are only six other numbers between 1 and 40,000,000 for which this is true (information from Victoria Kirkham).

Melpomene gave the sweet knowledge of the lyre to
   mortals;
Terpsichore, obligingly, offered skilfully made pipes;
Erato discovered the most delightful hymns to
   immortals;
erudite Polyhymnia found out the pleasures of dance
and gave harmony to every song;
Urania revealed the heavens and the dance
   of the celestial stars;
Thalia invented comedy and renowned mores.[9]

In addition to all this, we believe (and most others concur) that the Muses
themselves correspond to the stars and modes such that we may assign them
to the strings that begin the modes, one by one. First we put Thalia underground, as in subterrenean silence, as these verses express:

In the first song Thalia, who lies quiet
in the breast of the earth, sprouts nocturnal silence.

The comparison of the earth with silence because it is immobile occurs in
Marcus Tullius;[10] they compare it to the three-headed, underground Cerberus
lying at the feet of Apollo. The beginning of the hypodorian, the lowest mode,
and the moon, the heaviest planet inhabiting only the house of Cancer (as
astronomers say),[11] and Clio are assigned to the lowest string[12] by this poem:

Persephone and Clio breath and the hypodorian
is born; from this origin melody blossoms.

To the second string, called *hypate hypaton,* the beginning of the hypophrygian
mode, Mercury in the houses of Gemini and Virgo and also Calliope are customarily assigned by this poem:

The following string gives rise to hypophrygian,
which Calliope and the messenger of the gods bring
   forth.

The third string, called *parhypate hypaton,* Terpsichore consecrated to the
hypolydian and to Venus in the houses of Libra and Taurus; whence the verses:

The third string reveals the start of hypolydian;
Terpsichore dances to it and kind Paphos rules it.

Melpomene and the sun in the house of Leo have granted the fourth string,
lychanos hypaton, to the dorian mode by this poem:

9. Greek (i.e., Palatine) Anthology 9.504. There are many epigrams by Callimachus in this huge
   compilation, but this one on the Muses is no longer considered his work.
10. That is, Cicero; see Macrobius, *Commentarii in somnium Scipionis* 1.22–2.1 and Wind, *Pagan
   Mysteries,* p. 265.
11. The houses are the twelve regions of the zodiac, each associated with a constellation and its
   sign. In astrological teaching reaching back to Late Antiquity each planet is thought to exert its
   influence most strongly in one or two particular houses. These correspondences are given here
   by Gafori, starting with the moon and Cancer.
12. That is, *proslambanomenos* in Greek musical terminology. Gafori supplies the Greek names of
   the remaining strings in his text.

> Melpomene and Titan establish (I avow)
> the mode called dorian in the fourth position.

On the fifth string, called *hypate meson,* Erato and Mars in the houses of Aries and Scorpio have placed the phrygian mode. Hence the verses:

> Erato wants to prescribe the fifth string to phrygian,
> and Mars always loves war, not peace.

The sphere of Jupiter, holding steadfastly to the houses of Pisces and Sagittarius, and also Euterpe along with the lydian mode are included in the sixth string, *parhypate meson,* by this poem:

> The lydian mode governs Euterpe and Jupiter,
> which the sixth string, sweetly sounding, ordains.

On the seventh string, *lychanos meson,* Saturn in the houses of Aquarius and Capricorn and the Muse Polyhymnia have placed the mixolydian mode; hence the verses:

> On the seventh string live Saturn and also
> Polyhymnia; from it the mixolydian begins.

The eighth string, called *mese,* has consecrated Urania and the hypermixolydian to the starry sphere, as this poem declares:

> While the hypermixolydian contemplates the eighth
>   string,
> friendly to Urania, it turns the heavens well.

Aristides Quintilianus, at the end of Book II of his *De musica,* gave a correspondence of Muses and modes that is in some ways the opposite of this.[13] And Herodotus of Halicarnassus, who dedicated the nine books of his *Histories* to these same Muses, gave yet another order.[14] At Apollo's right side the Greeks usually placed the three young women called the Charities or Graces, attendants on Venus. Their names are Aglaia, meaning luster, Thalia, signifying youthful bloom, and Euphrosyne or joy.

All these things are shown in the following figure:[15]

---

13. 2.19. Here Gafori's understanding of Aristides was imperfect. Aristides names only three Muses, Polyhymnia, Erato, and Euterpe, and he associates them not with modes but with lesser forms of music for the kithara, lyre, and auloi respectively. See Aristides Quintilianus, *On Music,* trans. Thomas J. Mathiesen (New Haven: Yale University Press, 1983) pp. 155–56.
14. Gafori refers to the once conventional (but inauthentic) sectional division of Herodotus's *Histories* into nine "Muses." See *The Oxford Classical Dictionary* (Oxford: Clarendon Press, 1970), s.v. "Herodotus."
15. For interpretation of this famous woodcut beyond what Gafori makes explicit see esp. Wind, *Pagan Mysteries,* app. 6; James Haar, "The Frontispiece of Gafori's *Practica musicae* (1496)," *Renaissance Quarterly* 27 (1974): 7–22; and Claude Palisca, *Humanism in Italian Renaissance Musical Thought* (New Haven: Yale University Press, 1985), pp. 171–74.

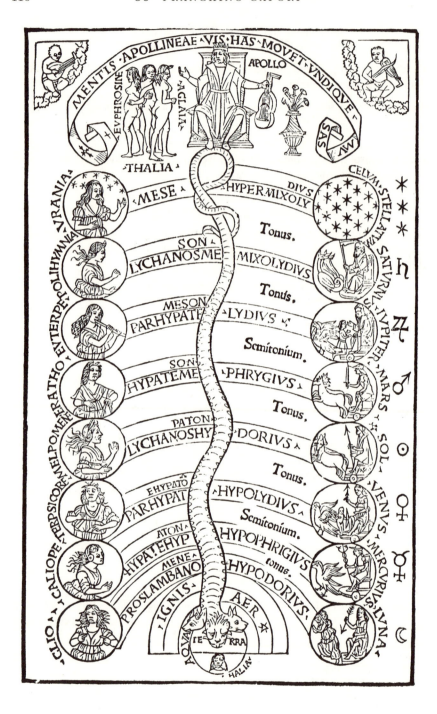

31   Pontus de Tyard

Among the Platonic themes dearest to Marsilio Ficino and his followers was the assertion (Plato, *Phaedrus* 265) that there were four sorts of divine madness by which the human soul might be seized and touched by divinity. One of these was the poetic furor or, as we might say, the furor of song or music. Ficino's writings on this topic gave rise to a literature extending through the sixteenth century on the heavenly sources of poetry and song. Pontus de Tyard's *First Solitaire or Prose on the Muses and Poetic Furor (Solitaire premier ou prose des Muses & de la fureur poétique)* elaborates this topic in the context of a work on music theory, often paraphrasing Ficino and occasionally taking over verbatim the views of his Florentine predecessor. The work takes the form of a dialogue between the Solitaire (representing Tyard himself) and his beloved Pasithée. The *Solitaire premier,* first published in 1552, was followed in 1555 by the *Solitaire second ou prose de la musique.* Both were reprinted in Tyard's *Discours philosophiques* in 1587.

In addition to his philosophical writings, Tyard is remembered for his poetry. Along with Ronsard and Baïf he was a member of the Pléiade, a circle of seven poets who strove to reform French literary usage and elevate the French lyric by imitating ancient models and Petrarch. Tyard was born in 1521 and died in 1605.

FROM *First Solitaire or Prose on the Muses and Poetic Furor*
(1552)

CHAPTER 3

. . . Platonic philosophers hold that when the soul descends into the body it is divided in various operations and loses the estimable unity that had enabled it to know and enjoy the sovereign one that is God. In this division and disunity its superior parts, sleeping and shrouded in a dull torpor, cede control to its inferior parts, which are always prey to perturbations. Therefore the whole soul lives full of a discord and disorder difficult to reconcile. So this is the task at

TEXT: Pontus de Tyard, *Oeuvres: Solitaire premier,* ed. Silvio F. Baridon (Geneva and Lille: Droz, 1950), pp. 12–13, 16–22. Translation by Gary Tomlinson. The first, fourth, and fifth paragraphs, and parts of the second and third as well, are virtual translations of Ficino's words in an account of divine furor he published twice with few alterations: first as his *Epitome* of Plato's *Ion* (mid-1460s; see *Opera omnia,* ed. M. Sancipriano and Paul Oskar Kristeller [4 vols., Turin: Bottega d'Erasmo, 1959] pp. 1281–84) and second as 7.13–14 of his commentary on Plato's *Symposium, De amore* (1468–69; *Opera omnia,* pp. 1361–62).

hand; this is where we must work to loosen the soul bogged in earthly mire
and to lift it up to join with the sovereign one, restoring it to its earlier unity.
Now, since the soul passes through four levels lowering itself into the body, it
is likewise necessary that its elevation pass from low to high through the same
four levels. As for the four levels of descent, the first and highest is angelic
understanding, the second intellectual reason, the third opinion, and the fourth
nature.[1]

•   •   •   •   •

    Thus to move up again four levels are necessary, and these levels can be
discerned in the illumination of the soul or elevation of the understanding . . .
known as divine furor. Divine furor, Pasithée, is the only stairway by which the
soul can find its way back to its original sovereign good and its ultimate happiness. . . . Man may be seized by divine furor in four ways. The first is by poetic
furor, which comes from the gift of the Muses. The second is by the knowledge
of the mysteries and secrets of religion, under the aegis of Bacchus. The third
is by the ravishment of prophecy or vatication or divination, under Apollo;
and the fourth is by the violence of amorous affection, under Love and Venus.
You must understand, Pasithée, that in these few words and these four types
are hidden all the highest and most sacred things human understanding can
aspire to, the true and certain knowledge of all disciplines that scholars seek
through long (and often futile) study. For we must believe that, without the
illumination of these divine rays, without the heat of this divine furor that lights
the torch of the soul, we cannot attain in any other way the knowledge of sound
doctrines and science. All the less can we elevate ourselves to a level of virtue,
freed from the base, corporeal shadows whose dim light is nourished by the
caprice of false and deceiving pleasures, where we could appreciate in our
minds the sovereign good. . . . Now the lowest point the soul reaches in its
descent is the body, to whose diverse and contrary parts it is so firmly attached
that it is forced to separate and distribute its powers in diverse and contrary
operations. Its superior part is asleep, stunned (as we might say) by so heavy a
fall, and its inferior part is agitated and full of perturbations, from which arise
a horrible discord, disorder, and unharmonious proportion. The soul seems
incapable of any just action unless by some means this horrible discord is transformed into a sweet symphony and this impertinent disorder reduced to a
measured equality, well ordered and proportioned. And to do this is the particular duty of poetic furor, awakening the sleeping part of the soul by the tones
of music; comforting the perturbed part by the suavity of sweet harmony; then
chasing away the dissonant discord by the well tuned diversity of musical

1. Ficino had adapted these ontological levels or grades of the universe from Plotinus; see Paul
   Oskar Kristeller, *The Philosophy of Marsilio Ficino,* trans. Virginia Conant (Gloucester, Mass.:
   Peter Smith, 1964), pp. 106–8.

accord; and finally reducing the disorder to a certain well and proportionately measured equality ordered by the graceful and grave facility of verses regulated by the careful observance of number and measure.

But this is, as yet, nothing; for it is necessary to efface the varying claims of diverse opinions caught up in the constant flux of a multitude of images and corporeal species; and it is necessary that the soul, now awakened and well ordered, call back into one its parts and powers so diversely diffused and separated. For this the holy communication of religious mysteries and secrets is needed, through whose purifications and devotional offices the soul gathers itself together and devotes itself completely to sacred dedication and utterly reverent intention, prostrating itself before the divinity it adores. When thus the diverse powers of the soul, formerly dispersed here and there in various exercises, are drawn up and gathered together in the single intention of rational understanding, the third furor is necessary to put aside such discursive intellectual ratiocinations concerning principles and conclusions and to lead the understanding back to union with the soul. This comes about through the ravishment of prophecies and divinations. Whoever is moved by the prophetic or divinatory furor is stolen away to interior comtemplation and joins his soul and all his spirits together, rising high above all human apprehension and natural reason to draw from the most intimate, profound, and hidden secrets of divinity the prediction of things which must come to pass. Finally, when all that is in the essence and in the nature of the soul is made one, it must (in order to return to its source) suddenly withdraw itself into the sovereign one, above all essences. This the great and celestial Venus accomplishes by love, that is to say by a fervent and incomparable desire that the soul, so elevated, has of enjoying the divine and eternal beauty.

· · · · ·

CHAPTER 4

The poetic furor comes from the Muses . . . and is a ravishment of the docile and insuperable soul in which it is awakened, moved, and incited by songs and other poems for the instruction of man. By ravishment of the soul I mean that the soul is occupied and entirely directed toward and intent on the holy and sacred Muses, who have found it to be docile and ready to receive the form they impress on it. That is, they have found it well prepared to be taken by that ravishment, by which from its softness it becomes insuperable. Then it cannot be stained or overtaken by any base or worldly thing but instead rises above and beyond all such vileness. Moreover it is awakened from bodily torpor and sleep to intellectual vigilance; it is summoned back from the shadows of ignorance to the light of truth, from death to life, from a deep and stolid forgetfulness to a remembrance of divine and celestial things; so that finally it is moved, impelled, and incited to express in verses the things it foresees and contemplates. Therefore no one should undertake recklessly to knock at the doors of poetry; for whomever the Muses had not graced with their furor and whomever God had not looked upon propitiously and favorably would approach in vain and make cold and wretched verses.

V

WRITINGS ON POLYPHONIC PRACTICE

32 Johannes Tinctoris

FROM *Liber de arte contrapuncti*
(1477)

BOOK 2

CHAPTER 19: THAT COUNTERPOINT IS OF TWO SORTS, NAMELY SIMPLE AND DIMINISHED.

Because, as we said at the beginning of the preceding book,[1] dissonances are sometimes admitted in counterpoint, it should be noted first that there are two sorts of counterpoint, simple and diminished. Simple counterpoint is that which is made by simply placing against a note another note of the same value. . . . This counterpoint is called simple because it is fashioned simply through the proportion of equality without any flowering of diversity. Diminished counterpoint is that which is created by placing two or more notes against one, sometimes dividing that note equally, sometimes unequally. . . . Counterpoint of this sort is called diminished because in it full notes are divided into various smaller parts. Hence some people metaphorically call it florid, for just as diversity of flowers makes the fields most delightful, so variety of proportions renders counterpoint most pleasant.

CHAPTER 20: THAT BOTH SIMPLE AND DIMINISHED COUNTERPOINT ARE MADE IN TWO WAYS, NAMELY IN WRITING AND IN THE MIND, AND HOW A COMPOSED PIECE DIFFERS FROM A COUNTERPOINT.

Furthermore, both simple and diminished counterpoint are made in two ways, in writing and in the mind. Counterpoint that is written is usually called a "composed piece" *[resfacta]*. But that which we put together in the mind we call a "counterpoint" pure and simple, and those who do this are said in common parlance to "sing over the book" *[super librum cantare]*. A composed piece differs from a counterpoint above all in that all parts of a composed piece, whether three, four, or more, are mutually bound to one another, so that the ordering and rule of consonances of any one part must be observed with

TEXT: Johannis Tinctoris, *Opera omnia,* ed. Albert Seay (2 vols., American Institute of Musicology, 1975), vol. 2, pp. 105–41. Translation by Gary Tomlinson. I have profited from the recent interpretations of these chapters cited below and also from Claude Palisca's unpublished translation of most of the chapters here and Klaus Jürgen Sachs's discussion of them in *The New Grove Dictionary of Music and Musicians,* s.v. "Counterpoint." Tinctoris's music examples are long; I have omitted those that are not required to understand his discussion.

1. 1.1.

respect to each and all the others. . . . But when two, three, four, or more sing together over the book, one is not subject to the other. Indeed it is enough that each of them be consonant with the tenor in regard to the rule and ordering of consonances. However, I do not consider it blameworthy but rather most laudable if the singers prudently avoid similarity among themselves in their choice and succession of consonances. In doing so they will make their harmony much fuller and sweeter.[2]

•   •   •   •   •

CHAPTER 22: HOW A COUNTERPOINT IS MADE ON A MEASURED MELODY.

A counterpoint is made on a measured melody when it is sung over a tenor measured in notes according to perfect or imperfect quantities. . . . A counterpoint resembling this is created on a plainchant when the notes of this plainchant are measured by means of the various quantities represented by the shapes of longs, breves, and semibreves. . . . There are still other counterpoints—though these are ever so rare—that are sung not only over a tenor but also over any other part of a composed piece. This sort of counterpoint requires much skill and practice. If it is done sweetly and expertly it deserves all the more praise for being so difficult.[3] Although all the preceding ways of making counterpoint, whether on a plainchant or on a measured melody, are examples of diminished counterpoint, it is possible in any of these ways to make simple counterpoint (that is, note against note of the same value). But to do this on a measured melody is altogether ridiculous and on a plainchant childish, except when the notes of the plainchant are sung more quickly as a semibreve of minor prolation, for then the words are distinctly enunciated and this kind of counterpoint yields great sweetness. . . .

2. This distinction between *res facta* and *cantare super librum* has in recent years stimulated much thought on the relations of written composition, performance of polyphony, and *contrapunctus* in the late fifteenth century; see esp. Margaret Bent, "*Resfacta* and *Cantare super librum*," *Journal of the American Musicological Society [JAMS]* 36 (1983): 371–91; Bonnie J. Blackburn, "On Compositional Process in the Fifteenth Century," *JAMS* 40 (1987): 210–84; David E. Cohen, "*Contrapunctus,* Improvisation, and *Res facta,*" paper presented at the 1989 national meeting of the American Musicological Society, Austin, Texas; and Rob C. Wegman, "From Maker to Composer: Improvisation and Musical Authorship in the Low Countries," *JAMS* 49 (1996): 409–79. From all this a summary of Tinctoris's categories might be hazarded. In *cantare super librum* he describes a widespread practice of singing polyphony over a written melody, typically a plainchant or the tenor of a separate piece of polyphony. (The "book," then, refers to the place where the written melody is found; the other parts are, in principle at least, unwritten.) *Res facta* refers to a piece of polyphony in principle fully written out; it touches on a sense crystalizing around 1500 of such a piece as an autonomous entity termed *compositio*. *Contrapunctus,* finally, is a word increasingly caught between the two practices; it is not yet conceived only as a set of techniques and rules to guide voice-leading in the making of a composition but instead both overlaps with and stands independent of the emerging category *compositio*.
3. On this special kind of "singing over the book," apparently using two parts from the written source, see Bent, "*Resfacta,*" pp. 388–89, and Blackburn, "Compositional Process," p. 256.

CHAPTER 23: THAT DISSONANCES MUST NOT BE ADMITTED IN SIMPLE COUNTERPOINT BUT ONLY IN DIMINISHED, AND FIRST, ON DISSONANCES ON THE PARTS OF THE MINIM IN EITHER PROLATION AND ON THE PARTS OF THE SEMIBREVE IN MINOR PROLATION.[4]

In simple counterpoint dissonances are simply and absolutely prohibited, but in diminished counterpoint they are sometimes permitted in moderation. Here it should be known that I ignore the compositions of older musicians, in which there were more dissonances than consonances. Nearly all more recent composers and also singers over the book place a consonance over the first or other part of a minim in the tenor, both in major and minor prolation; and moreover in minor prolation they place it either over the first or another part of the semibreve. They employ a dissonance of the same or a smaller note value over what immediately follows.[5] On the other hand, a dissonance is almost always used in major or minor prolation on the first part of the first of two minims on the same pitch, joined together or separate, or of a single minim, and also on the first part of two semibreves in minor prolation, joined or separated, when these immediately precede some perfect consonance.[6] However, if the tenor descends to a perfect consonance through several minims in major or minor prolation or several semibreves in minor prolation, a syncopated dissonance is very frequently admitted on the first part of any of these minims or semibreves, as is clear from the following example:[7]

4. Prolation refers to the relationship in mensural notation between semibreve and minim; the semibreve is worth three minims in major prolation, two in minor. Major prolation is signaled by a dot in the mensuration sign, minor prolation by its absence.
5. For example, for major prolation: music example, m. 1, supremum, m. 3 supremum and contratenor; for minor prolation: m. 16, supremum.
6. This stipulation recognizes cadential suspensions. For two minims on the same pitch see m. 8 (major prolation) and m. 22 (minor prolation). For two minims "joined together" see m. 4 (major) and m. 20 (minor). For a single minim Tinctoris gives no examples other than those involved at the end of chains of syncopations; see n. 7 below. For two semibreves in minor prolation see m. 26; for two semibreves joined together see m. 24.
7. This is the syncopated descent to a cadence frequently encountered in mid- and late-fifteenth-century polyphony. For minims see m. 12 (major) and m. 28 (minor); for semibreves in minor prolation, m. 32.

CHAPTER 24: ON DISSONANCES ALLOWED ON PARTS OF THE NOTE VALUES THAT DIRECT THE METER OF THE SONG AND ARE SUBJECT TO BINARY PROPORTION AND IMPERFECT QUANTITY.

Although we have already spoken about the dissonances allowed on parts of the semibreve in minor prolation, we must still explain how dissonances are allowed on the parts of all the other note values in meters that divide them

evenly into two parts.[8] Concerning the parts of minims in either prolation in
subduple proportion or where the tenor doubles its time, which amounts to
the same thing; or concerning the parts of the breve in imperfect tempus and
minor prolation in *cantus ad medium*[9] or in duple proportion, which are also
the same thing; or in singing the parts of longs in the same tempus and prolation in imperfect minor mode but in quadruple proportion; or in singing the
parts of maxims in the same tempus, prolation, and minor mode and in imperfect major mode in octuple proportion: when a consonance is placed over the
first or other part of such notes sung according to the aforementioned modes,
proportions, and quantities, then a dissonance of equal or lesser note value
may be placed on what follows. If two of these notes on the same pitch, joined
or separate, stand together before some perfect consonance, a dissonance is
sometimes permitted on the first part of the first of these. However, when a
descent is made into some perfect consonance through one or more of these
aforementioned notes, any of these frequently permits a syncopated dissonance
on its first part. . . .

●   ●   ●   ●   ●

CHAPTER 29: THAT MANY COMPOSERS NEVER EMPLOY A DISSONANCE THE LENGTH OF HALF THE NOTE VALUE THAT DIRECTS THE METER OF THE SONG BUT RATHER EMPLOY SHORTER DISSONANCES.

Many composers avoid dissonances so carefully that they never extend them
over a full half of the note value that directs the meter but only over a third,
fourth, or smaller part of it. In my opinion these composers should be imitated. . . .

●   ●   ●   ●   ●

CHAPTER 31: WHY SMALL DISSONANCES MAY BE USED BY MUSICIANS.

Nevertheless, in the manners described above small dissonances may sometimes be used by musicians, just as reasoned rhetorical figures are used by
orators for the sake of embellishment and effect. For a song is embellished
when it ascends or descends from one consonance to another by appropriate

8. That is, we must extend the rules of Chapter 23 to other note values, in mensurations that divide
   them in two, that might be brought by the use of proportion signs to take over the minim's or
   semibreve's usual role of carrying the beat. Thus in subduple proportion or where the tenor
   doubles its time *(crescit in duplo)* the minim carries the beat, in duple proportion the breve, in
   quadruple proportion the long, and in octuple proportion the maxim. Tinctoris's music example
   applies all these proportions to the tenor part only so that, for example, in the section showing
   octuple proportion the tenor's maxims have the same duration as semibreves in the other voices.
9. That is, cut time or *alla breve.*

means and by syncopations, which sometimes cannot be made without dissonances. These small dissonances do not present themselves so strongly to the ear when they are placed over the last parts of notes in the tenor as they do when placed over the first. . . .

CHAPTER 32: ON THE ARRANGEMENT OF ANY DISSONANCE.

Any dissonance should be arranged so that, whether ascending or descending, it comes after the consonance nearest to it, as for example a second after a unison or a third, a fourth after a third or a fifth, a seventh after a fifth or an octave, and so on. And any dissonance should be followed by a consonance that is only one or, very rarely, two steps removed from it. . . .[10]

10. That is, dissonances should be approached and left by step and most often with oblique motion between the parts. For exceptions to this rule in Tinctoris's music examples see Sachs, "Counterpoint."

33 Bartolomé Ramis de Pareia

The *Musica practica* of Bartolomé Ramis (or Ramos) de Pareia was printed in Bologna in 1482. Of the life of its author we know little. That he came from Baeza, near Madrid, and lectured in Bologna, after having previously lectured in Salamanca, is set forth in his book. Other sources tell us that he left Bologna sometime after 1484 and went to Rome, where he was still living in 1491. From his pupil Giovanni Spataro we also learn that Ramis withheld parts of his book from the printer with a view to lecturing on them publicly; as we have it, then, the *Musica practica* is only a fragment. A completion of the work, in a companion treatise called *Musica theorica,* was written at least in part but never published.

Among other innovations in *Musica practica* Ramis challenges the solmization practices passed down from the Middle Ages and associated especially with Guido of Arezzo. In place of the Guidonian system of six syllables matched to the notes of a hexachord, Ramis proposes eight new syllables matched to the octave. This does away with most of the mutations, or shifts of syllable (and hence hexachord) on a single pitch, called for by the Guidonian system. Although Ramis's syllables were never widely adopted, his system in general stands behind modern "fixed *do*" approaches.

The increasing complexities of solmization resulted from the increasingly frequent use of half-steps in positions where they were not naturally found in the three Guidonian hexachords (which started only on the notes C, F, and G). Singing these new half-steps in the old system required a proliferation of *mi–fa* mutations and hence a proliferation of new hexachords. (For example, to sing a–c♯–d where a–c–d is written requires the syllables *ut–mi–fa* rather than *re–*

fa–sol and assigns *ut* to a non-Guidonian position on a.) Ramis outlines these difficulties in his discussion of *musica ficta*.

FROM *Musica practica*
(1482)

TRACTATE 1

CHAPTER 4: SUBTLE APPLICATION OF THE GIVEN FIGURE FOR THE PRACTICE OF SINGERS

By making use of a tetrachord Guido, perhaps a better monk than a musician, included all these twenty letters[1] when he developed the hexachord. And he was moved to create such a hexachord in this way because number six is called perfect by mathematicians, for its aliquot parts, namely 1, 2, 3, when added together make six, and each string of the hexachord receives a name from the first six syllables of six lines of the hymn of St. John the Baptist, namely: Ut queant laxis. Resonare fibris. Mira gestorum. Famuli tuorum. Solve polluti. Labii reatum. Sancte Johannes.

If we have examined correctly the first syllable after each period we will extract these six vocables: *ut, re, mi, fa, sol, la,* and when put in a successive order each is a whole tone from the next except *fa,* because it is a semitone from *mi.* So two whole tones will be above and two below the semitone. And with the first letter *g,* which is called Γ, the syllable *ut* is written, forming a unit called *gamma ut;*[2] from letter *a* and syllable *re* a unit is formed which is called *a re;* also from letter *b* and syllable *mi* comes *b mi,* from letter *c* and syllable *fa,* comes *c fa,* from *d* and *sol, d sol,* and from *e* and *la, e la.*

In order to follow the Boethian doctrine, which divides the entire tonal series by tetrachords,[3] when Guido comes to the fourth place, namely *c fa,* he again creates another hexachord, another offspring as it were. But if the syllable *ut* is joined to *c fa* the entire arrangement is called *c fa ut,* and it continues with *d sol re* and *e la mi,* where the first hexachord ends. Since *fa,* however, follows in the order of letters, the syllable *ut* is also joined to the second tetrachord's *fa,* which is the fourth tone of the second tetrachord. And so when *f fa* occurs *ut* will receive such a name by being joined to it, with *g sol re* and *a la*

TEXT: Bartolomé Ramis de Pareia, *Musica practica*, ed. Clement A. Miller (American Institute of Musicology, 1993), pp. 55–57, 64–66, 74–75, and 93–94. Reprinted by permission. Translation by Clement A Miller. I have made some minor alterations in Miller's translation by comparing it with the facsimile of the original edition (Bologna, 1482) published in Madrid, 1983.

1. That is, the pitch-letters Γ (gamma), representing our G, to e″ two octaves and a major sixth above it; this span is the medieval or Guidonian gamut of pitches.
2. The source, by contraction, of our word "gamut."
3. *De institutione musica* 1.20.

mi following. And so that he would not seem ignorant of the similitude of the outer limits of the octave[4] he again begins to form a hexachord. And since in the aforementioned two tetrachords, that is, the second and third, we place two syllables, namely *sol* and *re*, with letter *g*, by adding *ut* to them the unit is named *g sol re ut*, and it is followed by *a la mi re*, where the second hexachord is completed. And where two tones, namely *fa mi* are joined together, with the first as ♭ *fa* and the second as square ♮ *mi*, we recognize that the one is higher than the other, just as the letters and syllables are shown to be unequal.[5] And thus the whole tone is divided into two semitones, and is followed by *c sol fa ut*, for just as the second hexachord is joined to the first in the same place, the entire unit is named in this way, that is, *c sol fa ut*, and is followed by *d la sol re*, then *e la mi, f fa ut, g sol re ut, a la mi re*, and ♭ *fa* square ♮ *mi*, just as before.

Hexachords can be multiplied indefinitely according to the extent of the instrument, but since an end must be reached somewhere in all knowledge, the hexachords now stop repeating and therefore another *ut* is not placed with *c sol fa*, but we move to *d la sol*, where we leave the sixth hexachord, while the seventh ends on the syllable *e la*. And so he set down seven hexachords[6] because of seven different tones, as it had seemed to him, just as the following

---

4. That is, Γ to g. [Tr.]
5. This is the distinction in pitch between *fa* of the third hexachord (our b-flat) and *mi* of the fourth (our b-natural).
6. The full Guidonian hexachordal system, giving pitch names by letter and solmization syllables, may be represented as follows:

Hexachord:	1	2	3	4	5	6	7
Pitch (low to high):							
Γ (G)	ut						
A	re						
B	mi						
c	fa	ut					
d	sol	re					
e	la	mi					
f		fa	ut				
g		sol	re	ut			
a		la	mi	re			
b			fa	mi			
c'			sol	fa	ut		
d'			la	sol	re		
e'				la	mi		
f'					fa	ut	
g'					sol	re	ut
a'					la	mi	re
b'						fa	mi
c"						sol	fa
d"						la	sol
e"							la

figure will show. Do you see the true figure of Guido? Indeed he himself does not, but he shows it through joints of the fingers in this way.[7]

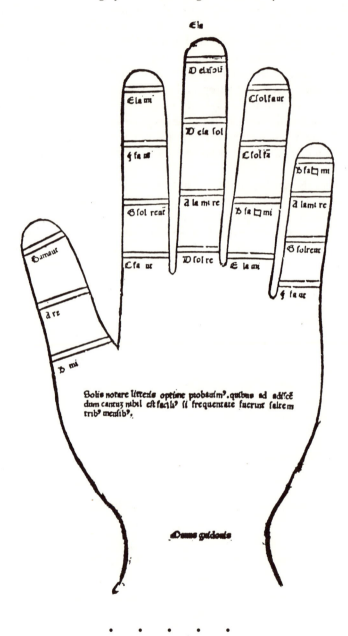

7. The text on the palm of the hand is: "We have shown that the best way to notate music is with letters alone; nothing is easier than learning how to sing with them if they have been practiced for at least three months." [Tr.]

CHAPTER 7: AN ACCURATE WAY OF CONNECTING A VOICE WITH AN INSTRUMENT

. . . In order, however, to memorize the sounds, each one is produced with a different name; this was customary among early writers. Odo said in the *Enchiriadis*: *noe, noananne, cane, agis*, which have no meaning.[8] Some used *tri, pro, de, nos, trite, ad*,[9] which indicated the bases of the modes, about which we will speak at the proper place. Others wrote only letters of the alphabet, namely: *a, b, c, d, e, f, g*, as Gregory, Augustine, Ambrose, and Bernard; but Guido used *ut, re, mi, fa, sol, la*, as we said earlier. Although he did not do this out of necessity, since he also showed all his examples with letters, his followers afterwards adhered so much to his syllables that they thought them entirely necessary to music, an idea which must be scorned.

We, therefore, who have labored a long time in nightly lucubrations and vigils to seek the truth of this art, arrange new syllables for individual strings and show the tones of the entire series,[10] so that on the lowest pitch *psal* is sung, on the next *li*, on the third *tur*, on the fourth *per*, on the fifth *vo*, on the sixth *ces*, on the seventh *is*, and on the eighth *tas*. And thus the connection of the syllables will be *psallitur per voces istas*,[11] for the entire series consists of eight syllables. We arrange them from low *c* to high *c* since they teach how to sing with perfection. Therefore they begin on letter *c* because the musical series begins on that letter, and the first semitone of two is included in the interval *r r* and the second sounds between the two *s s*. So the first is *e f* or *tur per*. But since the second semitone sometimes is formed from letter *a* to ♭, and sometimes from ♮ to high *c* on account of the synemmenon and diezeugmenon tetrachords,[12] because three semitones are located separately there, three places are indicated by letter *s*, that is, *ces, is, tas*. So with these syllables making sounds equivalent to the strings of an instrument we easily will be able to harmonize the natural instrument of voice with an instrument made by art. But if we wish to rise an octave higher we will place *psal* on the same sound as the first octave. Then one will have a dissyllabic *c*, namely, *tas-psal*,[13] and continue with *d li* and with *e tur* and the rest just as before. This must also be done in the low octave, because, as we often have said, a tone reappears after an octave,

---

8. These words occur in medieval treatises from the ninth century onward. For their relation to the modes see Michel Huglo, *Les tonaires* (Paris: Société française de musicologie, 1971), pp. 383–90; also "The Psalmodic Formula *Neannoe* and Its Origin," *The Musical Quarterly* 28 (1942): p. 93. [Tr.]

9. This version is based on an eleventh-century hymn. [Tr.]

10. A series that Ramis expanded and shifted from the Guidonian gamut to the three octaves from C to c″.

11. "It is sung through these syllables."

12. That is, the conjunction of the c–f tetrachord with the tetrachord starting on f ("synnemenon") yields b-flat, while the disjunction of the c–f tetrachord from the tetrachord starting on g ("diezeugmenon") yields b-natural. The conception and terminology, if not the specific pitches associated with them, are from Boethius, *De institutione musica* 1.20.

13. This is the only mutation that remains in Ramis's system.

and whenever we ascend or descend more than an octave we repeat a tone; thus the teaching is correct only by using these eight syllables.[14]

•   •   •   •   •

TRACTATE 2

CHAPTER 2: AN EXPLANATION OF *MUSICA FICTA*.

In order to have a fuller understanding of these signs and notes[15] we will investigate some things about them in greater detail. For some signs are accustomed to be placed in songs through which unequal differences of intervals are heard; one of these is written as round ♭, the other as square ♮. The first sign is called soft or round ♭, the second square or hard ♮. Square ♮ and round ♭ are named from the nature of the sign, but soft ♭ or hard ♮ are so named because, when those singing with the letters of Gregory make a semitone from *a* to *b*, they call it soft *b*. For when a leap is made in arsis and thesis, the voice softens

14. In 2.7 Ramis supplied a picture of his alternative to the Guidonian hand:

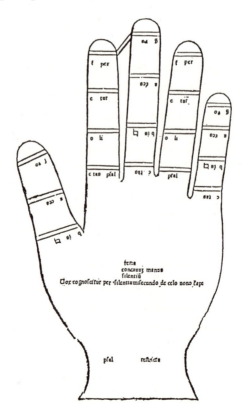

15. 2.1 discusses the notation of pitch with staves and clefs.

more in a semitone than in a whole tone, as for example from *a* to soft ♭ and from *a* to hard, square ♮. So also movement by a semiditone is softer than by a ditone, as *g* to soft ♭ and *g* to hard, square ♮; likewise a fourth is softer than a tritone, as *f* to soft ♭ and *f* to very hard, square ♮.

From these examples the error is clear of certain singers who say soft ♭ or square ♮. They err in two ways: first, because they sing with Guido's syllables and not Gregory's letters, thus saying neither soft ♭ or hard, square ♮ but *fa* or *mi*; second, they do not make the correct relationship, for when they say square ♮ they should correspondingly say round ♭ and when they say soft ♭ they should say hard ♮, and then the relationship will be correct. This was the custom among those singing with the letters of Gregory in early times; to them these letters are the proper names, just as synemmenon or diezeugmenon are proper to the Greeks. In our terminology the correct names in singing will be ♭ *is* in the conjunct tetrachord and *is* ♮ in the disjunct tetrachord; indeed, the syllables making a whole tone or semitone are common in all respects.

But elsewhere singers write whole tones or semitones with these signs not only on paramese,[16] for they say that wherever *fa* is found without *mi* then *mi* must be used, as in ♭ *fa* ♮ *mi*. The same occurs when *mi* is found without *fa*. Many call this musica ficta; of them Philipetus,[17] speaking rashly, says this: musica ficta is a single procedure. But he did not know that it should occur at least in two ways, for making *fa* from *mi* is different than making *mi* from *fa* (as will be shown a little later), since the tones do not correspond in the way in which they are naturally situated. Therefore, when *fa* is to be made from *mi*, they write with such a sign, namely, round ♭, but when *mi* is made from *fa* they write the sign, namely, square ♮ or else ♯.

Thus, according to them soft ♭ is located in five places, namely, on *b mi, e la mi,* the first *a la mi re,* high *e la mi,* and the second *a la mi re.* In these places we will say *fa* by lowering it a semitone from its original place. But we use ♮ or ♯ on *c fa ut, f fa ut, c sol fa ut,* high *f fa ut* and *c sol fa;* in those places we will say *mi* by raising it a semitone from its original position. They also call these procedures conjunctions, for just as when trite synemmenon is put after mese so that the whole tone of mese and paramese is to be divided into two semi-tones,[18] any whole tone located elsewhere should be divided in the same way. They add further that any of these conjunctions forms a hexachord, just as the others that were formed earlier; thus, just as after *f fa ut,* where *ut* is said, *g sol re ut* follows where *ut* is again placed, as already stated, so it occurs in each of the positions.[19] And they define a conjunction in this way: A conjunction is

---

16. For Ramis, the pitch b.
17. The reference is probably to Philippe de Vitry; see his *Ars contrapunctus* 2.1, in E. de Coussemaker, ed., *Scriptorum de musica medii aevi . . . nova series* (4 vols., Paris: A. Durand, 1864–76), vol. 3, p. 26.
18. That is, when the conjunct tetrachord f–b-flat calls for the interval a–b to be divided.
19. In other words, each mutation of *mi* to *fa* or *fa* to *mi* creates a hexachord beginning, respectively, a perfect fourth or major third beneath the pitch on which the mutation occurs.

making a whole tone from a semitone and a semitone from a whole tone, also a ditone from a semiditone and a semiditone from a ditone, and likewise with the other species. Here they speak correctly, because these conjunct hexachords occur in the manner of diezeugmenon and synemmenon tetrachords.

• • • • •

CHAPTER 7: REPROVING THE FOLLOWERS OF GUIDO AND SHOWING ACCURATELY THE TRUTH OF THE MATTER.

Having observed and examined the diversity of music, it now remains to be shown how whole tones may become semitones and the reverse. Regarding this it should be known, as John of Villanova[20] says, that a rising song desires the voice to be strengthened, and a descending song to become soft. Then he says that if a melody sounds *a c d* and does not return to *c,* although *re fa sol* should be said, as the order indicates, yet *ut mi fa* ought to be said, because *a c* is not the interval of a semiditone but of a ditone;[21] or if the melody is pronounced according to the other syllables, namely *re fa,* the ditone may be said to be understood. Again, if a melody may be formed as *g f g* and it does not return to *f,* a semitone is understood, even though *sol fa sol* or *re ut re* may be said. The same thing always holds true in forming synemmenon, when after a note placed on ♭ *fa* ♮ *mi* another note follows it on mese, whether it will have come from lower letters to synemmenon or will have reached it by descending from higher letters, especially if it will have repeated the same pitch many times.[22] It is also true if the melody will have made this movement *d b c d c d d,* and in its octaves; *b c* is a whole tone and *c d* is a semitone formed twice, and so either whole tones will replace semitones mentally or a mutation will be made of *mi* into *re,* which is a syllable of conjunctions.[23]

The same John also says a semiditone is made from a ditone in this way: if a melody may say *la fa sol sol* without returning to *fa,* either a semiditone will be mentally understood or a mutation may be made of *la* into *sol,* so that *lasol mi fa fa* may be said; in this way a diligent reader will be able to judge other syllables arranged in this manner. Such notes should be indicated with this sign, namely ♮ or ♯. For greater clarity, therefore, anyone who wishes to compose a song should zealously turn his attention to these things. . . .

20. Perhaps Ramis has Jehan des Murs in mind, though I cannot explain his association of Jehan with Villanova; the views that follow resemble Jehan's in his *Ars discantus* (see Coussemaker, *Scriptorum* vol. 3, pp. 71–73).
21. That is, the interval is not a minor but a major third. In modern terminology the c is altered to c-sharp, but note that for Ramis the interval a–c represents either our a–c or our a–c-sharp depending on the melodic context in which it is found and the syllables used to sing it.
22. That is, descending from b to a requires b-flat to be sung.
23. That is, a hexachord will be begun on a; in modern terms, the c's will be raised to c-sharps.

34 Pietro Aaron

Born about 1480 in Florence, Pietro Aaron (or Aron) was cantor at the Cathedral of Imola for a number of years until around 1522. Then he moved to Venice, where he seems to have remained until 1536. In that year he became a monk of the order of the Bearers of the Cross and entered the monastery of San Leonardo at Bergamo. He died about 1550.

Aaron's published works on music theory comprise the *Libri III de institutione harmonica* (1516), the *Toscanello in musica* (1523, with later revised editions), the *Treatise on the Nature and Recognition of All the Tones of Figured Song* (*Trattato della natura e cognitione di tutti gli tuoni di canto figurato,* 1525), the *Lucidario in musica* (1545), and the *Compendiolo di molti dubbi* (ca. 1549–50). The chapters from the *Trattato* given here take their general approach to identifying modes from the fourteenth-century *Lucidarium* of Marchetto of Padua and are anticipated in some particulars in treatises of Tinctoris. Nevertheless, they present the first systematic attempt to apply the modal theory of medieval plainsong to polyphonic repertories. In their numerous citations of individual pieces, they also reflect Aaron's familiarity with the printed collections of polyphony, especially those of Petrucci, that appeared in the first decades of the sixteenth century.

FROM *Treatise on the Nature and Recognition of All the Tones of Figured Song*

(1525)

I. An Explanation of the Finals of All the Tones

Just as it is a credit and an honor to any artificer to comprehend and to know and to have a precise understanding of the parts and reasonings of his art, so it

Text: The original edition (Venice, 1525). Translation by Oliver Strunk. References to practical examples and certain parentheses of the original are given as author's notes. The many examples that Aaron cites are listed below in alphabetical order, with his attributions, the indications of the tones to which he assigns them, and references to the following contemporary editions in which the works appear: *Harmonice musices Odhecaton A* (RISM 1501), *Canti B* (RISM 1502[2]), *Misse Petri de La Rue* (RISM L718; 1503), *Motetti C* (RISM 1504[1]), *Missarum Josquin liber secundus* (RISM J670; 1505), *Motetti a cinque libro primo* (RISM 1508[1]), *Missarum Josquin liber tertius* (RISM J673; 1514), *Motetti de la corona. Libro primo* (RISM 1514[1]), *Motetti de la corona libro secondo* (RISM 1519[1]), *Motetti de la corona. Libro tertio* (RISM 1519[2]), *Motetti libro primo* (RISM 1521[3]).

6 A l'audience	Hayne	Odhecaton 93
6 Allez regretz	Agricola	Odhecaton 57

is a disgrace and a reproach to him not to know and to be in error among the articles of his faculty. Therefore, when I examined and considered the excellence and grandeur of many, many authors, ancient and modern, there is no manner of doubt that did not assail me inwardly as I reflected on this undertaking, especially since I knew the matter to be most difficult, sublime, and lofty

5 Alma redemptoris	Josquin	Corona III
7 Ascendens Christus	Hylaere	Corona I
8 Beata Dei genitrix	Anon	Motetti C
1 / 2 Beata Dei genitrix	Mouton	Corona I
3 Benedic anima mea	Anon	Corona II
6 Brunette	Stokhem	Odhecaton 5
8 C'est possible	Anon	Odhecaton 72
2 Ce n'est pas	La Rue	Canti B
– Cela sans plus	Josquin	Odhecaton 61
6 Celeste beneficium	Mouton	Corona I
1 Clangat plebs flores	Regis	Motetti a 5
7 Comment peult	Josquin	Canti B
1 Congregati sunt	Mouton	Corona II
2 D'ung aultre amer	Orto	Canti B
2 D'ung aultre amer	Hayne	
2 De tous biens playne	Hayne	Odhecaton 20
8 Disant adieu madame	Anon	Odhecaton 89
8 E d'en revenez vous	Compère	Canti B
8 E la la la	Anon	Canti B
6 Egregie Christi	Févin	Corona I
1 Fors seulement	La Rue	Canti B
1 Gaude Barbara	Mouton	Corona I
1 Gaude Virgo	Festa	
8 Hélas hélas	Ninot	Canti B
1 Hélas qu'il est à mon gré	Japart	Odhecaton 30
5 Hélas que pourra devenir	Caron	Odhecaton 13
– Hélas m'amour	Anon	
5 Illuminare Jerusalem	Mouton	Corona II
3 Interveniat pro rege nostro	Jacotin	Corona II
7 Je cuide si ce temps	Anon	Odhecaton 2
1 Je déspite tous	Brumel	Canti B
6 Je ne demande	Busnois	Odhecaton 42
8 Je suis amie	Anon	Canti B
1 Judica me Deus	Caen	Corona II
1 L'homme armé	Josquin	Canti B
8 Ne l'oserai je dire	Anon	Odhecaton 29
– La dicuplaisant	Anon	
1 La plus des plus	Josquin	Odhecaton 64
5 La regretée	Hayne	Canti B
3 Laetatus sum	Eustachio	Corona I
– Le serviteur	Anon	Odhecaton 35
7 Madame hélas	Anon	Odhecaton 66
3 Malheur me bat	Ockeghem	Odhecaton 63
7 Mes pensées	Compère	Odhecaton 59
3 Michael archangele	Jacotin	Corona II
3 Miserere	Josquin	Corona III

to explain. None the less I intend to relate it to you, most gracious reader, not in a presumptuous or haughty style, but speaking humanely and at your feet. And knowing it to be exacting and strange, I judge that it was abandoned by the celebrated musicians already referred to not through ignorance but merely because it proved otherwise troublesome and exacting at the time. For it is clear that no writers of our age have explained how the many different modes are to be recognized, although to their greater credit they have treated of matters which cannot be readily understood. I, therefore, not moved by ambition of any kind, but as a humble man, have undertaken this task, hoping that in humanity and kindliness my readers will all excuse whatever errors I may make. I show briefly what I know to be necessary, for I see that many are deceived

1 Missa Ave maris stella	Josquin	Missarum II
1 Missa D'ung aultre amer	Josquin	Missarum II
– Missa de Beata Virgine	Josquin	Missarum III
5, 7 Missa de Beata Virgine	La Rue	Missae
2 Missa Hercules dux Ferrariae	Josquin	Missarum II
7 Missa Ut sol	Mouton	
7 Mittit ad Virginem	Anon	Motetti C
8 Mon mari m'a diffamée	Orto	Canti B
7 Multi sunt vocati	Zanetto [Giovanni del Lago]	
8 Myn morgem ghaf	Anon	Canti B
1 Nobilis progenie	Févin	Corona I
1 Nomine qui Domini	Caen	Corona II
3 Nunca fué pena mayor	Anon	Odhecaton 4
6 O admirabile commercium	Josquin	Motetti I
4 O Maria rogamus te	Anon	Motetti C
8 O venus bant	Josquin	Odhecaton 78
– Peccata mea Domine	Mouton	Corona II
1 Pour quoy fut fuie cette emprise	Anon	Canti B
1 Pourtant si mon	Busnois	
5 Quaeramus cum pastoribus	Mouton	Motetti I
1 Rogamus te Virgo Maria	Jacotin	Corona II
6 Sancta Trinitas	Févin	Corona I
8 Si dedero	Agricola	Odhecaton 56
2 Si mieulx	Compère	Odhecaton 51
5 Si sumpsero	Obrecht	Canti B
5 Stabat mater	Josquin	Corona III
6 Tempus meum	Févin	Corona I
2 Virgo celesti	Compère	Canti B
6 Vostre bergeronette	Compère	Odhecaton 41
1 Vulnerasti cor meum	Févin	Corona I

For careful analysis of the chapters translated here see Harold Powers, "Is Mode Real? Pietro Aron, the Octenary System, and Polyphony," *Basler Jahrbuch für historische Musikpraxis* 16 (1992): 9–52, and Cristle Collins Judd, "Reading Aron reading Petrucci: The Music Examples of the *Trattato della natura et cognitione di tutti gli tuoni* (1525)," *Early Music History* 14 (1995): 121–52. I have made several changes in Strunk's chart by comparison with Judd's Tables.

about the true understanding, and regarding this I hope in some measure to satisfy them.

First I intend to explain what is meant by "final" and what by "species" and whether the final is always necessary and rational for the recognition of the tone or whether the tones are sometimes to be recognized from their species. Then I shall show what part the singer ought to examine and how composers ought to proceed in their compositions in accordance with their intentions, touching also on certain other secrets which will surely afford you no little delight.

I say, then, that the final being diverse, that is, regular or irregular, it follows that each tone has a similarly diverse form. From this it follows that at one time the final governs and at another time the species. "Final" I define in this way: a final is simply a magisterial ending in music, introduced in order that the tone may be recognized. Musicians conclude such an ending regularly or irregularly in order that the nature and form of each tone may be the better understood. Thus the positions D *sol re,* E *la mi,* F *fa ut,* and G *sol re ut* have been constituted regular finals or ending steps for the first and second, third and fourth, fifth and sixth, and seventh and eighth tones, while the steps Gamma *ut,* A *re,* ♮ *mi,* C *fa ut,* A *la mi re,* B *fa* ♮ *mi,* and C *sol fa ut* are called irregular. In accordance with this understanding, the final remains necessary, rational, and governing to every tone on the above-named regular steps.

The species, then, will govern sometimes regularly and sometimes irregularly. "Species" is simply the arrangement of the sounds of the genus, varied in definite prescribed ways, as shown in the example.

| The first diapente and diatessaron | The second diapente and diatessaron | The third diapente and diatessaron | The fourth diapente and diatessaron |

It follows, then, that the final is also necessary in the above-named irregular positions, namely A *la mi re,* B *fa* ♮ *mi,* and C *sol fa ut.* Here we shall consider it in two ways: first, with respect to confinality; second, with respect to the differences of the Saeculorum.[1] Thus, if a composition[2] ends in the position called A *la mi re* and there is no flat in the signature, the final will be common to the first and second tones with respect to confinality and also to the third with respect to difference, provided—as you will understand from what fol-

---

1. The confinals of the eight tones are, for Aaron, the pitches a fifth above (or a fourth below) the established finals. He seems not to have thought it necessary to list the differences. These are the variable formulas used to end the eight psalm tones associated with the eight modes of chant theory; see Powers, "Is Mode Real?", p. 25. Aaron calls them "the differences of the Saeculorum" because the last word of the Lesser Doxology that ends psalm recitations is *saeculorum.*
2. I speak always of masses, motets, canzoni, frottole, strambotti, madrigali, sonetti, and capitoli. [Au.]

lows—that the *processo* in the composition be suited and appropriate to confi-nality or difference.[3] But if the composition has a flat in the signature, the final will be in my opinion neither necessary nor rational with respect to confinality, for it is clear that the form will differ from its previous state. For this reason, such compositions are to be judged by their species. The same will obviously apply to compositions ending on B *fa* ♮ *mi,* C *sol fa ut,* and all other steps on which the species may occur.

Therefore, the cognition derived from species is necessary understanding and not arbitrary to music. First, because this cognition is by definition true and necessary. Besides this, understanding that is necessary has something essential about it; but the cognition of species is essential and therefore necessary. Besides this, that which demands necessary cognition is *per se;* but the cogni-tion of species is cognition *per se* and therefore necessary. Nor is it an objection that we are for the most part accustomed to base our cognition of music on the final, for I reply that this has been for the sake of readier understanding, inas-much as those things that are at the end are customarily more closely observed than those that are at the beginning and in the middle.

And that our conclusion is true, we may demonstrate with these and other similar arguments. We say that man is defined as an animal rational and mortal; it is certain that rational and mortal are two differences for knowing what man is; of these, one is final and considered according to the end of man, namely mortal—the other is formal and considered according to the specific and for-mal being of living man, namely rational; the latter makes the essence of man better known than the former, which considers him according to his end, namely that man is mortal, for this is common both to man and to the other animals. Thus the cognition of the end is not cognition *per se* and therefore not always necessary. And this is demonstrated by certain compositions which, having the ordinary and regular final, but lacking the ascent and descent of some of its species, are not said to be of any tone but (as was shown in Chapter 30 of the first book of another work of mine, *De institutione harmonica*) are merely called *Canti euphoniaci.*

---

3. As Aaron explains in Chapter 8, suitable and appropriate *processo* turns largely on the choice of proper steps for medial cadences. In Chapters 9 to 12 these are said to be as follows: for the first tone—D, F, G, and a; for the second—A, C, D, F, G, and a; for the third—E, F, G, a, ♮, and c; for the fourth—C, D, E, F, G, and a; for the fifth—F, a, and c; for the sixth—C, D, F, a, and c; for the seventh—G, a, ♮, c, and d; for the eighth—D, F, G, and c. *Processo* (Latin *processus*) is a difficult but important term in Medieval and Renaissance discussions of mode, and I have chosen to mark this complexity throughout Aaron's chapters here by leaving it untranslated. For Aaron, *processo* signifies in part the range or compass of a given tenor melody. But it also connotes less quantifiable elements: the way the melody moves through its range, the pitch areas it emphasizes, the medial cadential points it gravitates toward, and others. In this way the term cuts to the heart of Medieval and Renaissance conceptions of mode, which did not involve reified scales so much as manners of exploring and exploiting particular segments extracted from the Guidonian gamut of pitches.

2. How the Singer Ought to Judge the Tone

The tenor being the firm and stable part, the part, that is, that holds and comprehends the whole concentus of the harmony, the singer must judge the tone by means of this part only. For we see that when a tenor and its cantus are far apart it causes, not pleasure, but little sweetness to those who hear it, something which arises from the distance that lies between the cantus and the contrabassus. The tenor being for this reason better suited to the natural *processi* and more easily handled, every composition[4] is in my opinion to be judged by its tenor. For in the tenor the natural form is more readily considered than in the soprano, where, should you wish to form the seventh tone, you would need to find its diatessaron through the accidental course.[5] Thus we prescribe this manner and order for all compositions written at the composer's pleasure, whether upon a plainsong or without regard for one, also for compositions for five, six, seven, and more voices, in which it is usual to write a first and principal tenor. Each of the added parts will be governed by the nature of the tenor, and by means of the tenor the tone will be recognized unless the plainsong itself, which is primary and principal to such a recognition, be in some other part.[6]

3. Ways of Recognizing the Tone of Different Compositions

Reflecting alone for days and days, I recalled certain projects often in my mind. Wherefore, gracious reader, had not your gentle aspect and my eager wish for the desired end constrained me, I should more lightly have lowered the sails at the hard-won port. But since I think that you by no means blamed it, I wish to pursue the enterprise begun, not for those who turn a thing over and over, but solely for those unfamiliar with this fare. Thus, having reached this point, I am left somewhat in doubt. Yet I intend rather to go on reasoning

4. Whether Introit, Kyrie, Gloria, Gradual, Alleluia, Credo, Offertory, Sanctus, Agnus Dei, Post-communion, Respond, Deo gratias, Psalm, Hymn, Magnificat, motet, canzone, frottola, bergerette, strambotto, madrigal, or capitolo. [Au.]

5. We see, in other words, that when a tenor and its cantus belong to the same tone—and unless this is the case, the cantus can have no bearing on the tonality of the composition—they will lie far apart and the resulting texture will be disagreeable, particularly in view of the disparity between the cantus and the contrabassus. Thus the usual thing will be to make the tenor authentic and the cantus plagal, or vice versa, leaving the tenor as the sole determining factor. Aside from this, "in view of the inconvenience of the upward range," the cantus will seldom ascend to the octave above the final in the seventh tone or (see chap. 5 below) in the transposed third. Aaron's "accidental course" refers to pitches above the Guidonian gamut.

6. Cf. Johannes Tinctoris, *Liber de natura et proprietate tonorum* 24: "When some mass or chanson or any other composition you please is made up of various parts, belonging to different tones, if you ask without qualification to what tone such a composition belongs, the person asked ought to reply without qualification according to the quality of the tenor, for in every composition this is the principal part and the basis of the whole relationship. But if it be asked specifically to what tone some single part of such a composition belongs, the person asked will reply specifically, 'To such and such a tone.

with you, seeking a rule by means of which you may arrive at a clear understanding of each of the tones in question.

In so far as compositions end in the positions D *sol re*, E *la mi*, F *fa ut*, and G *sol re ut*, they are to be judged according to their finals, and by means of these their true and proper species[7] will be recognized. These are the steps called regular to the first, second, third, fourth, fifth, sixth, seventh, and eighth tones, and on these steps the final will be necessary, rational, and governing.

Let me explain this to you more fully. First consider those compositions that have their final on D *sol re* and that at the beginning or in their course proceed with the species of the third, fourth, fifth, sixth, seventh, or eighth tone; all these are in my opinion to be judged only from their proper and regular final, even though they contain contradictory and unsuitable *processi*, for no other tone has a difference ending on this step. And as to those ending on E *la mi*, these are in my opinion subject in the same way only to their own form. Such compositions are best said to belong to mixed tones *(toni commisti)*.[8]

But those compositions that end in the position called F *fa ut* are in my opinion subject not only to their own final and species but also to the nature and form of the first and fourth tones, in view of the difference which these tones sometimes exhibit on this step. Understand, however, that this is when they proceed in the way suited to the first and fourth tones, for otherwise they will remain of the fifth or sixth. Certain others end on G *sol re ut;* these are in my opinion subject to the seventh and eighth tones and also to the first, second, third, and fourth, as you will understand from what follows.[9]

Certain other compositions end on the irregular steps A *la mi re*, B *fa ♮ mi*, and C *sol fa ut;* these we shall consider according to their *processo*, their species, and the differences of the Saeculorum, for these considerations will govern them and yield the true recognition of the tone.

Certain other compositions end on D *la sol re*, E *la mi*, F *fa ut*, and G *sol re ut;*[10] these steps are of the same nature as the regular steps previously named.

Certain other compositions, although they end regularly, have a flat signature; these are to be judged according to their species (excepting those ending on D *sol re* and F *fa ut*, etc.), for the final will now be neither necessary nor rational to the recognition of the tone.

Certain other compositions proceed at the beginning and in their course with the species suited to a given tone but end with species that contradict it;

7. Namely, from D *sol re* to the first A *la mi re* and from thence to D *la sol re*, from E *la mi* to B *fa ♮ mi* and from thence to high E *la mi*, from F *fa ut* to C *sol fa ut* and from thence to high F *fa ut*, and from low G *sol re ut* to D *la sol re* and from thence to the second G *sol re ut*. [Au.]

8. Cf. Johannes Tinctoris, *Terminorum musicae diffinitorium* 18: 'A *tonus commixtus* is one which, if authentic, is mixed with a tone other than its plagal, if plagal, with a tone other than its authentic."

9. Aaron does not refer again to the possibility of endings on F in the first and fourth tones or on G (as difference) in the first, second, and fourth; for the ending on G in the third, see chap. 5 below.

10. I.e., an octave above the regular finals D *sol re* etc.

these are to be judged according to the species and differences previously mentioned, excepting (as was noted above) those ending on the regular finals.

Certain other compositions have an irregular end and an inharmonious *processo* without any complete diapente by means of which their true form might be recognized; these are to be judged by means of some species of diatessaron or by their own finals.

One will also find compositions arbitrarily written without regard to form or regular manner, comparable indeed to players of the game called *alleta,* who agree upon a certain goal at which they will take refuge and, chasing one after another, run back to that place or goal and are safe; of the composers of such works as these we say that they turn aimlessly round and round, progressing and digressing beyond the nature and the primary order that they have in mind until, by some trick, they arrive at an end of their own. Such harmonies or compositions can in my opinion be judged only by means of the final, and then only when they end without a flat signature.

In certain other compositions this signature appears only in the contrabassus, in others only in the tenor; such an arrangement is in our opinion neither permissible nor suitable in a harmony or composition unless it is used deliberately and introduced with art.[11]

Certain other compositions have a flat signature on low E *la mi,* the first A *la mi re,* B *fa ♮ mi,* and high E *la mi;* whether they end regularly or irregularly, these are in my opinion to be judged according to the species, not according to the final.[12]

4. An Explanation of the First and Second Tones

Every composition in which the tenor ends on D *sol re* is unhesitatingly to be assigned to the first or second tone, the more readily if the soprano ends on D *la sol re* with the regular and rational final, clearly showing the natural form.[13] The same is also true of certain other compositions with a flat signature; the nature of these remains unchanged, in my opinion, for only the diatessaron,

11. As by the excellent Josquin in the Patrem of his Mass of Our Lady and in a similar way by the divine Alexander [Agricola] in many of his compositions. [Au.] As published in vol. 42 of *Das Chorwerk,* the Credo of Josquin's *Missa de Beata Virgine* has no signatures whatever. But it is clear from Aaron's comment and from the composition itself that the Tenor secundus, following the Tenor in canon at the fifth below, should have the signature one flat.

12. For example, "Cela sans plus" by Josquin, "Peccata mea Domine" by Jean Mouton (in the *Motetti de la corona*), "Le serviteur," "Hélas m'amour," "La dicuplaisant," &c. [Au.] Cf. Johannes Tinctoris, *Liber de natura et proprietate tonorum* 24: "If some one were to say to me, speaking in general, 'Tinctoris, I ask you to what tone the chanson *Le serviteur* belongs,' I would reply, 'Generally speaking, to the first tone irregular,' since the tenor, or principal part, of this chanson belongs to this tone. But if he were to ask specifically to what tone the superius or contratenor belongs, I would reply specifically that the one and the other belong to the second tone irregular. But there is no one who doubts that a specific question about the tenor is to be answered as was the general one."

13. As in the motets "Rogamus te virgo Maria" by Jacotin, "Judica me Deus" by A. Caen, "Congregati sunt" and "Beata Dei genitrix" by Jean Mouton, and "Clangat plebs flores" by Regis. [Au.]

formed by the interval A *la mi re* to D *la sol re,* is altered. Seeing then that the diapente primary and natural to the tone is left intact, such compositions are also to be assigned to the first tone.[14]

And if sometimes, as has become the custom, the composer prolongs his work, amusing himself with additional progressions, you will, in my opinion, need to consider whether the final, as altered by the composer, is suited to and in keeping or out of keeping with his composition, for if reason guides him in what is suited to the tone he will at least see to it that some one part (namely, the tenor or cantus) sustains the final, while the others proceed as required by the tone, regular or irregular, with pleasing and appropriate progressions like those shown below, or in some more varied manner according to his pleasure and disposition.

OPTIONAL ENDING FOR THE FIRST AND SECOND TONES:

But since some will say, perhaps, that the position D *sol re* is common also to the second tone, I shall tell you that in figured music you will very seldom find a tenor with the *processo* and downward range suited and appropriate to the second tone ended in this way. Nevertheless, a composer may wish to proceed in accordance with the nature of the second tone; he will then take care to proceed at the beginning and in the course of his composition with some regard for its proper form, as observed and comprehended in the psalms and the Magnificat, where he is restricted and subject to the manner and order proper to the second tone.

Certain other compositions end on the step G *sol re ut;* with a flat signature, these are in my opinion only to be understood as of the first or second tone, even though this is the step ordinary and regular to the seventh and eighth. For this signature (or figure) alters the form or structure proper and natural to the seventh and eighth tones; at the same time, having acquired the species belonging to the first and second, the final becomes inactive and on this step is left arbitrary and as it were regular *per se,* not suited to the seventh and eighth tones, but necessary to the first and second.[15]

Certain other compositions, ending on this same step, are said to be of the

14. As in the motet "Nomine qui Domini" by A. Caen, "Pour quoy fut fuie cette emprise," &c. [Au.]

15. This is demonstrated by the following masses and motets, which are of the first tone in view of their *processo,* structure, and complete diapason: *Ave maris stella* and *D'ung aultre amer* by Josquin, "Nobilis progenie" and "Vulnerasti cor meum" by Févin, &c. [Au.]

second tone; these are readily recognized by their extended downward range.[16] And if this consideration seems to you not always to the purpose, do not be surprised, for composers sometimes observe the *processo* of a given tone at the beginning and in the course of a composition, ending then in accordance with the difference of the plainsong, as you will understand from what follows.

Certain other tenors end on A *la mi re;* here you will need to consider and examine whether their *processo* is suited and rational to such an ending, for if a tenor ends irregularly in the first or second tone, not proceeding with its proper form, it may easily not belong to it, even though this step is one of its irregular finals and an ending of its Saeculorum or difference. As you will understand from what follows, this is because the third and fourth tones also use this step as a difference. For this reason, then, you will assign such a tenor to the first or second tone only when you find the proper form.[17]

Certain other compositions end on D *la sol re;* these are in my opinion to be assigned in the same way to the first and second tones, for it is clearly evident that from D *la sol re* to its diapason is the proper form of the first diapente and diatessaron, namely *re–la* and *re–sol.* When they ascend as far as the fifth or sixth step, and especially when they ascend still further, they will be of the first tone.[18] But when they lack this extension to the upper limit of the diapente, proceeding rather in the lower register, they will be of the second tone and not of the first. This opinion of mine is supported by the venerable Father Zanetto, a musician of Venice.[19]

5. AN EXPLANATION OF THE THIRD AND FOURTH TONES

The few who fish these waters are in the habit of saying that every composition ending in the position E *la mi* is to be assigned to the fourth tone. They forget that this step is common also to the third, and in so doing seem to me to involve themselves in no little difficulty. Seeing that the difference often ends on this step in the fourth tone, many, thinking only of the ending of its Saeculorum, judge a composition to belong to it. Thus the greatest confusion may easily arise. It is accordingly necessary to consider at various times the final, the upward and downward range, the *processo,* the intonations, and the

16. For example, "Virgo celesti" by Loyset Compère, "D'ung aultre amer" and "De tous biens playne" by Hayne, "Ce n'est pas" by Pierre de La Rue, and "D'ung aultre amer" by Orto. [Au.]

17. As in "La plus de plus" by Josquin, which is of the first tone in view of the course of its diapente and its upward range, or in "Si mieulx" by Loyset Compère, which is of the second, as will be readily evident. [Au.]

18. Whether with a flat signature, as in "Pourtant si mon" by Antoine Busnois, "Gaude virgo," a motet by Costanzo Festa, "L'homme armé" *et sic de singulis* by Josquin, and "Hélas qu'il est à mon gré" by Japart; or without, as in "Fors seulement" by Pierre de La Rue, "Je déspite tous" by Brumel, and "Gaude Barbara" by Jean Mouton. [Au.]

19. For example, the mass *Hercules dux Ferrariae,* composed by Josquin, and many other works which I shall not enumerate, since you will readily understand them from their similarity to this one. [Au.] "Father Zanetto" is the music theorist and composer Giovanni del Lago; see Bonnie Blackburn, Edward Lowinsky, and Clement Miller, *A Correspondence of Renaissance Musicians* (Oxford: Clarendon Press, 1991), p. 129, n. 10.

differences, which, since they are of different sorts, end naturally in different ways.[20]

OPTIONAL ENDING FOR THE THIRD AND FOURTH TONES:

Certain other compositions ending in the position G *sol re ut* are said to be of the third tone, even though this is the step ordinary and regular to the seventh and eighth. You will need to give your most careful consideration to these and, above all, to their *processo*, for unless they have the form and order due and appropriate to the third tone, with this final they will never be assigned to it, but rather to the seventh or eighth. But where the natural form is found, they will always be assigned to the third tone, and not to the seventh or eighth, in view of their form and difference.[21] This opinion is likewise supported by the venerable Father Zanetto, Venetian musician.

You will also find certain other compositions ending on A *la mi re;* when these observe the appropriate *processo* they will be assigned to the third tone.[22] But when they have a flat signature, they are in my opinion to be assigned to the third tone the more readily, even though at the beginning and in their course they fail to proceed in the due and appropriate way, for it is evident that the regular structure of the tone[23] will prevail. But because of the inconvenience of their upward range, few such pieces will be found, unless written for equal voices or *voci mutate*.[24] So compositions of this sort are to be assigned to the third or fourth tone in view of their species and downward range, not because of their difference or *processo*. Thus it may be inferred that, in view of their extended downward range, they will in preference be assigned to the fourth tone.[25]

20. Thus, in the motet "Michael archangele" by Jacotin, the first part is in my opinion of the irregular third tone while the second ends in the regular third tone, not in the fourth; the same is true of "Malheur me bat" by Ockeghem, "Interveniat pro rege nostro" by Jacotin, and many other compositions, similar to these and having the regular final and the required *processo* and upward range. [Au.]
21. For example, "Nunca fué pena mayor," &c. [Au.]
22. For example, "Miserere mei Deus" by Josquin, "Laetatus sum" by Eustachio, "Benedic anima mea Dominum," in which the first part ends on the confinal, the second on the final, and the third on the difference, &c. [Au.]
23. Namely, *mi-mi* and *mi-la*, arising from the interval A *la mi re* to high E *la mi,* to which is added the upper diatessaron *mi-la*. [Au.]
24. That is, for a group of voices restricted to a similar, in this case high, compass. The more common term for such a group is *voci pari*.
25. For example, "O Maria rogamus te" in the *Motetti C* and many others which you will readily recognize on the same principle. [Au.]

6. An Explanation of the Fifth and Sixth Tones

Spurred on by your affection and with my goal in sight, I turn to the question about which you may have been in doubt. Thus, in beginning this part of my explanation, I ask you to observe that compositions ending in the position F *fa ut* are to be assigned to the fifth or sixth tone. On this point I should like to remove any remaining uncertainty, for seeing that such compositions very often—indeed, almost always—have the flat signature and that the form of the tone is altered, it would be easy for you to believe the contrary, in view of certain opinions that I have expressed above.[26] Know, then, that in compositions such as these the older composers were more concerned with facility than with proper form and correct structure. For the fifth and sixth tones often require the help of the b-flat, although always to use it would be contrary to the tendencies of the mediations of these tones as laid down by the ancients. This opinion is likewise supported by the previously mentioned Venetian, Father Zanetto. For this reason, then, the older composers altered the third diapente, giving it the nature of the fourth, in order that the tritone which would otherwise occur in running through it might not cause inconvenience or harshness in their music.[27]

OPTIONAL ENDING FOR THE FIFTH AND SIXTH TONES:

And if certain other compositions, ending on A *la mi re,* are to be assigned to the fifth tone, know that at the beginning and in their course these must observe a *processo* suited to it; lacking this, the difference will have little force and, as previously explained, they may easily be of some other tone. Nevertheless, the composer may if he pleases observe this tone, but what is necessary

26. The reader, that is, having been told that in the D and F modes the flat signature does not effect a transformation (chap. 3), and having seen that the explanation of this given for the D modes (chap. 4) will not apply to the F, will have anticipated a difficulty at this point.

27. This is uniformly demonstrated in the following compositions of the fifth tone, compositions which cannot be otherwise assigned in view of their upward range and *processo:* "Stabat mater dolorosa" and "Alma redemptoris" by Josquin, "Hélas que pourra devenir" by Caron, "Quaeramus cum pastoribus" and "Illuminare illuminare Jerusalem" by Jean Mouton, and the Sanctus and Agnus Dei of the Mass of Our Lady by Pierre de La Rue. Those which do not have frequent *processo* in this high range, falling short of the diapente or hexachord, are to be assigned to the sixth tone as regularly ended, for example, "Brunette" by Stokhem, "Vostre bergeronette" by Compère, "Je ne demande" by Busnois, "Allez regretz" by Agricola, "A l'audience" by Hayne, "Sancta Trinitas unus Deus" and "Tempus meum est ut revertar ad eum" by Févin, "Celeste beneficium" by Jean Mouton, "'Egregie Christi" by Févin, &c. [Au.]

will be recognized more clearly in the psalms and the Magnificat. The sixth tone we do not concede on this step, for it has neither the form nor the difference.

Certain other compositions ending on B *fa* ♮ *mi* are said to be of the fifth tone, but we do not approve this in the absence of the flat signature (or figure) which on this step produces the proper structure both ascending and descending. Here, then, the final is rational, necessary, and governing, and in this way the proper form is recognized.[28]

Certain other compositions, ending on C *sol fa ut,* are said to be of the fifth tone, both with and without the flat signature;[29] this is solely in view of the difference which the plainsong sometimes exhibits here. The sixth tone is lacking on this step, even though it is the confinal of the fifth and sixth tones regularly ended, for the step can bear no form or difference appropriate to it.

7. AN EXPLANATION OF THE SEVENTH AND EIGHTH TONES

Certain persons have held that the seventh and eighth tones may end regularly and irregularly on three steps, namely Gamma *ut,* C *fa ut,* and G *sol re ut,* and regarding these endings many advance many different opinions, especially regarding those on Gamma *ut* and C *fa ut.* Compositions ending on these steps they assign rather to the seventh tone than to the eighth, and this because such a composition seldom if ever descends as the plagal form requires. In view of this confusion I shall tell you that I cannot admit such opinions, for it is clear that these compositions continue to observe the natural requirements of the proper and regular tones. Those ending on Gamma *ut,* in view of their acquired form, peculiar to the seventh tone, I take to be of this tone and not of the eighth when they are without the flat signature, but of the first or second when they have it. But those ending on C *fa ut,* for the reason given above and also because they do not have the proper diatessaron, I assign to the eighth tone and not to the seventh.[30] This opinion is likewise held by the previously mentioned musician, Father Zanetto.

Certain other compositions end in the position G *sol re ut;* these are naturally and regularly to be assigned to the seventh tone or to the eighth in view of their proper final and natural form.[31]

---

28. As demonstrated in the chanson "La regretée," composed by Hayne, which is of the fifth tone in view of its species, cadences, and upward range; or in "O admirabile commercium" by Josquin, which is said to be of the sixth, as are certain others similar to it, although there are few of these. [Au.]

29. For example, "Si sumpsero" by Obrecht. [Au.]

30. As demonstrated in the following compositions: "Mon mari m'a diffamée" by Orto and the chanson called "E la la la"; following the same principle you will understand the rest. [Au.]

31. Thus the mass *Ut sol* by Jean Mouton and the Gloria of Our Lady by Pierre de La Rue are in our opinion to be assigned to the seventh tone in view of their species, their final, and their extended upward range; the same applies to "Multi sunt vocati pauci vero electi" by the venerable Father Zanetto of Venice and "Ascendens Christus in altum" by Hylaere. But "Si dedero" by Alexander Agricola and "C'est possible que l'homme peut" will be of the eighth tone in view

OPTIONAL ENDING FOR THE SEVENTH AND EIGHTH TONES:

Certain other compositions end in the position C *sol fa ut;* these are in my opinion to be assigned in the same way to the seventh tone or to the eighth in view of their difference and *processo,* the difference often ending on this step. Thus, if such a composition proceeds in the appropriate way it will most certainly be of the seventh tone or of the eighth in view of its final, still more reasonably so if it has the flat signature, for this will give it the proper structure, namely *ut–sol* and *re–sol,* the form peculiar to the seventh and eighth tones.[32]

Following these principles in your examinations and reflecting on the method set forth above, you will have a clear understanding of any other composition or tone suited and appropriate to figured music.

---

of their final and their *processo;* the same is true of "O venus bant" by Josquin, "Disant adieu-madame," "Je suis amie," "Myn morghem ghaf," "Hélas hélas" by Ninot, "E d'en revenez vous" by Compère, "Beata Dei genitrix," and many others which you will recognize on the same principle. [Au.]

32. Thus "Mes pensées" by Compère, "Madame hélas," "Comment peult" by Josquin, and "Mittit ad virginem" can be assigned only to the seventh tone, and also "Je cuide si ce temps"; and "Ne l'oserai je dire" will be of the eighth tone and not of the seventh, as its form and extended downward *processo* will show you. [Au.]

35 Heinrich Glarean

Heinrich Glarean (known as Glareanus), one of the great humanist-scholars of the sixteenth century, was born in the canton of Glarus in Switzerland in 1488 and died in Freiburg in 1563. A friend of Erasmus of Rotterdam, Glarean was a philosopher, theologian, philologist, historian, poet, and musical scholar. Already in 1512 he was crowned poet laureate by Emperor Maximilian I. Among his works of musical interest, the most important is the *Dodecachordon* (literally, the *Instrument of Twelve Strings*). Here he advocated a system of twelve modes, adding four new modes to the existing eight: Aeolian, Hypoaeolian, Ionian, and Hypoionian. True to Glarean's humanist background, his discussion of the modes incorporates classical learning much more than Aaron's. Glarean rationalized his twelve-mode system by a scrupulous analysis, along ancient lines, of the pertinent octave species and their formation out of the conjunction of different species of fifth and fourth. He selected the names for his new modes after carefully scrutinizing ancient authorities and their varying terminologies. Nevertheless, his new modes, like Aaron's, had an empirical basis as well. This is clear from his use of Gregorian chant to exemplify the twelve-mode system (which also made a broader ideological point: Glarean was a staunch Catholic and resisted movements of Protestant reform). Glarean's empiricism is evident also in his presentation of numerous full compositions by composers of his time to exemplify his theory and in his observations that modern polyphonic practice tended to the frequent use of the octave species that we would call the major and natural minor modes.

Glarean's twelve-mode system was very influential. Zarlino embraced it in his *Istitutioni harmoniche* without mentioning Glarean and, later, went Glarean one better by renumbering his modes from the Ionian, beginning on C, rather than from the conventional starting-point, Dorian-D. In the present excerpt Glarean combines a paean to his favorite composer, Josquin Desprez, with an exemplification by means of Josquin's works of the mixture of authentic and plagal modal pairs.

FROM *Dodecachordon*
(1547)

BOOK 3

CHAPTER 24: EXAMPLES OF THE PAIRED COMBINATIONS OF THE MODES TOGETHER WITH AN ENCOMIUM OF JOSQUIN DESPREZ

So much for our examples of the twelve modes in that varied sort of music not (at least in our opinion) inappropriately called mensural, examples cited with all possible brevity from various authors in proof of those things that have seemed to us in need of proof. It now remains for us to give examples of these same modes in combination,[1] not commonplace examples, to be sure, but weighty ones elegantly illustrating the matter. And since in our preceding book[2] we have sufficiently discussed the actual nature of these combinations, we shall refrain from re-examining it here. All our examples will be in the order seen in our last book; thus, having begun with Dorian and Hypodorian, we shall then add examples of the other paired combinations, briefly expressing our opinion about these, partly to show others a better way of judging and, as it were, to open men's eyes, partly to make known the merits of the ingenious

---

TEXT: The original edition (Basle, 1547). Glarean gives the complete musical texts of the seven examples discussed in this chapter. These are omitted here. Translation by Oliver Strunk.

1. Examples, that is, in which the tenor or principal part has the combined plagal and authentic range.
2. 2.28–35.

in this art, merits which to certain sufficiently hostile judges seem common-place, but which to us seem considerable and most worthy of admiration.

Now in this class of authors and in this great crowd of the ingenious there stands out as by far pre-eminent in temperament, conscientiousness, and industry (or I am mistaken in my feeling) Jodocus à Prato, whom people play-fully (ὑποκοριστικῶς) call in his Belgian mother-tongue Josquin, as though they were to say "Little Jodocus." If this man, besides that native bent and strength of character by which he was distinguished, had had an understanding of the twelve modes and of the truth of musical theory, nature could have brought forth nothing more majestic and magnificent in this art; so versatile was his temperament in every respect, so armed with natural acumen and force, that there is nothing he could not have done in this profession. But moderation was wanting for the most part and, with learning, judgment; thus in certain places in his compositions he did not, as he should have, soberly repress the violent impulses of his unbridled temperament. Yet let this petty fault be condoned in view of the man's other incomparable gifts.

No one has more effectively expressed the passions of the soul in music than this symphonist, no one has more felicitously begun, no one has been able to compete in grace and facility on an equal footing with him, just as there is no Latin poet superior in the epic to Maro. For just as Maro, with his natural facility, was accustomed to adapt his poem to his subject so as to set weighty matters before the eyes of his readers with close-packed spondees, fleeting ones with unmixed dactyls, to use words suited to his every subject, in short, to undertake nothing inappropriately,[3] as Flaccus says of Homer, so our Jos-quin, where his matter requires it, now advances with impetuous and precipi-tate notes, now intones his subject in long-drawn tones, and, to sum up, has brought forth nothing that was not delightful to the ear and approved as inge-nious by the learned, nothing, in short, that was not acceptable and pleasing, even when it seemed less erudite, to those who listened to it with judgment. In most of his works he is the magnificent virtuoso, as in the *Missa super voces musicales* and the *Missa ad fugam;* in some he is the mocker, as in the *Missa La sol fa re mi;* in some he extends himself in rivalry,[4] as in the *Missa de Beata Virgine;* although others have also frequently attempted all these things, they have not with the same felicity met with a corresponding success in their undertakings.

This was for us the reason why in this, the consummation of our work, we have by preference cited examples by this man. And although his talent is beyond description, more easily admired than properly explained, he still seems preferable to others, not only for his talent, but also for his diligence in emending his works. For those who have known him say that he brought his things forth with much hesitation and with corrections of all sorts, and that he

3. Maro is Virgil. Compare the similar remarks by Zarlino in no. 2 above, p. 17.
4. With Antoine Brumel; see below at n. 20.

gave no composition to the public unless he had kept it by him for several years, the opposite of what we said Jacob Obrecht is reported to have done. Hence some not inappropriately maintain that the one may justly be compared to Virgil, the other to Ovid. But if we admit this, to whom shall we more fittingly compare Pierre de La Rue, an astonishingly delightful composer, than to Horace, Isaac than perhaps to Lucan, Févin than to Claudianus, Brumel to Statius? Yet I should seem foolish, and rightly, if I were to speak with so little taste of these men, and perhaps I should deserve to hear that popular saying, "Shoemaker, stick to your last!" Hence I proceed to the explanation and judging of the examples.

Of the first combination, that of Dorian and Hypodorian, let our example be the melody "Victimae paschali laudes," on the Blessed Resurrection of Christ, as set by this same author Josquin, a melody that we have mentioned twice before and that we have further cited as an example of this combination in our second book.[5] In it, it will rightly be judged ingenious that the given theme is heard thus divided by intervals among the four voices, as is most fitting.[6] In its first part, the highest voice, borrowed from some well-known song,[7] presents the Hypodorian mode with an added ditone below. In the following part it is Dorian with an added diatessaron above. Here the ending is on the highest step of the diapason, whereas just the other way it ought to have been on the lowest; this part, however, is also borrowed,[8] and on this account he has not wished to alter it. The tenor is extended a ditone lower than the Hypodorian form requires, but the author does this with his usual license. The borrowed melodies he combines with other ancient ones, appropriately in the same mode, for melodies in other modes would not agree to this extent. At the same time, it was not difficult for this author to combine melodies belonging to different modes, even to do so gracefully, for he composed scarcely a single mass, be its mode what it may, without bringing in the Aeolian mode in the Nicene Creed,[9] something that others have attempted also, but not always with the same success. Each voice has something worthy of note, thus the tenor its stability, the bass its wonderful gravity, although I scarcely know whether it pleases everyone that he ascends as he does in the bass at the word "Galilaea." That this proceeds from the wantonness of his temperament we cannot deny; thus we must accept it gracefully as an addition. The cantus has an ancient flavor; the seventh note from the end is heard alone, with all the other voices pausing. Yet, in comparison with the genius of the man, all these things are wholly unimportant. Let us go on, then, to other examples.

5. 1.14 and 2.29.
6. Josquin treats the plainsong as a "wandering cantus firmus," giving stanza 1 to the tenor and, in stanza 2, l. 1 to the alto, l. 2 to the bass, l. 3 to the tenor, and so forth.
7. It is the superius of Ockeghem's chanson "D'ung aultre amer."
8. It is the superius of Hayne's chanson "De tous biens playne."
9. That is, without interpolating the Gregorian Credo, officially of Mode IV but assigned by Glarean (2.17) to the Aeolian mode.

Here, in the motet "De profundis," I wish everyone to observe closely what the beginning is like and with how much passion and how much majesty the composer has given us the opening words; instead of transposing the modes from their natural positions to the higher register (as is elsewhere the usual custom), he has combined the systems of the two; at the same time, with astonishing and carefully studied elegance, he has thrown the phrase into violent disorder, usurping now the leap of the Lydian, now that of the Ionian, until at length, by means of these most beautiful refinements, he glides, creeping unobserved and without offending the ear, from Dorian to Phrygian.[10] That this is difficult to do, especially in these two modes, the Dorian and Phrygian, we have already shown.[11] Thus, contrary to the nature of the modes, he has ended the combined systems of the Dorian and Hypodorian on E, the seat of the Phrygian. Yet there are other compositions in which he has done this also (nor is he alone in it), evidently from an immoderate love of novelty and an excessive eagerness to win a little glory for being unusual, a fault to which the more ingenious professors of the arts are in general so much given that, be it ever so peculiar to the symphonists, they still share it in common with many others. None the less the motet remains between A and d, respecting the limits of the Dorian and Hypodorian systems. And although by his unusual procedure he has sought nothing else, he has at least made it plain that, through the force of his temperament, he could bring it about that the charge customarily brought against the ancient musicians, namely, of progressing "From Dorian to Phrygian,"[12] would be brought in vain against him by whom it was so learnedly accomplished, without the slightest offense to the ear. But enough of this motet.[13]

The second combination is that of the Hypophrygian and Phrygian modes, extending from B to e. But the combination rarely descends in this way to B without descending also to A; thus it usually lies between C and e. Yet our Josquin, in setting the Genealogy of Christ Our Saviour according to the Evangelists Matthew and Luke for four voices in harmony in this combination, descends to A *re* and ascends to f, adding here a semitone and there a tone,

10. The word "phrase" *(phrasis)* has for Glarean the special meaning "melodic idiom"; the "phrase" of a given mode consists for him partly in its tendency to emphasize its natural arithmetic or harmonic division at the fourth or fifth, partly in its use of certain characteristic tone-successions taken over from plainsong. Compare 1.13, where the leaps characteristic of the eight modes of plainsong are discussed and illustrated; also 2.36. The leap characteristic of the Lydian mode is that from a to c; by Ionian leap Glarean must mean that from e to g.
11. 2.11, where the present example is also mentioned.
12. Ἀπὸ δορίου ἐπὶ φρύγιον. The proverb is also found in Gafori, *De harmonia musicorum instrumentorum opus* 4.2, and seems to harken back to Aristotle's story of Philoxenus attempting to compose a dithyramb in Dorian but being forced by the nature of the genre back to Phrygian; see *Politics* 1342b.
13. Despite the range of its tenor, by which Glarean has evidently been misled, Josquin's "De profundis" is clearly Hypophrygian, or combined Phrygian and Hypophrygian; cf. Zarlino, *Istitutioni harmoniche* 4.23.

and this with his usual license.[14] The first one, according to Matthew, he has arranged in accordance with the true final close of the mode, namely on E; we show it here. The second one, taken from Luke, he has forced to end on G, but without altering the phrase of the modes at the time, and this also with his usual license.[15] The motet has great majesty, and it is wonderful that from material so sterile, namely, from a bare catalogue of men, he has been able to fashion as many delights as though it had been some fertile narrative. Many other things might be said, but let some of these be left for others to discuss.

The third combination, that of Lydian and Hypolydian, is unusual in this our age, for, as we have often remarked in the foregoing, all compositions in these modes are forced into the Ionian.[16] But in our example, the Agnus Dei from the *Missa Fortuna desperata*, the reader may first admire the way in which a Lydian has been made from an Ionian, for the whole mass is sung in the Ionian mode. This is doubtless due to the bass, plunged into the lowest diapason. For in other compositions, as often as the tenor is Hypodorian, the bass is usually Dorian or Aeolian; again, just as a Phrygian tenor often has an Aeolian bass and cantus, here an Ionian bass has a Lydian tenor and alto.[17] But it is doubtful whether the author has done this by design or by accident. Aside from this, he talks nonsense with his canon, following the custom of the singers.[18] For who except Oedipus himself would understand such a riddle of the sphinx? He has humored the common singers, obeying the maxim, Ἀλωπεκίζειν πρὸς ἑτέραν ἀλώπεκα; that is, *Cum vulpe vulpinare tu quoque invicem,* as Master Erasmus has learnedly translated it, or, as the vulgar inelegantly put it, "Howl with the wolves, if you want to get along with them."[19]

The fourth combination is that of the Mixolydian and its plagal, the Hypo-mixolydian; in our age it is seldom used. Nevertheless, once the symphonists

14. *Werken, Motetten* (Amsterdam, 1926), vol. 1, pp. 59–69 (Matthew) and 70–81 (Luke). The tenor descends to A in the Luke genealogy only.

15. On this ending see 2.36, also no. 34 above (Aaron), chap. 5, p. 147

16. No. 34 above (Aaron), chap. 6, p. 148.

17. See 3.13 on the "mysterious relationship" of the modes, where the present example is also mentioned. Here, as there, Glarean clearly has three distinct sorts of relationship in mind: 1) the natural relationship of any authentic mode to the plagal mode having the same final; 2) the special relationship of Phrygian to Aeolian, as a result of which a Phrygian composition may have marked Aeolian characteristics or an Aeolian composition a Phrygian final cadence; as an example of this relationship Glarean gives in 3.19 the motet "Tulerunt Dominum meum"; cf. Zarlino, *Istitutioni harmoniche* 4.30; 3) the peculiar relationship of D-Dorian to D-Aeolian (transposed Aeolian) and of F-Lydian to F-Ionian (transposed Ionian), of which the present example is an illustration.

18. In Agnus 1 the bass is to invert his part at an eleventh lower than written and multiply the durations by four (double augmentation). Petrucci's editions, followed by Glarean, hint at this in the following distich, which Glarean heads "the riddle of the sphinx": *In gradus undenos descendant multiplicantes / Consimilique modo crescant Antipodes uno* (Let them descend by eleven steps with multiplied measure; then once more in like manner increase, to antipodes changing).

19. See Desiderius Eramus, *Adagia* 1.2.28.

had perceived the magnificence of these modes from ancient examples of ecclesiastical melody, roused as it were with enthusiasm, they tried in a certain most praiseworthy rivalry to do their utmost with the melody "Et in terra pax" on the Most Blessed Virgin and Queen of Heaven, Mary, Mother of Jesus Christ, above all Antoine Brumel and our Josquin Desprez, at a time when both were verging toward extreme old age.[20] Brumel, in his setting, has spared no pains to show the singers his skill, nay, he has strained every fiber of his temperament to leave behind for later generations a specimen of his ingenuity. Yet, in my opinion at least, Josquin has by far surpassed him in natural force and ingenious penetration and has so borne himself in the contest that nature, mother of all, as though wishing to form from the four elements her most perfect creation, seems to me to have brought her utmost powers into play in order that it might be impossible to invent a better music. And thus the major-ity of the learned have not hesitated to award the first place to this composition, especially Joannes Vannius,[21] whom we have mentioned in connection with the Hypomixolydian mode and to whose judgment we gladly subscribe, both because he gave it before us and because he outdid us in this matter by far. At the beginning, the tenor descends once to the Hypomixolydian diatessaron, otherwise the entire melody is Mixolydian, not Hypomixolydian. To me, the greatest passion seems to have been expressed at the word "Primogenitus" in the first part of the setting; others prefer the second part. But there is no part whatever that does not contain something that you may greatly admire.

Of the fifth combination, that of Aeolian and Hypoaeolian, we should not again be giving the same example if we had been able to obtain or discover another one anywhere among the symphonists of our age. Although in our previous book[22] we also produced other examples of the combination, this one[23] was by far the most enlightening, as one by many treated yet by all perverted and transposed from its natural position, even mutilated or altered with respect to its two diatessarons above and below, namely by Brumel and Josquin in their two so celebrated masses of the Virgin Mary, Mother of God; for this reason we have earnestly entreated that excellent man, Master Gregor Meyer, the distinguished organist of the cathedral at Solothurn in Switzerland, to treat the theme worthily, with all the skill at his command, in its natural position and with the two diatessarons proper to and born with the body of the melody. In truth, we imagine this melody to be some splendid bird, whose body is the diapente *re–la* and whose two wings are the diatessarons *mi–la*. To sew to this body wings other than those with which it was born would be fool-ish, surely, unless like Aesop's crow it was to fly with strange plumage. We have

20. The Glorias of both Josquin's and Brumel's masses *De beata virgine* paraphrase Gloria IX, for the Mass on the Feast of the Blessed Virgin Mary; for the chant see *Gradual sacrosanctae romanae ecclesiae*, p. 30°.
21. This is Johannes Wannenmacher, Swiss choirmaster and composer.
22. 2.33
23. The Gregorian Kyrie "Cum jubilo" (*Gradual . . . romanae ecclesiae*, p. 29°).

prevailed upon him and, in all friendliness toward me and readiness to further liberal studies, he has sent us what we wanted; of this we now desire to make the reader a sharer. We do not at all hesitate to insert this composition among those of Josquin, such praise has been given to it; namely, the opinion of that learned man, Master John Alus, canon of the same cathedral and preacher of the Divine Word, who thinks that it would be no small ornament to the more serious studies, such as theology and sacred letters, if to these were added a knowledge of languages and of the mathematical disciplines, and that among these last it would most befit a priest of Holy Church if he knew music. Nor was the man mistaken in his opinion, for he had become versed in musical knowledge. We had his support in this work when he lived with us at Freiburg at the foot of the Black Forest and often refreshed us, now playing the organ, now joining to this the singing of things by Josquin. And so, since he has given the highest praise to this composition of our Gregor, he has easily won our approval and has been responsible for its coming into men's hands as worthy of the ears of the learned.

Of the sixth combination, that of Hyperaeolian and Hyperphrygian, we have deliberately omitted an example, for none is to be found anywhere and it would be foolish to invent one, especially with so great a choice of modes; the tenor, too, would have an outrageous ambitus, actually exceeding all the remaining combinations of the modes by an apotome. Aside from this, in our previous book we have given an invented example, less for imitation than for illustration, so that the matter might be understood, not so that something of the sort might be attempted by anyone, a thing we find that no one has attempted.[24]

Of the seventh and last combination, namely of Ionian and Hypoionian, our example, "Planxit autem David," is again by Josquin Desprez, the author of the examples of all the other combinations except the fifth. Of its beginning some will no doubt exclaim: "The mountain has labored and brought forth a mouse!" But they will not have considered that, throughout the motet, there is preserved what befits the mourner, who is wont at first to cry out frequently, then to murmur to himself, turning little by little to sorrowful complaints, thereupon to subside or sometimes, when passion breaks out anew, to raise his voice again, shouting out a cry. All these things we see most beautifully observed in this composition, as will be evident to the attentive reader. Nor is there in it anything unworthy of its author; by the gods, he has everywhere expressed the passion in a wonderful way, thus, at the very beginning of the tenor, at the word "Jonathan."

24. See 2.34.

36 Gioseffo Zarlino

FROM *Istitutioni harmoniche*
(1558)

BOOK THREE

26. WHAT IS SOUGHT IN EVERY COMPOSITION; AND FIRST, OF THE SUBJECT[1]

I shall come now to the discussion of counterpoint, but before I begin this discussion it must be understood that in every good counterpoint, or in every good composition, there are required many things, and one may say that it would be imperfect if one of them were lacking.

The first of these is the subject, without which one can do nothing. For just as the builder, in all his operations, looks always toward the end and founds his work upon some matter which he calls the subject, so the musician in his operations, looking toward the end which prompts him to work, discovers the matter or subject upon which he founds his composition. Thus he perfects his work in conformity with his chosen end. Or again, just as the poet, prompted by such an end to improve or to delight (as Horace shows so clearly in his *Art of Poetry*, when he says:

> Poets aim either to benefit, or to amuse,
> or to utter words at once both pleasing and helpful to life),[2]

takes as the subject of his poem some history or fable, discovered by himself or borrowed from others, which he adorns and polishes with various manners, as he may prefer, leaving out nothing that might be fit or worthy to delight the minds of his hearers, in such a way that he takes on something of the magnificent and marvelous; so the musician, apart from being prompted by the same end to improve or to delight the minds of his listeners with harmonious accents, takes the subject and founds upon it his composition, which he adorns with various modulations and various harmonies in such a way that he offers welcome pleasure to his hearers.

TEXT: The edition published as the first volume of the *Opere* (Venice, 1589), collated with the first and second editions (Venice, 1558 and 1562). The postils of the original and some of the additions of 1589 are given as author's notes. Translation by Oliver Strunk.

1. The first half of this chapter is literally translated by Pietro Cerone in his *El melopeo y maestro* (Naples, 1613), 12.1.
2. Ll. 333–34; trans. H. Rushton Fairclough, *Horace: Satires, Epistles and Ars Poetica* (Cambridge, Mass.: Harvard University Press, 1966), 479.

The second condition is that the composition should be principally composed of consonances; in addition, it should incidentally include many dissonances, suitably arranged in accordance with the rules which I propose to give later on.

The third is that the procedure of the parts should be good, that is, that the modulations[3] should proceed by true and legitimate intervals arising from the sonorous numbers,[4] so that through them may be acquired the usage of good harmonies.

The fourth condition to be sought is that the modulations and the concentus be varied, for harmony[5] has no other source than the diversity of the modulations and the diversity of the consonances variously combined.

The fifth is that the composition should be subjected to a prescribed and determined harmony, mode, or tone (call it as we will), and that it should not be disordered.

The sixth and last (aside from the others which might be added) is that the harmony it contains should be so adapted to the speech, that is, to the words, that in joyous matters the harmony will not be mournful, and vice versa, that in mournful ones the harmony will not be joyful.

3. "A movement made from one sound to another by means of various intervals" (2.14). Zarlino distinguishes two sorts of modulation: "improper," as in plainsong, and "proper," as in figured music. "Proper modulation" has these further divisions: first, sol-fa or solmization; second, the modulation of artificial instruments; third, modulation in which words are adapted to the musical figures.

4. "Sonorous number is number related to voices and to sounds" (1.19). For Zarlino, the sonorous (or harmonic) numbers are specifically the numbers 1 to 6, with their products and their squares. As he says in 1.15, the six-part number has its parts so proportioned that, when any two of them are taken, their relation gives us the ratio or form of one of the musical consonances, simple or composite. And these parts are so ordered that, if we take six strings stretched subject to the ratio of the numbers 1 to 6, when we strike them all together, our ear perceives no discrepancy and takes the highest pleasure in the harmony that arises; the opposite is the case if the order is changed in any respect. It should be noted that Zarlino does not say that the lengths of the strings correspond to the numbers 1 to 6; he says that they correspond to the ratios of these numbers. The relative lengths, as given in the *Dimostrationi armoniche* 3, *Definitione* 44, are 60, 30, 20, 15, 12, and 10; the resulting harmony will consist of unison, octave, twelfth, fifteenth, seventeenth, and nineteenth.

5. In 2.12 Zarlino defines harmony as having two varieties, "proper" and "improper." "Proper harmony" is a combination or mixture of low and high sounds, divided or not divided by intermediate sounds, which impresses the ear agreeably; it arises from the parts of a composition through the procedure which they make in accord with one another until they attain their end, and it has the power to dispose the soul to various passions. "Proper harmony" arises not only from consonances, but also from dissonances. It has two divisions: "perfect," as in the singing of many parts, and "imperfect," as in the singing of two parts only. "Improper harmony" arises when two sounds distant from one another with respect to the low and the high are heard divided by other intermediate sounds so that they give out an agreeable concentus, subject to several proportions. Musicians call such a combination a harmony. But, Zarlino says, it ought rather to be called a harmonious consonance, for it contains no modulation, and although its extremes are divided, it has no power to move the soul. "Improper harmony" has also two divisions: "simple," as in a combination of consonances arranged in harmonic proportion, and "by extension of meaning" *(ad un certo modo),* as in a combination otherwise arranged.

To assure a perfect understanding of the whole, I shall discuss these things separately as they become suited to my purpose and to my needs.

Beginning with the first, then, I say that, in every musical composition, what we call the subject is that part from which the composer derives the invention to make the other parts of the work, however many they may be. Such a subject may take many forms, as the composer may prefer and in accordance with the loftiness of his imagination: it may be his own invention, that is, it may be that he has discovered it of himself; again, it may be that he has borrowed it from the works of others, adapting it to his work and adorning it with various parts and various modulations. And such a subject may be of several kinds: it may be a tenor or some other part of any composition you please, whether of plainsong or of figured music; again, it may be two or more parts of which one follows another in consequence[6] or in some other way, for the various forms of such subjects are innumerable.

When the composer has discovered his subject, he will write the other parts in the way which we shall see later on. When this is done, our practical musicians call the manner of composing "making counterpoint."

But when the composer has not first discovered his subject, that part which he first puts into execution or with which he begins his work, whatever it may be or however it may begin, whether high, low, or intermediate, will always be the subject to which he will then adapt the other parts in consequence or in some other way, as he prefers, adapting the harmony to the words as the matter they contain demands. And when the composer goes on to derive the subject from the parts of the work, that is, when he derives one part from another and goes on to write the work all at once, as we shall see elsewhere, that small part which he derives without the others and upon which he then composes the parts of his composition will always be called the subject. This manner of composing practical musicians call "composing from fantasy," although it may also be called "counterpointing," or as they say, "making counterpoint."

27. THAT COMPOSITIONS SHOULD BE MADE UP PRIMARILY OF CONSONANCES, AND SECONDARILY AND INCIDENTALLY OF DISSONANCES

And although every composition, every counterpoint, and in a word every harmony is made up primarily and principally of consonances, dissonances are used secondarily and incidentally for the sake of greater beauty and elegance. Taken by themselves, these are not very acceptable to the ear; arranged as they

6. "Consequence we define as a certain repetition or return of a part or the whole of a modulation; it arises from an order and arrangement of many musical figures which the composer makes in one part of his composition and from which, after a certain and limited space of time, there follow one or more other parts, low, high, intermediate, or in the same sound, at the diapason, diapente, diatessaron, or unison, these proceeding one after another by the same intervals. Imitation we shall define as a repetition or return which does not proceed by the same intervals but by wholly different ones, only the movements made by the parts and the figures being similar" (3.54). Each has two varieties, strict and free, and may be either in direct or in contrary motion.

regularly should be and in accordance with the precepts which we shall give, the ear tolerates them to such an extent that, far from being offended, it receives from them great pleasure and delight.

From this, among many other advantages, the musician derives two of no little value: we have already stated the first, namely, that with their aid he may pass from one consonance to another;[7] the second is that a dissonance causes the consonance which immediately follows it to seem more acceptable. Thus it is perceived and recognized with greater pleasure by the ear, just as after darkness light is more acceptable and delightful to the eye, and after the bitter the sweet is more luscious and palatable. And from everyday experience with sounds we learn that if a dissonance offends the ear for a certain length of time, the consonance which follows is made more acceptable and more sweet.

Thus the ancient musicians judged that they should admit in composition not only the consonances which they called perfect and those which they called imperfect, but dissonances also, knowing that their compositions would thus attain to greater beauty and elegance than they would without them. For if they were made up entirely of consonances, although beautiful sounds and good effects would issue from them, they would still be somehow imperfect, both as sound and as composition, seeing that (the consonances not being blended with dissonances) they would lack the great elegance that dissonance affords.

And although I have said that the composer is to use consonances principally and dissonances incidentally, he is not to understand by this that he is to use them in his counterpoints or compositions as they come to hand, without any rule or any order, for this would lead to confusion; on the contrary, he must take care to use them in a regular and orderly manner so that the whole will be profitable. Above all (apart from other things) he must keep in mind the two considerations upon which (in my judgment) all the beauty, all the elegance, and all the excellence of music depend: the movements which the parts of the composition make in ascending or descending in similar or contrary motion, and the arrangement of the consonances in their proper places in the harmonies. Of these things I propose with God's help to speak as may suit my purpose, for this has always been my chief intention.

And to introduce this discussion I propose to explain certain rules laid down by the ancients, who recognized the importance of such matters; teaching by means of these the regular procedure to be followed in using the consonances and dissonances one after another in composition, they went on to give rules about the movements, which they did imperfectly. Thus I shall state and explain these rules in order, and from this explanation I shall go on to show with evident reason what is to be done and how the rules are to be understood, adding also certain further rules, not only useful but also most necessary to those who seek to train themselves in a regular and well-ordered way of composing music of any kind in a learned and elegant manner, with good reasons

7. 3. 17.

and good foundations. In this way everyone may know in what part to arrange the consonances and in what place to use the major and the minor in his compositions.

·   ·   ·   ·   ·

29. THAT TWO CONSONANCES SUBJECT TO THE SAME PROPORTION ARE NOT TO BE USED ONE AFTER ANOTHER, ASCENDING OR DESCENDING, WITHOUT A MEAN[8]

The ancient composers also avoided using one after another two perfect consonances of the same genus or species, their extremes subject to the same proportion, the modulations moving one step or more; thus they avoided using two or more unisons, two or more octaves, or two or more fifths, as seen in the following examples:

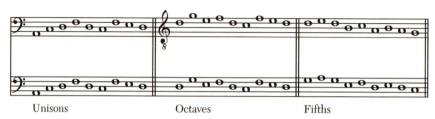

Unisons   Octaves   Fifths

For they knew very well that harmony can arise only from things that are among themselves diverse, discordant, and contrary, and not from things that are in complete agreement. Now if harmony arises from variety such as this, it is not sufficient that in music the parts of the composition be at a distance from one another with respect to the low and the high; the modulations must also be varied in their movements and must contain various consonances, subject to various proportions. And the more harmonious we judge a composition to be, the more we will find, between its several parts, different distances with respect to the low and the high, different movements, and different proportions. Perhaps the ancients saw that when consonances were not put together in the manner I have described, they were similar in their procedure and similar in the form of their proportions, although sometimes varied in their extremes with respect to the low and the high. Knowing, then, that such similarity can generate no variety in the concentus and judging (as was true) that perfect harmony consists in variety, not so much in the positions or distances of the parts of the composition as in the movements, the modulations, and the proportions, they held that in taking one after another two consonances similar in proportion, they were varying the position from low to high, or vice versa, without producing any good harmony, even though the extremes did vary one from another. Thus they did not wish that in composition two or more perfect consonances subject

8. Having concluded the discussion of his first and second requirements, Zarlino now skips over to the fourth, leaving the third for Chapters 30 and 31.

to the same proportion should be taken one after another, the parts ascending or descending together, without the mediation of another interval.

The unisons they especially avoided, for these sounds have no extremes and are neither different in position, nor at a distance from one another, nor productive of any variety in the procedure, but wholly similar in every respect. Nor in singing them does one find any difference with respect to the low and the high, for there is no interval between the one sound and the other, the sounds of the one part being in the same places as those of the other, as may be seen in the example above and in the definition given in Chapter 11, on the unison. Nor does one find any variety in the modulation, for the one part sings the very intervals by which the other proceeds.

The same might be said of two or more octaves, if it were not that their extremes differ from one another with respect to the low and the high; thus, being somewhat varied in its extremes, the octave affords the ear somewhat more pleasure than the unison.

And the same may be said of two or more fifths; since these progress by similar steps and proportions, some of the ancients were of the opinion that to a certain extent they gave rise rather to dissonance than to harmony or consonance.

Thus they held it as true that whenever one had arrived at perfect consonance one had attained the end and the perfection toward which music tends, and in order not to give the ear too much of this perfection they did not wish it repeated over and over again.

The truth and excellence of this admirable and useful admonition are confirmed by the operations of Nature, for in bringing into being the individuals of each species she makes them similar to one another in general, yet different in some particular, a difference or variety affording much pleasure to our senses. This admirable order the composer ought to imitate, for the more his operations resemble those of our great mother, the more he will be esteemed. And to this course the numbers and proportions invite him, for in their natural order one will not find two similar proportions following one another immediately, such as the progressions 1:1:1 or 2:2:2 or others like them, which would give the forms of two unisons, still less the progression 1:2:4:8, which is not harmonic but geometric and would give the forms of three consecutive octaves, and still less the progression 4:6:9, which would give the forms of two consecutive fifths. Thus he ought under no conditions to take one after another two unisons, or two octaves, or two fifths, since the natural cause of the consonances, which is the harmonic number, does not in its progression or natural order contain two similar proportions one after another without a mean, as may be seen in Chapter 15 of Part I. For although these consonances, taken in this manner, would obviously cause no dissonance between the parts, a certain heaviness would be heard which would displease.

For all these reasons, then, we ought under no conditions to offend against this rule, that is, we ought never to use the consonances one after another in the way described above; on the contrary, we should seek always to vary the sounds, the consonances, the movements, and the intervals, and in this way, from the variety of these things, we shall come to make a good and perfect harmony. Nor need it concern us that some have sought to do the opposite, rather (as we see from their compositions) from presumption and on their own authority than for any reason that they have had. For we ought not to imitate those who offend impertinently against the good manners and good rules of an art or science without giving any reason for doing so; we ought to imitate those who have conformed, conforming ourselves to them and embracing them as good masters, always avoiding the dreary and taking the good. And I say this for this reason: just as the sight of a picture is more delightful to the eye when it is painted with various colors than when it is painted with one color only, so the ear takes more pleasure and delight in the varied consonances which the more diligent composer puts into his compositions than in the simple and unvaried.

This the more diligent ancient musicians, to whom we are so much indebted, wished observed, and to it we add that, for the reasons already given, the composer ought not to use two or more imperfect consonances one after another, ascending or descending together, without a mean, such as two major or minor thirds, or two major or minor sixths, as seen in the example:

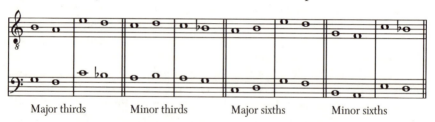

Major thirds   Minor thirds   Major sixths   Minor sixths

For not only do these offend against what I have said about the perfect consonances, but their procedure causes a certain bitterness to be heard, since there is altogether lacking in their modulations the interval of the major semitone, in which lies all the good in music and without which every modulation and every harmony is harsh, bitter, and as it were inconsonant. Another reason for this bitterness is that there is no harmonic relationship[9] between the parts or sounds of two major thirds or of two minor sixths, which makes these somewhat more dreary than the others, as we shall see later on. Thus in every progression or modulation which the parts make in singing together we ought to take special care that wherever possible at least one of them has or moves by the interval of the major semitone, so that the modulation and the harmony which arise from the movements which the parts of the composition make together may be more delightful and more sweet.[10] This is easily managed if the consonances

9. Non-harmonic relationship or, as we should call it, false relation is defined and discussed in Chapters 30 and 31.
10. "The semitone is indeed the salt (so to speak), the condiment, and the cause of every good modulation and every good harmony" (3.10, with reference to the role of the semitone in the

taken one after another are diverse in species, so that after the major third or sixth will follow the minor, or vice versa, or so that after the major third will follow the minor sixth, or after the latter the former, and after the minor third the major sixth, or in the same way after the major sixth the minor third.[11] Nor is there more reason for forbidding the use, one after another, of two perfect consonances than of two imperfect ones, for although the former are perfect consonances, each of the latter is found to be perfect in its proportion. And just as it may not be said with truth that one man is more man than another, so also it may not be said that a major or minor third or sixth taken below is greater or less than another taken above, or vice versa. Thus, since it is forbidden to use two perfect consonances of the same species one after another, we ought still less to use two imperfect ones of the same proportion, seeing that they are less consonant than the perfect.

But when two minor thirds, and similarly two major sixths, are used one after another, ascending or descending together by step, they may be tolerated, for although the major semitone is not heard in their modulations, and the thirds are naturally somewhat mournful and the sixths somewhat harsh, the slight difference that is heard in the movements of the parts gives a certain variety. For the lower part always ascends or descends by a minor tone and the upper by a major, or vice versa,[12] and this affords a certain satisfaction to the ear, the more so since the sounds of the parts stand in a harmonic relationship to one another. But when the parts move by leap we ought by no means to use two or more similar consonances one after another, ascending or descending, for apart from not observing the conditions touched on above, the sounds of the parts will not stand in a harmonic relationship to one another, as seen below:

Example of thirds   Example of sixths

Thus, to avoid the errors that may occur when it becomes necessary to take two thirds or two sixths one after another, we shall take care to take first the

progressions major sixth to octave, major third to fifth, minor sixth to fifth, minor third to unison. "Guido places the semitone in the center of each of his hexachords, as though in the most worthy and most honored place, the seat of Virtue (as they say), for its excellence and nobility are such that without it every composition would be harsh and unbearable to hear, nor can one have any perfect harmony except by means of it" (3.19).

11. As in the first part of the musical example at the end of the present chapter.

12. In Zarlino's scale the minor tones are those from D to E and from G to A; all the others are major, including the tone b-flat to c.

major and then the minor, or vice versa, taking them in whatever manner we wish, with movements by step or by leap, for everything will now agree. And we ought also to take care that, in taking the third after the sixth or the sixth after the third, we make one of them major and the other minor, as we can when there is movement in each of the parts, above and below. But when there is no movement in one or other of them, this rule cannot be observed without departing from the rules which, for the well-being of the composition, we shall give later on. Thus after the major third we shall have to take the major sixth and after the minor third the minor sixth, or vice versa, as seen in the example below:

Example of everything that has been said

We shall add that, it being forbidden to take two perfect or imperfect consonances in the way we have described, we ought also not to take two fourths in any composition whatever, as some do in certain short sections of their *canzoni* which they call *falso bordone,* for the fourth is without a doubt a perfect consonance.[13] But I shall discuss this point when I show how to compose for more than two voices.

30. WHEN THE PARTS OF A CANTILENA HAVE BETWEEN THEM A HARMONIC RELATIONSHIP AND HOW WE MAY USE THE SEMIDIAPENTE AND THE TRITONE IN COMPOSITION

Before going on, I propose to explain what I have said above about the parts of the composition, namely, that sounds sometimes have and sometimes have not a harmonic relationship between them. It must first be understood that to say that the parts of a composition do not have between them a harmonic relationship is to say that between two consonances that two parts make one

13. "I am well aware that with many the authority of those who have taken this liberty will count more than the arguments I have put forward against it; let them do their worst by saying that what I hold in little esteem has been practised by many, for they are not capable of reason and do not wish to be." (3.61.).

after another in singing, ascending or descending together, or ascending and descending together, there comes to be heard the augmented diapason, or the semidiapente, or the tritone. This occurs in the crossing of the first figure or note of the upper part with the second figure or note of the lower, or of the first of the lower with the second of the upper. Such a relationship, then, can occur only when we have at least four figures or notes, namely, the two lower and the two upper figures or notes of two consonances, as seen here:[14]

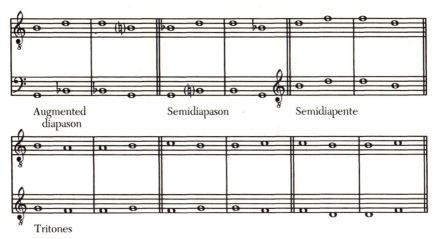

Augmented
diapason

Semidiapason

Semidiapente

Tritones

Thus, in order that our compositions may be correct and purged of every error, we shall seek to avoid these relationships as much as we can, especially when we compose for two voices, since these give rise to a certain fastidiousness in discriminating ears. For intervals like these do not occur among the sonorous numbers and are not sung in any sort of composition, even though some have held a contrary opinion. But be this as it may, they are most difficult to sing and they make a dreary effect.

And I am much astonished by those who have not hesitated at all to require the singing or modulation of these intervals in the parts of their compositions, and I cannot imagine why they have done so. And although it is not so bad to find this in the relationship between two modulations as to find it in the modulation of a single part, the same evil that was heard in the single part is now heard divided between two, and it gives the same offense to the ear. For unless the evil is diminished, little or nothing relieves the offensive nature of a fault, even though it be more offensive from one than from many.

Thus, in a composition for several voices, those intervals that are not admit-

---

14. But when two parts ascend together and the one or the other makes a movement which involves the semitone, it seems that because of this movement they are tolerated by the ear, as are the first cases of the augmented diapason and the semidiapente in the first and third sections of the example. [Au.] (This sentence is not found in earlier editions of the *Istitutioni* and has accordingly been made a note.)

ted in modulation are to be so avoided that they will not be heard as relation-ships between the parts. This will have been done when the parts can be interchanged by means of harmonically proportioned intervals of the diatonic genus, that is, when we can ascend from the first sound of the lower part to the following sound of the upper, or vice versa, by a legitimate and singable interval. But this will not be the case when non-harmonic relationships are heard between the parts of the composition, whatever it may be, among four sounds arranged in the manner explained, for these cannot be changed unless with great disadvantage, as the intervals of the last example are changed in the example below:

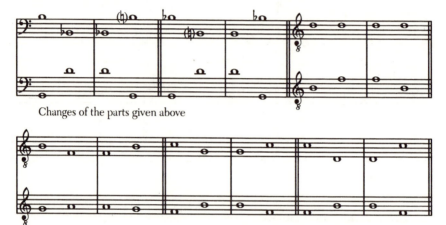

Changes of the parts given above

Thus, whenever the parts of a composition or cantilena cannot be so inter-changed that from this change there arises a procedure by true and legitimate singable intervals, we ought to avoid it, especially if our compositions are to be correct and purged of every error. But in compositions for more than two voices it is often impossible to avoid such things and not to run into intricacies of this kind. For it sometimes happens that the composer will write upon a subject which repeatedly invites him to offend against this precept; thus, when necessity compels him, he will ignore it, as when he sees that the parts of his composition cannot be sung with comfort or when he wishes to adapt a conse-quent which may be sung with comfort, as we shall see elsewhere.[15] But when necessity compels him to offend, he ought at least to take care that he does so between diatonic steps and in steps which are natural and proper to the mode, for these do not give rise to so dreary an effect as do those which are accidental, being indicated within the composition by the signs ♮, ♯, and ♭.

Take note that I call those errors "natural" which arise in the way shown in the first example above, and that I call those "accidental" which arise when, between the true steps of the mode, there is inserted a step of another order,

15. 3.55, 63.

this step being the cause of the difficulty, as may happen in the Fifth Mode,[16] where the central step ♮ is often rejected in favor of the accidental ♭. Thus, between the ♭ and the ♮ preceding or following it, there will arise some one of the disorders in question, as seen in the first of the examples below. And this is the less agreeable since the ♮, which is the principal step of the mode, is absent from its proper place while the ♭, which is accidental, is present in its stead.

And although, for the reasons already given, we ought not to use these intervals in composition in this way, we may sometimes use the semidiapente as a single percussion if immediately after it we come to the ditone, for, as seen in the third of the examples below, the parts may be interchanged without disadvantage. This the better modern musicians observe, just as some of the more ancient observed it in the past.[17] And we are permitted to use not only the semidiapente, but in some cases the tritone also, as we shall see at the proper time. It will, however, be more advantageous to use the semidiapente than the tritone, for the consonances will then stand in their proper places, a thing which will not occur when the tritone is used. And we ought to take care that, in the parts involved, the semidiapente or tritone is immediately preceded by a consonance, no matter whether perfect or imperfect, for through the force of the preceding and following consonances the semidiapente comes to be tempered in such a way that, instead of making a dreary effect, it makes a good one, as experience proves and as is heard in the examples that follow.

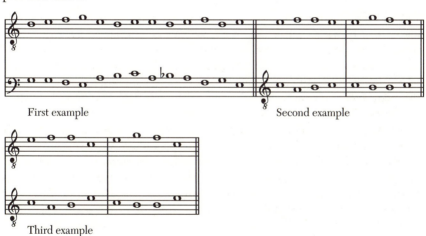

First example   Second example

Third example

16. The Third Mode of the ecclesiastical system (Glarean's Phrygian). Having adopted Glarean's twelve modes in the earlier editions of the *Istitutioni* (1558 and 1562), by 1571, when the *Dimostrationi* were first published, Zarlino had persuaded himself to renumber them, counting the authentic and plagal forms of the C mode as First and Second, and so forth. The various arguments for this renumbering are set forth in the *Dimostrationi* (5, Def. 8). The principal argument is that, in numbering the species of any interval, the point of departure ought to be the natural scale resulting from the harmonic numbers.

17. 3.61.

31. WHAT CONSIDERATION IS TO BE PAID TO RELATED INTERVALS IN COMPOSITIONS FOR MORE THAN TWO VOICES

Aside from this, the composer should bear in mind that, when they occur in counterpoints without being combined with other intervals, such relationships as the tritone, the semidiapente, the semidiapason, and the others that are similar to them are counted among the things in music that can afford little pleasure. Thus we should oblige ourselves not to use them in simple compositions, which (as I have said) are those for two voices, or in other compositions when two parts sing alone, for the same effects will obviously be heard in these. This is because there will not in either case be present what we have called "perfect harmony," in which a body of consonances and harmonies is heard, the extreme sounds being divided by other mean sounds; on the contrary, there will be present only what we have called "imperfect harmony," in which only two parts are heard singing together, no other sound dividing.[18] And since the sense of hearing grasps two parts more fully than three or four, we ought to vary the harmony between the two as much as we can and to take care not to use these relationships, a thing which may be done without any difficulty.

But in compositions for more than two voices this consideration is not so necessary, both because we cannot always observe it without great inconvenience, and because variety now consists not only in the changing of consonances, but also in the changing of harmonies and positions, a thing which is not true of compositions for two voices.

And I say this for this reason: just as there are ingredients in medicines and other electuaries, bitter and even poisonous in themselves, but indubitably health-giving and less harsh when combined with other ingredients, so many things which in themselves are harsh and harmful become good and healthful when combined with others. Thus it is with these relationships in music. And there are other intervals which in themselves give little pleasure, but when combined with others make marvelous effects.

We ought, then, to consider these relationships in one way when we are about to use them simply and in another when we are about to use them in combination. For the variety of the harmony in such combinations consists not only in the variety of the consonances which occur between the parts, but also in the variety of the harmonies, which arises from the position of the sound forming the third or tenth above the lowest part of the composition. Either this is minor and the resulting harmony is ordered by or resembles the arithmetical proportion or mean, or it is major and the harmony is ordered by or resembles the harmonic.[19]

18. For "perfect" and "imperfect" harmony, Zarlino has "proper" and "improper," an obvious slip; cf. n. 5 above.
19. "Not with respect to the order of the proportions, which is actually arithmetic, but with respect to the proportions of the parts when the mean term has been interposed, for these are of the same quantity and proportion as are those produced by a harmonic mean term or divisor,

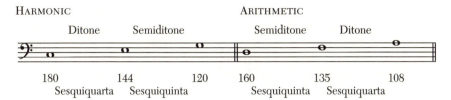

HARMONIC			ARITHMETIC		
Ditone	Semiditone		Semiditone	Ditone	
180	144	120	160	135	108
Sesquiquarta	Sesquiquinta		Sesquiquinta	Sesquiquarta	

On this variety depend the whole diversity and perfection of the harmonies. For (as I shall say elsewhere)[20] in the perfect composition the fifth and third, or their extensions, must always be actively present, seeing that apart from these two consonances the ear can desire no sound that falls between their extremes or beyond them and yet is wholly distinct and different from those that lie within the extremes of these two consonances combined. For in this combination occur all the different sounds that can form different harmonies. But since the extremes of the fifth are invariable and always placed subject to the same proportion, apart from certain cases in which the fifth is used imperfectly, the extremes of the thirds are given different positions. I do not say different in proportion; I say different in position, for (as I have said elsewhere[21]) when the major third is placed below, the harmony is made joyful and when it is placed above, the harmony is made mournful. Thus, from the different positions of the thirds which are placed in counterpoint between the extremes of the fifth or above the octave, the variety of harmony arises.

If, then, we wish to vary the harmony and to observe in so far as possible the rule laid down in Chapter 29 (although this is not so necessary in compositions for more than two voices as it is in those for two) we must take the different thirds in such a way that, after first taking the major third, which forms the harmonic mean, we then take the minor, which forms the arithmetical. This we would not be able to observe so easily if we were to take the non-harmonic relationships into consideration, for while we were seeking to avoid them, we would be continuing the concentus in one division for some time without the mediation of the other; thus to no purpose we would cause the composition to sound mournful to words that carry joyfulness with them or to sound joyful to words that treat of mournful matters. I do not go so far as to say that the composer may not take two arithmetical divisions one after another, but I do

---

although in the opposite order." (1.15.) The harmonic mean between two numbers (x and z) is a number (y) such that the difference between it and the smaller number (y−x) is the same fraction of the smaller (x) as the difference between it and the larger number (z−y) is of the larger (z). In Zarlino's example, 144 is the perfect harmonic mean between 120 and 180 because 24 (i.e., 144−120) is one fifth of 120 and 36 (i.e., 180−144) is one fifth of 180. The arithmetic mean between two numbers is larger than one by the same numerical amount as it is smaller than the other. Zarlino's 135 is only an approximate arithmetic mean between 108 and 160, as Zarlino recognizes at the end of his chapter. The exact arithmetic mean would be 134 (i.e., 160−134=134−108). See also Plato, *Timaeus*, SR 1.

20. 3.59.
21. Chapter 10. [Au.]

say that he ought not to continue in this division for long, since to do so would make the concentus very melancholy. But to take two harmonic divisions one after another can never give offense, provided they be formed from natural steps, and with some judgment and purpose from accidental ones, for when its parts are thus arranged in order, harmony attains its ultimate end and makes its best effect.

But when two parts ascend or descend by one step or two steps we ought to use different divisions, especially when the tritone or semidiapente falls as a relationship between the two parts involved, that is, when in ascending or descending one step two major thirds are taken one after another, and when ascending or descending two steps two minor ones. But when the relationship is that of the semidiatessaron,[22] and it occurs between accidental signs, such as the ♯ and the ♭, or when only one of these signs is present, we need not avoid it at all, for the two divisions being harmonic it is obvious that they will make a good effect, even though they are not varied.

Nor need this astonish anyone, for if he will carefully examine the consonances arranged in the two orders, he will discover that the order which is arithmetical or resembles the arithmetical departs a little from the perfection of harmony, its parts being arranged out of their natural positions; on the other hand he will discover that the harmony which arises from or resembles the harmonic division is perfectly consonant, its parts being arranged and subject to the proper order of this proportion and according to the order which the sonorous numbers maintain in their natural succession, to be seen in Chapter 15 of Part I.

Let this be enough for the present; at another time, perhaps, I shall touch on this again in order that what I have said may be better understood.

·   ·   ·   ·   ·

40. THE PROCEDURE TO BE FOLLOWED IN WRITING SIMPLE COUNTERPOINTS FOR TWO VOICES, SUCH AS ARE CALLED NOTE AGAINST NOTE

To come now to the application of the rules that I have given, I shall show the procedure to be followed in writing counterpoints, beginning with those which are written simply and for two voices, note against note. From these the

---

22. For *semidiatessaron* (diminished fourth) we ought probably to read *diapente superflua* (augmented fifth); diminished fourths, fifths, and octaves occur as false relations between minor consonances, augmented ones between major consonances. Zarlino has already shown how the diminished fourth and augmented fifth occur as false relations in the third musical example of Chap. 29.

Semidiatessaron   Augmented diapente

composer may go on to diminished counterpoints and to the usage of other compositions.[23] Wishing then to observe what has been observed by all good writers and compilers on every other subject, I shall with reason begin with simple things, both to make the reader more submissive and to avoid confusion.

First observing what was said above in Chapter 26, the composer will choose a tenor from any plainsong he pleases, and this will be the subject of his composition, that is, of his counterpoint. Then he will examine it carefully and will see in what mode it is composed, so that he may make the appropriate cadences in their proper places and may know from these the nature of his composition. For if inadvertently he were to make these inappropriately and out of their places, mixing those of one mode with those of another, the end of his composition would come to be dissonant with the beginning and the middle.

But assuming that the chosen subject is the plainsong tenor given below, which is subject to the Third Mode,[24] he will above all else observe what was said in Chapter 28 above about the procedure in beginning a composition. Thus we shall place the first figure or note of our counterpoint at such an interval from the first of the subject that they will have between them one of the perfect consonances. This done, we shall combine the second note of our counterpoint with the second of the subject in a consonance, either perfect or imperfect, but in any case different from the preceding one, so that we shall not be offending against what was said in Chapter 29, always having an eye to what was laid down in Chapter 38[25] and observing the teaching of Chapter 37,[26] taking care that the parts of the composition are as conjunct as possible and that they make no large leaps, so that the interval between them will not be too great. This done, we shall come to the third figure or note of our counterpoint and combine it with the third of the subject, varying not only the steps or positions but also the consonances, taking perfect consonance after imperfect, or vice versa, or taking one after another two perfect consonances or two imperfect ones different in species, according to the rules given in Chapter 33[27] and 34.[28] We shall do the same with the fourth note of our counterpoint and the fourth of the subject, and with the fifth, the sixth, and the others in order until we come to the end, where, following the rule given in the preceding chapter, we shall conclude our counterpoint with one of the perfect consonances.

But above all else we must take care that the contrapuntal part is not only varied in its different movements, touching different steps, now high, now low,

---

23. For simple and diminished counterpoint see no. 32 above (Tinctoris), p. 123.
24. The First Mode of the ecclesiastical system (Glarean's Dorian).
25. How we ought to proceed from one consonance to another.
26. That we ought to avoid as much as we can those movements that are made by leap, and in a similar way those distances that may occur between the parts of a composition.
27. When two or more perfect or imperfect consonances, subject to different forms and taken one immediately after another, are conceded.
28. That we do well to take imperfect consonance after perfect, or vice versa.

and now intermediate, but that it is varied also in its consonances with the subject. And we should see to it that the contrapuntal part sings well and proceeds in so far as possible by step, since there lies in this a part of the beauty of counterpoint. And added to the many other things that one may ask (as we shall see), this will bring it to its perfection.

Thus he who will first exercise himself in this simple manner of composing may afterwards go on easily and quickly to greater things. For seeking to write various counterpoints and compositions upon a single subject, now below and now above, he will make himself thoroughly familiar with the steps and with the intervals of each consonance; then, following the precepts which I am about to give, he will be able to go on to the diminution of the figures, that is, to diminished counterpoint, writing the contrapuntal parts sometimes in consequence with his subject and sometimes imitating them or writing them in other ways, as we shall see; and from this he will be able to go on to compositions for more voices, so that, aided by our directions and by his own talents, he will in a short time become a good composer. . . .

Thus the musician must also seek to vary his counterpoint upon the subject, and if he can invent many passages he will choose the one that is best, most suited to his purpose, and most capable of making his counterpoint sonorous and orderly; the others he will set aside. And when he has invented a passage such as might be appropriate for a cadence, if it is not at the moment to his purpose he will reserve it for some other more suitable place. This he will do if the clause or period in the words or speech has not come to an end, for he must always wait until each of these is finished; in a similar way he will take care that it is in the proper place and that the mode in which his composition stands requires it.

He who wishes to begin in the right way with the art of counterpoint must observe all these things. But above everything else he must industriously exercise himself in this sort of composition in order that he may thus arrive more easily at the practice of diminished counterpoint, in which, as we shall see later on, there are many other things that he may use. And in order that he may have some understanding of all that I have said, I shall give below some varied counterpoints, note against note, upon the subject already mentioned; once he has examined these, he will readily understand the things that I shall show later on[29] and will be able to work with greater ease.

Be advised, however, that to write counterpoint, note against note, appears to be and actually is somewhat more difficult than to write it diminished, for the one has not that liberty which the other has, seeing that in the one each note or figure may have one consonance only, while in the other it may have many of them, blended with dissonances according to the composer's pleasure and good judgment. Thus in the first sort the composer cannot at his pleasure arrange the parts so well that they will be without leaps, especially if he wishes

29. 3.42–44.

to write upon a single subject many counterpoints which will be different throughout. But this need not discourage him, for if the root tastes somewhat bitter, he will before long enjoy the fruits which spring from it, and these are sweet, luscious, and palatable. Thus virtue (as the wise affirm) has to do with the difficult and not with the easy.

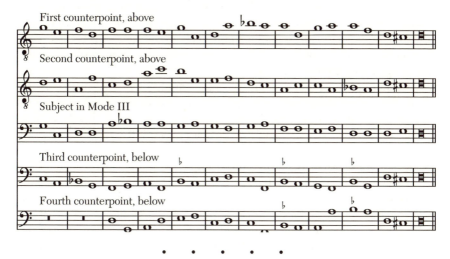

71. ON THE BENEFIT WHICH GOOD HARMONIES DERIVE FROM THE ACCIDENTS ENUMERATED

And now, before going further, let us determine to what extent good and sonorous harmonies derive benefit from the accidents enumerated.[30] And adopting a somewhat lofty manner of speaking for the sake of greater clarity: if the true object of sensation is the body which moves it through the mediation of the sensory organ, it must be understood that, in so far as we consider such bodies according to the different reasons of their movements, we must necessarily postulate in sensation different powers. For considered in so far as it may be seen, an object is called visible and may not be perceived by any other sense than vision. These objects are in fact of two sorts, for they are either primary, as is the color which we see before anything else, or they are commensurate (or shall we say proportionate), and not color, and inherent in many things that are not colored, such as the fire, the moon, the sun, the stars, and other similar things. Indeed these objects have for this reason no proper name; they are simply called visible, and this includes all those things that are visible through light, such as all the luminous bodies, which are those that I have named above. In so far as an object may be heard, as are the voices and the sounds, it is called audible and may not be perceived by any other sense than hearing. The same

---

30. In 3.67–70, on mode, time, prolation, perfection, imperfection, and the various species and effects of the point or dot.

might also be said of the other kinds of objects. Such objects are called sensible particulars, since no one of them may be perceived by more than one of the senses which we have named.

To be sure, there are certain objects which are called common and which may be perceived by several senses; thus movement, rest, number, shape, and size may manifestly be seen, heard, and touched. Then there are certain other objects which are sensible by accident and which may not be perceived except through the mediation of something else; such are the sonorous bodies, which cannot be heard except through the mediation of the sound which is made in the air, as I have shown in Part II.[31]

The more pleasing and sweet these objects are to their particular sense, the more they are proportioned to it, and vice versa; thus the eye, looking at the sun, is offended, for this object is not proportioned to it. And what the philosophers say is true—that excess in the sensible object, if it does not corrupt the sense, at least corrupts the instrument.[32]

If, then, the particular sensible objects may not be perceived or judged by any other sense than that peculiar to them, as sound is by hearing, as color is by vision, and as the others are in order, let those who strive so hard and take such pains to introduce these intricacies into their compositions tell me (if they will) what and how much pleasure and benefit these may afford to the sense and whether these compositions of theirs are more beautiful and more sonorous than those that do not have such things, which are exclusively visible and fall under no other sense than vision and may not be heard in any way, since they are not common objects, perceptible to several senses, as were those mentioned above. If they have judgment, I know that they will reply that these things afford no benefit at all, for when they have been reduced to simple, ordinary notation and stripped of their ciphers, whatever and however great the harmony heard before, such and as great will be the harmony heard afterward. If, then, they are of no benefit at all in the formation of good harmonies, and if they afford no benefit at all to the sense, why to no purpose multiply the singer's duties and augment his vexations with things of this kind? For when he ought to be intent on singing cheerfully such compositions as are to the purpose, he must stand ready to consider chimeras of this sort, falling (according to the various accidents) under mode, time, and prolation, and he must allow nothing written to pass until he has examined it closely, seeing that if he does otherwise he will be thought (if I may say so) an awkward fellow and an ignoramus. And if these things afford no benefit, as they in truth do not, it seems to me sheer madness that anyone of lofty intelligence should have to end his studies and to waste his time and to vex himself about such irrelevant matters. Thus I counsel everyone to disregard these ciphers and to give his attention rather to those things that are productive of good harmonies and sweet ones.

31. Chapter 10. [Au.]
32. Aristotle, *De anima* [i.e., 424a, 435b]. [Au.]

Perhaps someone will say: "Is it not a fine thing to see a tenor well ordered under the signs of mode, time, and prolation, as contrived by the ancient musicians, who gave their attention to almost nothing else?"

It is indeed a fine thing, especially when it is written or painted, and miniatured too, by the hand of an outstanding scribe and miniaturist, using good inks, fine colors, and proportioned measures, and when (as I have seen) there is added to it a coat of arms, a miter, or a cardinal's hat, together with some other splendid object. But of what importance is this if a composition having a tenor written simply and without any intricacy is just as sonorous or as graceless as though it were full of such things?

Thus one may say with truth that this way of composing is simply an unnecessary multiplying of difficulty, and not a multiplying of harmony, and that it affords no benefit at all, since, as the philosophers hold, things are vainly multiplied when there is no purpose. For music, being the science which treats of the sounds and the voices, which are the particular objects of hearing, contemplates only the concord which arises from the strings and the voices (as Ammonius says[33]) and considers nothing else. Thus it seems to me that everything in music that is contemplative without being directed toward this end is vain and useless. For since music was indeed discovered to improve and to delight, as we have said at other times,[34] nothing in music has validity except the voices and the sounds which arise from the strings. These, as Aurelius Cassiodorus imagines, are so named because they move our hearts, a thing he shows most elegantly with the two Latin words *chordae* and *corda*.[35] Thus it is by this path that we perceive the improvement and delight that we derive from hearing harmonies and melodies.

From what has been said we may conclude, then, that this way of composing is not only useless but also harmful, as a loss of time, more precious than anything else, and that the points, lines, circles, semicircles, and other similar things depicted on the page are subject to the sense of vision and not to that of hearing, and that these are matters considered by the geometer, while the sounds and the voices (being in truth the particular objects of hearing) are matters primarily considered by the musician, although he incidentally considers many others.

Here, perhaps, someone will wish to reprehend and censure me, seeing that many learned and most celebrated ancient musicians, whose fame still lives among us, have practiced this way of composing and that I now wish to censure them.

To this I reply that if these critics will consider the matter, they will find that those compositions that are wrapped round with such restraints afford no greater benefit than they would if they were bare and plain, without any difficulty at all, and they will see that they complain with little reason, and they will

---

33. *In Praedicamentis.* [Au.]
34. 1.3. [Au.]
35. *Variae* 2.40 (Ad Boetium patricium). [Au.]

understand that they themselves are to be censured, as persons opposed to truth. For although the ancients followed this fashion, they were well aware that such accidents can afford no augmentation or diminution of the harmony. But they practiced such things to show that they were not ignorant of the speculations put forward by certain idle theorists of that day, seeing that the contemplative part of the science then consisted rather in the contemplation of accidents of this sort than in the contemplation of the sounds, the voices, and the other things discussed in Parts I and II of these my labors.

And of this we have the testimony of many books, written by various authors; these treat of nothing but circles and semicircles, with and without points, whole or divided not only once but two and three times, and in them one sees so many points, pauses, colors, ciphers, signs, numbers against numbers, and other strange things that they sometimes appear to be the books of a bewildered merchant. Nor does one read in these books anything that might lead to the understanding of anything subject to the judgment of the sense of hearing, as are the voices and sounds from which the harmonies and melodies arise; they treat only of the things that we have named. And although the fame of some of these musicians still lives honorably among us, they have acquired their reputation, not with such chimeras, but with the good harmonies, the harmonious concentus, and the beautiful inventions which are seen and heard in their works. And although they disordered these with their intricacies, they obliged themselves also, if not through speculation, at least with the aid of practice and their judgment, to reduce their harmonies to the ultimate perfection they could give them, even if the matter was misunderstood and abused by many others, as the many errors committed by the practical musicians in their works bear witness.

Then as to the rational, that is, speculative part, we see that there were few who kept to the good road, for apart from what Boethius wrote in Latin about our science, and this too we find imperfect, there has been no one (leaving Franchino[36] and Faber Stapulensis[37] to one side, for one may say that they were commentators on Boethius) who has gone further in speculating on things pertaining to music, discovering the true proportions of the musical intervals, except Lodovico Fogliano[38] of Modena,[39] who having perhaps considered what Ptolemy left written on the syntonic diatonic,[40] spared no pains in writing a

36. Zarlino refers here to Franchino Gafori's *Theoricum opus musice discipline* (Naples, 1480).
37. *Musica libris quatuor demonstrata* (Paris, 1496). The philosopher Faber is better known by the French version of his name, Jacques Lefèvre d'Étaples.
38. *Musica theorica* (Venice, 1529)
39. A note for the malicious. [Au.] (This note, which does not appear in the earlier editions of the *Istitutioni*, is aimed at Vincenzo Galilei, who in his *Dialogo della musica antica, et della moderna* [Florence, 1581], accuses Zarlino of appropriating Fogliano's ideas without giving him credit for them. Zarlino's defense may be seen in his *Sopplimenti* 3.2.)
40. In the syntonic diatonic of Ptolemy, the tetrachords of the Greater Perfect System are divided in the proportions 16:15, 9:8, 10:9. One of Zarlino's principal theses is that this division is the natural and inevitable one and the one actually used in the practical vocal music of his time.

Latin book on this branch of the science, showing as well as he could the true proportions of the intervals involved. The rest of the theoretical musicians, clinging to what Boethius wrote of these matters, did not wish or were not able to go further and gave themselves over to describing the things that we have named; these they made subject to the quantitative genus, as they called it, under which come mode, time, and prolation, as may be seen in the *Recaneto di musica*,[41] the *Toscanello*,[42] the *Scintille*,[43] and a thousand other similar books.

Besides this there are also conflicting opinions on these questions and long disputations, of which there is no end, then many tracts, invectives, and apologies, written by certain musicians against certain others, in which (although one reads them a thousand times), having read, reread, and examined them, one finds nothing but the innumerable villanies and slanders which they immodestly address to one another (O what shame!) and in the end so little good that one is dumbfounded.

But we may in truth excuse these writers. There were sophists in those days, just as there were sophists in the time of Socrates and Plato, and they were as much esteemed, and this quantitative genus of theirs (one may truly call it an *Arte sofistica* in music and its musicians sophists) was as much practiced in its time as was sophistry in the time of the philosophers in question. Thus we ought continually to praise God and to thank Him that little by little (I know not how) this thing is almost spent and extinct and that He has put us into an age concerned only with the multiplying of good concentus and good melodies, the true end toward which the musician ought to direct his every work.

·   ·   ·   ·   ·

BOOK FOUR

32. HOW THE HARMONIES ARE ADAPTED TO THE WORDS PLACED BENEATH THEM

Seeing that the time and place require it, it now remains to be determined how one ought to combine the harmonies with the words placed beneath them. I say "to combine the harmonies with the words" for this reason: although (following Plato's opinion) we have said in Part II[44] that melody is a combination of speech, harmony, and rhythm,[45] and although it seems that in such a combination no one of these things is prior to another, Plato gives speech the first place and makes the other two parts subservient to it, for after he has shown the whole by means of the parts, he says that harmony and rhythm ought to follow speech. And this is the obligation. For if in speech, whether by

41. The *Recanetum de musica aurea*, by Stefano Vanneo (Rome, 1533).
42. The *Toscanello in musica*, by Pietro Aaron (Venice, 1523).
43. The *Scintille di musica* by G. M. Lanfranco (Brescia, 1533).
44. Chapter 12.
45. *Republic* 3 [i.e. 398c]. [Au.]

way of narrative or of imitation (and these occur in speech), matters may be treated that are joyful or mournful, and grave or without gravity, and again modest or lascivious, we must also make a choice of a harmony and a rhythm similar to the nature of the matters contained in the speech in order that from the combination of these things, put together with proportion, may result a melody suited to the purpose.

We ought indeed to listen to what Horace says in his epistle on the *Art of Poetry*:

A theme for Comedy refuses to be set forth in verses of Tragedy;[46]

and to what Ovid says in this connection:

Achilles must not be told of in the numbers of Callimachus;
Cydippe suits not thy utterance, Homer.[47]

For if the poet is not permitted to write a comedy in tragic verse, the musician will also not be permitted to combine unsuitably these two things, namely, harmony and words.[48] Thus it will be inappropriate if in a joyful matter he uses a mournful harmony and a grave rhythm, neither where funereal and tearful matters are treated is he permitted to use a joyful harmony and a rhythm that is light or rapid, call it as we will. On the contrary, he must use joyful harmonies and rapid rhythms in joyful matters, and in mournful ones, mournful harmonies and grave rhythms, so that everything may be done with proportion.

He who has studied what I have written in Part III and has considered the nature of the mode in which he wishes to write his composition will, I think, know precisely how to do this. In so far as he can, he must take care to accompany each word in such a way that, if it denotes harshness, hardness, cruelty, bitterness, and other things of this sort, the harmony will be similar, that is, somewhat hard and harsh, but so that it does not offend. In the same way, if any word expresses complaint, grief, affliction, sighs, tears, and other things of this sort, the harmony will be full of sadness.[49]

Wishing to express effects of the first sort, he will do best to accustom himself to arrange the parts of his composition so that they proceed with such movements as are without the semitone, as are those of the tone and ditone, allowing the major sixth or thirteenth, which are naturally somewhat harsh, to be heard above the lowest tone of the concentus, and accompanying these with the syncope of the fourth or eleventh above this same tone, using rather slow movements; with these he may use the syncope of the seventh. But wishing to

---

46. L. 89. Trans. Fairclough, p. 459.

47. *Remediorum amoris*, 381–382. [Au.] Trans. J. H. Mozley in Ovid, *The Art of Love, and Other Poems* (London: Heinemann, 1929), p. 205.

48. The "Rules to be observed in dittying" given by Thomas Morley on pages 177 and 178 of his *Plaine and Easie Introduction* (London, 1597) are in effect an abridged translation of the remainder of this chapter.

49. Even though this is censured by some of our modern Aristarchs. [Au.] (Namely, Vincenzo Galilei, on pp. 88 and 89 of his *Dialogo della musica antica, et della moderna* [see no. 37 below, pp. 185–87]) But as to this, see Chapter II of Book VIII of our *Sopplimenti*. [Au.]

express effects of the second sort, he will use (always observing the rules that have been given) such movements as proceed by the semitone or semiditone or in some other similar way, often taking above the lowest tone of his composition the minor sixth or thirteenth, which are naturally soft and sweet, especially when they are combined in the right ways and with discretion and judgment.

Note, however, that the expression of these effects is to be attributed not only to the consonances that we have named, used as we have directed, but also to the movements that the parts make in singing, which are of two sorts— natural and accidental. The natural movements are those made between the natural steps of the music, where no sign or accidental step intervenes, and these have more virility than those made by means of the accidental steps, marked with the signs ♯ and ♭, which are indeed accidental and somewhat languid. In the same way there arises from the accidental movements a sort of interval called accidental, while from the natural movements arise the intervals called natural. We ought then to bear in mind that the natural movements make the music somewhat more sonorous and virile, while the accidental ones make it softer and somewhat more languid. Thus the natural movements may serve to express effects of our first sort, and the accidental ones may serve for the rest, so that combining with some judgment the intervals of the major and minor consonances and the natural and accidental movements, we will succeed in imitating the words with a thoroughly suitable harmony.

Then as to the observance of the rhythms, the primary consideration is the matter contained in the words: if this is joyful, we ought to proceed with swift and vigorous movements, that is, with figures carrying swiftness, such as the minim and semiminim; if it is mournful, we ought to proceed with slow and lingering movements.

Thus Adriano has taught us to express the one sort and the other in many compositions, among them "I vidi in terra angelici costumi," "Aspro core e selvaggio," and "Ove ch'i posi gli occhi," all written for six voices, "Quando fra l'altre donne" and "Giunto m'ha Amor" for five voices, and innumerable others.[50]

And although the ancients understood rhythms in another way than the moderns do, as is clear from many passages in Plato, we ought not only to keep this consideration in mind but also to take care that we adapt the words of the speech to the musical figures in such a way and with such rhythms that nothing barbarous is heard, not making short syllables long and long syllables short as is done every day in innumerable compositions, a truly shameful thing.[51] Nor do we find this vice only in figured music but, as is obvious to every man of

---

50. The works named here are all madrigals from Adriano Willaert's *Musica nova*. Zarlino was not the first writer to hold up this collection as exemplary of appropriate relations between music and words; see no. 13 above (Doni), pp. 55–57.

51. But as to this, what has been said in Chapter 13 of Book VIII of our *Sopplimenti* [On the three sorts of accents: grammatical, rhetorical, and musical] ought by all means to be carefully considered, so that all may go well and no error be committed. [Au.]

judgment, in plainsong also, for there are few chants that are not filled with barbarous things of this kind. Thus over and over again we hear length given to the penultimate syllables of such words as *Domínus, Angélus, Filíus, miracúlum, gloría,* and many others, syllables which are properly short and fleeting. To correct this would be a most praiseworthy undertaking and an easy one, for by changing it a very little, one would make the chant most suitable, nor would this change its original form, since this consists solely of many figures or notes in ligature, placed under the short syllables in question and inappropriately making them long when a single figure would suffice.

In a similar way we ought to take care not to separate the parts of the speech from one another with rests, so long as a clause, or any part of it, is incomplete and the sense of the words imperfect, a thing done by some of little intelligence, and unless a period is complete and the sense of the words perfect we ought not to make a cadence, especially one of the principal ones, or to use a rest larger than that of the minim, nor should the rest of the minim be used within the intermediate points. For this is in truth a vicious thing, and for all that it is practiced by some little repentent practical musicians of our time, anyone inclined to heed the matter may easily observe and understand it.

Thus, since the matter is of great importance, the composer ought to open his eyes and not keep them closed so that he may not be thought ignorant of a thing so necessary, and he ought to take care to use the rest of the minim or semiminim (whichever suits his purpose) at the head of the intermediate points of the speech, for these have the force of commas, while at the head of the periods he may use whatever quantity of rest he chooses, for it seems to me that when the rests are used in this manner one may best distinguish the members of the period from one another and without any difficulty hear the perfect sense of the words.

33. THE PROCEDURE TO BE FOLLOWED IN PLACING THE MUSICAL FIGURES UNDER THE WORDS[52]

Who will ever be able to recite, unless with great difficulty, the disorder and the inelegance that many practical musicians support and have supported and the confusion that they have caused in suitably adapting the musical figures to the words of the speech? When I reflect that a science that has brought law and good order to other things is in this respect so disorderly that it is barely tolerable, I cannot help complaining, for some compositions are indeed dumbfounding to hear and to see. It is not only that in the declamation of the words one hears confused periods, incomplete clauses, unsuitable cadences, singing without order, innumerable errors in applying the harmonies to the words, little regard for mode, badly accommodated parts, passages without beauty, rhythms without proportion, movements without purpose, figures badly numbered in time and prolation, and a thousand other disorders; one also finds the

52. Here as above Zarlino uses the word *figura* to mean "note."

musical figures so adapted to the words that the singer cannot determine or discover a suitable way of performing them. Now he sees two syllables under many figures, now under two figures many syllables. Now he hears the singer of another part who, at some point where the words require it, uses the apostrophe or elides the vowels; wishing to do the same in his part, he succeeds in missing the beautiful and elegant manner of singing and in putting a figure that carries length under a short syllable, or vice versa. Now he hears the singers of the other parts make a syllable long which in his must necessarily be short. Thus, hearing all this diversity, he does not know what to do and remains thoroughly bewildered and confused.

And since the whole consists in adapting the musical figures to the words beneath them, and since in composition it is required that the musical figures be used to mark and note the pitches so that the sounds and the voices may be properly performed in every modulation; and seeing that it is by means of such figures that we perform the rhythm, that is, the length and brevity of the syllables of the speech, and that over these syllables there are often put, not one, two, or three, but even more such figures, as may be required by the accents suitably arranged in the speech; therefore, in order that no confusion may arise in adapting the figures to the syllables and to the words, and wishing (if I can) to end all this disorder, to the many rules I have already given in various places in accordance with the requirements of my materials, I now add these, which will serve both the composer and the singer and will at the same time be to my purpose.

1. A suitable figure is to be placed below each long or short syllable so that nothing barbarous will be heard. For in figured music each musical figure that stands alone and is not in ligature (apart from the semiminim and all those that are smaller than the semiminim) carries its own syllable with it. This rule is observed in plainsong also, for to each square figure is adapted a syllable of its own, excepting for the middle notes, which are sometimes treated like minims or even semiminims, as may be seen in many chants, especially in the chant for the Nicene Creed, "Credo in unum Deum," which they call the Credo cardinale.[53]

2. Not more than one syllable, and that at the beginning, is to be adapted to each ligature of several notes or figures, whether in figured music or in plainsong.

3. No syllable is to be adapted to the dot placed after the figures of figured music, although this is sung.

4. It is not usual to place a syllable below a semiminim, or below those figures that are smaller than the semiminim, or below the figure immediately following.

5. It is not customary to place any syllable below the figures immediately following a dotted semibreve or dotted minim, when these following figures

53. Credo IV.

are valued at less than the dots, as are semiminims after a dotted semibreve or chromas after a dotted minim; the same is true of the figures that immediately follow these.

6. Should it be necessary to place a syllable below a semiminim, one may also place another syllable below the figure following.

7. At the beginning of a composition, or after any rest in the middle, the first figure, whatever it may be, must necessarily carry with it a syllable.

8. In plainsong no word or syllable is ever repeated, although one sometimes hears this done, a thing indeed to be censured; in figured music such repetitions are sometimes tolerated—not of a syllable or of a word, but of some part of the speech whose sense is complete. This may be done when there are figures in such quantity that words may be repeated conveniently. But to repeat a thing many times over does not, in my opinion, go over well, unless it be done to give greater emphasis to words that have in them some grave sense and are worthy of consideration.

9. When all the syllables of a period or of one part of the speech have been adapted to the musical figures and there remain only the penultimate syllable and the last, the penultimate syllable will have the privilege of bearing a number of small figures—two, three, or some other quantity—provided, however, that it be long and not short, for if it were short a barbarism would occur. Singing in this way, there arises what many call a *neuma,* which occurs when many figures are sung above a single syllable. But when figures are placed in this way, they offend against our first rule.

10. The final syllable of the speech will fall below the final figure of the composition, if our rules are observed.

Seeing that the reader will find innumerable examples of all these things if he will examine the learned works of Adriano and of those who have been and are his disciples and observers of the good rules, I shall go on without giving further examples to the discussion of the ligatures formed from certain of the musical figures, for these are useful in this connection.

37 Vincenzo Galilei

Vincenzo Galilei, father of the famous astronomer and natural philosopher Galileo Galilei, was born near Florence in the late 1520s. A fine lutenist, he enjoyed the patronage of the Florentine nobleman Giovanni de' Bardi and studied with Gioseffo Zarlino in Venice. He spent most of the 1560s in Pisa and returned to Florence in 1572. During that year he became acquainted with the researches into ancient Greek music that Girolamo Mei, a Florentine expatriate, was pursuing in Rome. The influence of Mei's views, especially regarding tuning systems, modes, and the means by which music moves the affections, led Galilei to question the contrapuntal practice of his day and brought him into open conflict with Zarlino. Galilei expressed his views in the *Dialogue on Ancient and Modern Music* (*Dialogo della musica antica, et della moderna*, 1581). Zarlino replied in his *Sopplimenti musicali* of 1588, and Galilei continued the exchange in his *Discorso intorno all'opere di Messer Gioseffo Zarlino* of 1589.

The excerpt below from the *Dialogo* is Galilei's famous chastisement of the expressive means associated especially, if not exclusively, with the contemporary madrigal. Its sentiments were inspired by letters Mei wrote to Galilei in the 1570s (especially no. 41 below, pp. 207–17) and shared by Galilei's patron Giovanni de' Bardi, who expressed similar concerns—if with greater urbanity— in a letter of ca. 1578 titled *Discorso sopra la musica, e'l cantar bene*. Both Galilei and Bardi thus aligned themselves with Renaissance traditions of solo song reaching back to Serafino Aquilano and beyond, and it is significant that Bardi's *Discorso* was addressed to Giulio Caccini, foremost exponent of solo song in the years around 1600.

FROM *Dialogue on Ancient and Modern Music*
(1581)

Bardi: Finally I come as I promised to the treatment of the most important and principal part of music, the imitation of the conceptions that are derived from the words. After disposing of this question I shall speak to you about the principles observed by the ancient musicians.

Our practical contrapuntists say, or rather hold to be certain, that they have expressed the conceptions of the mind in the proper manner and have imitated the words whenever, in setting to music a sonnet, *canzone, romanzo,* madrigal, or other poem in which there occurs a line saying, for example:

> Bitter heart and savage, and cruel will,[1]

which is the first line of one of the sonnets of Petrarch, they have caused many sevenths, fourths, seconds, and major sixths to be sung between the parts and by means of these have made a rough, harsh, and unpleasant sound in the ears of the listeners.[2]

TEXT: The original edition (Venice, 1581). Some of the postils and one parenthesis of the original are given as author's notes. Translation by Oliver Strunk. The interlocutors of Galilei's dialogue are Giovanni de' Bardi and Piero Strozzi.

1. Petrarch, *Rime* 245, l. 1: *Aspro core et selvaggio et cruda voglia;* it will be recalled that Willaert's setting of this poem was cited by Zarlino in his *Istitutioni* 4.32 as a model of correct musical expression. See no. 36 above, p. 181.
2. Zarlino, *Istitutioni*, 3.66 and 4.32. [Au.] See no. 36 above (Zarlino), pp. 180–81.

The sound is indeed not unlike that given by the cithara of Orpheus in the hands of Neantius, the son of Pittacus, the tyrant of the Greek island of Lesbos, where flourished the greatest and most esteemed musicians of the world, in honor of whose greatness it had been deposited there, we read, after the death of the remarkable cithara player Pericletus, the glorious winner in the Carneian festival of the Lacedaemonians. When this Neantius played upon the cithara in question, it was revealed by his lack of skill that the strings were partly of wolf-gut and partly of lamb-gut, and because of this imperfection[3]—or because of the transgression he had committed in taking the sacred cithara from the temple by deceit, believing that the virtue of playing it well resided in it by magic, as in Bradamante's lance that of throwing to the ground whomsoever she touched with it[4]—he received, when he played it, condign punishment, being devoured by dogs. This was his only resemblance to the learned poet, sage priest, and unique musician who as you know was slain by the Bacchantes.

At another time they will say that they are imitating the words when among the conceptions of these there are any meaning "to flee" or "to fly"; these they will declaim with the greatest rapidity and the least grace imaginable. In connection with words meaning "to disappear," "to swoon," "to die," or actually "to be extinguished" they have made the parts break off so abruptly, that instead of inducing the passion corresponding to any of these, they have aroused laughter and at other times contempt in the listeners, who felt that they were being ridiculed. Then with words meaning "alone," "two," or "together" they have caused one lone part, or two, or all the parts together to sing with unheard-of elegance. Others, in the singing of this particular line from one of the sestinas of Petrarch:

> And with the lame ox he will be pursuing Laura,[5]

have declaimed it to staggering, wavering, syncopated notes as though they had the hiccups. And when, as sometimes happens, the conceptions they have had in hand made mention of the rolling of the drum, or of the sound of the trumpet or any other such instrument, they have sought to represent its sound in their music, without minding at all that they were pronouncing these words in some unheard-of manner. Finding words denoting diversity of color, such as "dark" or "light" hair and similar expressions, they have put black or white notes beneath them to express this sort of conception craftily and gracefully, as they say, meanwhile making the sense of hearing subject to the accidents of color and shape, the particular objects of sight and, in solid bodies, of touch. Nor has there been any lack of those who, still more corrupt, have sought to portray with notes the words "azure" and "violet" according to their sound, just as the stringmakers nowadays color their gut strings. At another time, finding the line:

3. Fracastoro, *De sympathia et antipathia rerum,* i. [Au.]
4. Ariosto, *Orlando furioso* 8.17 and 30.15.
5. *Rime* 239 l. 36: *Et col bue zoppo andrem cacciando l'aura* (Galilei writes *andrà* and *Laura*).

> He descended into hell, into the lap of Pluto,

they have made one part of the composition descend in such a way that the singer has sounded more like someone groaning to frighten children and terrify them than like anyone singing sense. In the opposite way, finding this one:

> This one aspires to the stars,

in declaiming it they have ascended to a height that no one shrieking from excessive pain, internal or external, has ever reached. And coming, as sometimes happens, to words meaning "weep," "laugh," "sing," "shout," "shriek," or to "false deceits," "harsh chains," "hard bonds," "rugged mount," "unyielding rock," "cruel woman," and the like, to say nothing of their sighs, unusual forms, and so on, they have declaimed them, to color their absurd and vain designs, in manners more outlandish than those of any far-off barbarian.

Unhappy men, they do not perceive that if Isocrates or Corax or any of the other famous orators had ever, in an oration, uttered two of these words in such a fashion, they would have moved all their hearers to laughter and contempt and would besides this have been derided and despised by them as men foolish, abject, and worthless. And yet they wonder that the music of their times produces none of the notable effects that ancient music produced, when, quite the other way, they would have more cause for amazement if it were to produce any of them, seeing that their music is so remote from the ancient music and so unlike it as actually to be its contrary and its mortal enemy, as has been said and proved and will be proved still more, and seeing that it has no means enabling it even to think of producing such effects, let alone to obtain them. For its sole aim is to delight the ear, while that of ancient music is to induce in another the same passion that one feels oneself.[6] No person of judgment understands the expression of the conceptions of the mind by means of words in this ridiculous manner, but in another, far removed and very different.

Strozzi: I pray you, tell me how.

Bardi: In the same way that, among many others, those two famous orators that I mentioned a little while ago expressed them, and afterwards every musician of repute. And if they wish to understand the manner of it, I shall content myself with showing them how and from whom they can learn with little pain and trouble and with the greatest pleasure, and it will be thus: when they go for their amusement to the tragedies and comedies that the mummers act, let them a few times leave off their immoderate laughing, and instead be so good as to observe, when one quiet gentleman speaks with another, in what manner he speaks, how high or low his voice is pitched, with what volume of sound, with what sort of accents and gestures, and with what rapidity or slowness his words are uttered. Let them mark a little what difference obtains in all these things when one of them speaks with one of his servants, or one of these with another; let them observe the prince when he chances to be conversing with

6. Galilei borrows this important distinction from Girolamo Mei; see no. 41 below, p. 213.

one of his subjects and vassals; when with the petitioner who is entreating his favor; how the man infuriated or excited speaks; the married woman, the girl, the mere child, the clever harlot, the lover speaking to his mistress as he seeks to persuade her to grant his wishes, the man who laments, the one who cries out, the timid man, and the man exultant with joy. From these variations of circumstance, if they observe them attentively and examine them with care, they will be able to select the norm of what is fitting for the expression of any other conception whatever that can call for their handling.[7]

Every brute beast has the natural faculty of communicating its pleasure and its pain of body and mind, at least to those of its own species, nor was voice given to them by nature for any other purpose. And among rational animals there are some so stupid that, since they do not know, thanks to their worthlessness, how to make practical application of this faculty and how to profit by it on occasion, they believe that they are without it naturally.[8]

When the ancient musician sang any poem whatever, he first considered very diligently the character of the person speaking: his age, his sex, with whom he was speaking, and the effect he sought to produce by this means; and these conceptions, previously clothed by the poet in chosen words suited to such a need, the musician then expressed in the tone[9] and with the accents and gestures, the quantity and quality of sound, and the rhythm appropriate to that action and to such a person. For this reason we read of Timotheus, who in the opinion of Suidas was a player of the aulos and not of the cithara,[10] that when he roused the great Alexander with the difficult mode of Minerva to combat with the armies of his foes, not only did the circumstances mentioned reveal themselves in the rhythms, the words, and the conceptions of the entire song in conformity with his desire, but in my opinion at least, his habit, the aspect of his countenance, and each particular gesture and member must have shown

7. "*O bel discorso,* truly worthy of the great man he imagines himself to be! From it we may gather that what he actually wishes is to reduce music greatly in dignity and reputation, when, to learn imitation, he bids us go to hear the zanies in tragedies and comedies and to become out-and-out actors and buffoons. What has the musician to do with those who recite tragedies and comedies?" (Zarlino, *Sopplimenti* 8.11).

8. "Thus in his opinion it is a shameful thing to be more man than beast, or at least to be more the modest man than the buffoon, because at the right time and place the songs of the buffoon may move his listeners to laughter. It is not perceived that such imitations belong rather to the orator than to the musician and that when the singer uses such means, he ought rather to be called an actor or a buffoon, than a singer. Everyone knows that the orator who wishes to move the passions must study them and must imitate not only the actor but any other sort of person who might help him to this end. This the great orator Cicero did, practicing continually with the actor Roscius and the poet Architus. But in this case, what becomes the orator does not become the musician." (Zarlino, *Sopplimenti* 8.11).

9. Galilei is using the word "tone" *(tono)* in its technical sense, as a translation of the Greek *tonos* Mei had helped him to understand. See no. 41 below, pp. 213–14.

10. *Lexicon,* under Timotheus: "When on one occasion Timotheus the aulos-player played on the aulos the nome of Athena called Orthios, they say that Alexander was so moved that, as he listened, he sprang to arms and said that this should be the royal aulos-music." See also no. 10 above (Castiglione), pp. 48–49, n. 2.

on this occasion that he was burning with desire to fight, to overcome, and to conquer the enemy. For this reason Alexander was forced to cry out for his arms and to say that this should be the song of kings.[11] And rightly, for provided the impediments have been removed, if the musician has not the power to direct the minds of his listeners to their benefit, his science and knowledge are to be reputed null and vain, since the art of music was instituted and numbered among the liberal arts for no other purpose.

11. "So that this Timotheus of his ought, if not to be, at least to seem the most perfect of zanies and buffoons. But who ever heard finer or sweeter discourse than this, all stuff and nonsense? Thus, leaving the *zanni*, the *zannini*, and the *zannoli* to one side, we shall now explain how one ought to speak in an imitation made by means of music" (Zarlino, *Sopplimenti* 8.11). Zarlino goes on to a discussion of the references to music at the beginning of Aristotle's *Poetics*.

38 Joachim Burmeister

The idea of *musica poetica* was a distinctive contribution by German music theorists of the Renaissance. In the hands of Nicolaus Listenius, Heinrich Faber, Gallus Dressler, and other writers, it came, across the sixteenth century, to focus attention more and more on the compositional process and organizational techniques that resulted in a finished piece of music, as distinct from the more abstract procedures of melody and voice-leading that tended to preoccupy writers on counterpoint. The phrase *musica poetica* thus reflected the meaning of its Greek source—*poiein,* to make—rather than a concern with the rapprochement of music and poetry.

Joachim Burmeister's treatise *Musica poetica* of 1606 represents a culmination, of sorts, of this tradition. In it, as in two earlier treatises where he dealt with closely similar materials (*Hypomnematum musicae poeticae,* 1599, and *Musica autoschediastike,* 1601), he conceives the structure of a musical work by analogy to that of a classical oration. He divides the work into exordium, body, and peroration, and distinguishes the smaller affective periods that make up these sections. He studies the "ornaments" or musical gestures of the work as individual rhetorical figures, even borrowing names for them from the verbal figures of ancient and modern rhetoricians. And, near the end of the treatise, he presents a discussion from this perspective of the organization or *dispositio* of a complete motet by Orlando di Lasso. Burmeister's striking term for this treatment of large-scale rhetorical organization is "analysis." Burmeister's analysis emphasizes the division of a work into smaller constituent parts; in this it remains faithful to ancient rhetoricians' treatments of orations and reflects the original sense of his term, from the Greek *analyein,* to unloose, loosen, dissolve. Burmeister's approach certainly singles out techniques that are basic to various polyphonic styles of the late sixteenth century and no doubt captures as well widespread organizational practices. Many motets, madrigals, and chansons clearly show his three-section arrangement.

Burmeister's rhetorical orientation in such matters came to him naturally. Born at Lüneburg in 1564 and trained there by the rhetorician Lucas Lossius, cantor of two churches at Rostock from 1589, he earned his master's degree from the University of Rostock in 1593. From then until his death in 1629 he devoted himself to the teaching of Latin and Greek classics in the town school there.

FROM *Musica poetica*
(1606)

CHAPTER 15: THE ANALYSIS OR ARRANGEMENT[1] OF A MUSICAL PIECE

Musical analysis is the examination of a piece belonging to a certain mode and to a certain type of polyphony. The piece is to be divided into its affections or periods, so that the artfulness with which each period takes shape can be studied and adopted for imitation. There are five areas of analysis: (1) investigation of the mode; (2) investigation of the melodic genus; (3) investigation of the type of polyphony; (4) consideration of the quality; (5) sectioning of the piece into affections or periods.

Investigation of mode is the consideration of those aspects which are essential for understanding the constitution and identification of the mode, whether this be in pitch connections already made or still to be made.

Investigation of melodic genus is the examination of the interval of the fourth, whereby one studies how it is comprised of smaller intervals and used in a piece, and what character it bears.

Investigation of type of polyphony is the comparison of sounds in terms of duration or value.

Consideration of quality is the inquiry as to whether the melodic pitches display the *diezeugmenon* system, which is *cantus durus*, or the *synemmenon* system, which is *cantus mollis*.[2]

Sectioning of the piece into affections means its division into periods for the

---

TEXT: Joachim Burmeister, *Musica Poetica*, ed. Benito Rivera (New Haven: Yale University Press, 1993), pp. 201–7. Copyright 1993 by Yale University; reprinted by permission. Translation by Benito Rivera. I have adapted and abridged Rivera's annotations.

1. Arrangement or *dispositio* is the second in the traditional list of five functions in rhetoric: *inventio, dispositio, elocutio, memoria,* and *pronuntiatio.* See *Rhetorica ad Herennium* 1.2.3. "Dispositio is the suitable arrangement of the parts of the oration and of the arguments. It fulfills the function of bringing so much clarity to the speech that even if you have invented the best ideas, none of them will be worth anything when you do not proceed suitably or intelligently." Phillip Melanchthon, *Institutiones rhetoricae* (Strasbourg, 1523), fol. 22v. [Tr.]

2. That is, whether they display b-natural and hence use the "hard" hexachord starting from g *(cantus durus)* or b-flat and hence use the "soft" hexachord starting from f *(cantus mollis).* See no. 33 above (Ramis), p. 133, n. 12.

purpose of studying its artfulness and using it as a model for imitation. A piece has three parts: (1) the exordium, (2) the body of the piece, (3) the ending.[3]

The exordium is the first period or affection of the piece. It is often adorned by fugue, so that the ears and mind of the listener are rendered attentive to the song, and his good will is won over. The exordium extends up to the point where the fugal subject ends with the introduction of a true cadence or of a harmonic passage having the marks of a cadence. This is seen to happen where a new subject definitely different from the fugal subject is introduced. However, examples do not confirm that all musical pieces should always begin with the ornament of fugue. With this in mind, let the music student follow common practice and what it allows. Sometimes *noëma*[4] takes place in the exordium. When this happens, it should be for the sake of an aphoristic text[5] or for other purposes which common practice will show.

The body of the musical piece is the series of affections or periods between the exordium and the ending. In this section, textual passages similar to the various arguments of the *confirmatio* in rhetoric are instilled in the listener's mind in order that the proposition be more clearly grasped and considered.

The body should not be protracted too much, lest that which is overextended arouse the listener's displeasure. For everything that is excessive is odious and usually turns into a vice.

The ending is the principal cadence where either all the musical movement ceases or where one or two voices stop while the others continue with a brief passage called *supplementum.* By means of this, the forthcoming close in the music is more clearly impressed on the listeners' awareness.

EXAMPLE OF AN ANALYSIS OF ORLANDO'S FIVE-VOICE COMPOSITION *IN ME TRANSIERUNT*[6]

This elegant and splendid harmonic piece by Orlando di Lasso, *In me transierunt*, is delimited by the authentic Phrygian mode. For the ambitus of the whole combined system of all the voices is *B* to *ee*. The ambitus of the

3. Classical authors varied in their numbering of the parts of an oration. *Rhetorica ad Herennium* 1.3.4 lists six parts: *exordium, narratio, divisio, confirmatio, confutatio,* and *conclusio.* The broader threefold division was obviously inspired by Aristotle's injunction that a tragic drama or epic poem, to be a unified whole, must have a beginning *(arche)*, middle *(meson)*, and end *(teleute; Poetics* 7.3 and 23.1). Chapters 12–14 of Gallus Dressler, *Praecepta musicae poëticae* (Magdeburg, 1564), provide guidelines on the structuring of the *exordium, medium,* and *finis.* [Tr.]

4. In rhetorical theory *noëma* is a figure of brief, subtle speech, an aphorism, or a *sententia.* Burmeister's *noëma* is one of the sixteen harmonic, six melodic, and four mixed figures he defines in Chapter 12, "Musical Ornaments or Figures," from which the definitions in the following notes are derived (see Rivera, pp. 154–97). *Noëma* is homophony or note-against-note texture. Evidently Burmeister associated this texture with *sententiae* or aphorisms because of its ability to make the words stand out.

5. *Textus sententiosus.* According to Cicero the exordium of a speech ought to be "sententiosus" *(De inventione* 1.18.25). [Tr.]

6. Here Burmeister investigates in order all five "areas of analysis" he specified at the beginning of the chapter. For Lasso's motet, see Orlando di Lasso, *Sämtliche Werke,* ed. Franz Haberl and

individual voices are as follows. The discant is bounded by *e* and *ee*, the tenor by *E* and *e*, the bass by ♯*B* and ♯*b*, the alto by ♯*b* and ♯*bb*. The basis of temperament is authentic, because the diapente from *E* to ♮ or ♯*b* is clearly there.[7] Furthermore, the affinal cadence, which is fully formed as a *hexaphonal* cadence, is located where the diapente is divided into two equal parts.[8] The ambitus of the alto and bass is plagal, because their ambitus is mediated at the place which allows the diatessaron to be positioned in the lower part and the diapente in the higher. Fully formed cadences, especially *triphonal* ones, are located where through the long tradition of this mode they are wont to be found and encountered. The two semitones likewise appear in their proper places. For the place of the lower semitone is in the first, bottom interval of the authentic ambitus. The place of the upper semitone is analogously the same as that of the lower.[9] The harmony has its authentic and principal ending on *E*, which is, as is usually the case, the lowest note of the tenor's ambitus. The second point of consideration is that the piece pertains to the diatonic genus of melody, because its intervals are mostly formed by tone, tone, and semitone. Third, it belongs to the fractured type of polyphony. For the pitches are combined with one another in unequal values. Fourth, it pertains to the *diezeugmenon* quality. For throughout the piece a disjunction of tetrachords occurs at *a* and *b*.

This harmonic piece can be divided very appropriately into nine periods. The first comprises the exordium, which is adorned by two figures: *fuga realis* and *hypallage*.[10] Seven inner periods comprise the body of the piece, similar to the *confirmatio* of a speech (if one may thus compare one cognate art with another). The first of these is adorned with *hypotyposis, climax,* and *anadiplosis;*[11] the second is likewise, and to those figures may be added *anaph-*

Adolf Sandberger (21 vols., Leipzig: Breitkopf & Härtel, 1894–1926), vol. 9, pp. 49–52. For a discussion of Burmeister's analysis including a labeling of his figures in Lasso's score, see Claude V. Palisca, "*Ut Oratoria musica:* The Rhetorical Basis of Musical Mannerism," in Palisca, *Studies in the History of Italian Music and Music Theory* (Oxford: Clarendon Press, 1994), pp. 282–311; for the most part I have followed below Palisca's division of the motet.

7. In *Musica autoschediastike*, fols. L4r–v, Burmeister correctly identified A and ee, rather than ♯B and ee, as the boundary notes of the piece. Nevertheless he maintained that the diapente E–B was prominent. [Tr.]

8. That is, on G.

9. That is, in the first interval of the diatessaron, B–C.

10. "*Fuga realis* is that disposition of harmony wherein all the voices imitate, by using identical or similar intervals, a certain subject *[affectio]* drawn from one voice. . . ." Hypallage, in rhetorical theory various kinds of metonymic exchange, is in Burmeister's musical usage an imitation using an inversion of the original material. See mm. 1–20.

11. Mm. 20–26. Hypotyposis, in rhetorical theory a particularly vivid description, is for Burmeister an ornament vividly depicting the sense of the words or, more simply, a madrigalism. Climax, a gradual buildup through increasingly emphatic words or phrases, is melodic sequence. Anadiplosis, the repetition of a word at the end of one line to begin the next, is for Burmeister a technique whereby a largely homophonic passage (or *noëma*) involving one semichoir is restated twice more by other groupings of voices.

ora;[12] the third is adorned by *hypotyposis* and *mimesis;*[13] the fourth likewise, with the addition of *pathopoeia;*[14] the fifth by *fuga realis;*[15] the sixth by *anadiplosis* and *noëma;*[16] the seventh by *noëma* and *mimesis.*[17] The final, namely, the ninth, period is like the epilogue of a speech. This harmony displays a principal ending, otherwise called a *supplementum* of the final cadence, which very often includes the ornament of *auxesis;* here the principal ending is protracted through a series of concords built on pitches which establish the mode, and which the polyphonic piece as a whole is wont to articulate more often than the other pitches.[18]

12. Mm. 26–32. Anaphora, the use of the same word or phrase to begin several verses or sentences, is for Burmeister melodic imitation involving only some of the voices.
13. Mm. 32–41. Mimesis is similar to anadiplosis but involves only one restatement of the *noëma.*
14. Mm. 41–52. Pathopoeia, a general term for figures that arouse passion, is for Burmeister a musical arousing of emotions by the use of semitones not proper to the mode or melodic genus of the piece—i.e., chromaticism.
15. See mm. 52–67.
16. See mm. 67–73.
17. See mm. 73–77.
18. Mm. 78–87. Auxesis, an ordering of words or phrases so as to intensify meaning, is for Burmeister a mainly homophonic declamation of a word or words repeated two, three, or more times with "growing harmony," i.e., fuller and fuller scoring.

39 Pietro Pontio

Pietro Pontio, born at Parma in 1532, served as chapelmaster in cathedrals of Bergamo, Parma, and Milan for most of his career. He died at Parma in 1595. A prolific composer of Masses and other sacred works, Pontio is best remembered for his two dialogues on music theory and composition, the *Ragionamento di musica* (Discussion on Music) of 1588 and the *Dialogo . . . ove si tratta della theorica et prattica di musica* (Dialogue . . . That Treats the Theory and Practice of Music) of 1595. In both works Pontio reveals an approach to contrapuntal practice much indebted to Zarlino.

Particularly interesting is the final section of the *Ragionamento,* in which Pontio distinguishes different polyphonic genres according to the rhythms, textures, uses of preexistent materials, and expressive demeanors appropriate to them. Here Pontio displays the increasingly strict, even schematic sense of generic propriety that characterized many arts at the end of the Renaissance, including poetry, drama, and painting. He also reveals an attentiveness to large-scale compositional organization generally akin to Joachim Burmeister's (see no. 38 above, pp. 189–91), if with none of the German classicist's rhetorical orientation. Pontio's guidelines were widely disseminated, not only in his own *Ragionamento* but also in the sprawling treatise *El melopeo y maestro* of 1613 by Pietro Cerone, where they are repeated and elaborated.

FROM *Ragionamento di musica*
(1588)

BOOK 4

•   •   •   •   •

Paolo: You have heard so many things the contrapuntist or composer must consider regarding the manner of singing, the needs of the singer, and the propriety of the composition. Doubtless we can hardly talk about and enumerate all the things that must be considered in composing; but at least the ones discussed above will allow you to make a composition with many fewer errors than those circulating these days by various composers. It remains now to show you the manner or style (as we might say) to be employed in making a motet, a mass, and other compositions that originate, as I have said, in florid counterpoint. And with this may you content yourself.

Hettore: I am content with whatever pleases you, and I would very much welcome your showing me the manner of making a motet or other composition. Indeed I desire no more of you than this, since you have already instructed me in so many things pertinent to musical artifice. Please, therefore, speak.

Paolo: I do so willingly. The manner or style (as we wish to call it) for making a motet is grave and tranquil. The parts, especially the bass, move with gravity, and the composer should maintain such ordering of the parts from beginning to end. Likewise the individual subjects should be grave, even if nowadays some composers make motets and other sacred works in which this is not true. In these sometimes they put the parts together with quick, even very quick motion, using syncopated minims instead of syncopated semibreves and even semiminim and quaver rests, all of which are not suitable to the gravity of motets, so that their works almost seem madrigals or canzoni. If this happened once it would not be worth mention; but these composers proceed in this manner straight through to the end, so that in my judgment theirs is the style of madrigals, not motets, observing no gravity at all. One can see such gravity well observed by Jacquet,[1] Morales, Adriano,[2] Gombert, Palestrina, Phinot, and many other excellent composers whom I pass over for the sake of brevity. . . .

You may observe gravity and the grave style in this manner: When two parts sing together and there is in one a figure in breves, the other should move in a figure of minims or semiminims or semibreves on the upbeat, and not in quavers or semiquavers or even continuously in semiminims, which in their very

TEXT: The facsimile of the edition of 1588, ed. Suzanne Clercx (Kassel: Bärenreiter, 1959), pp. 153–61. Translation by Gary Tomlinson. For a translation of Cerone's reuse of this material see Oliver Strunk, *Source Readings in Music History* (New York: Norton, 1950), no. 28.

1. Jacquet of Mantua.
2. Willaert.

quick motion would rob the melody of all gravity. In making a motet for three voices, when in two parts there is a breve or two semibreves on the downbeat the third part should move in a figure in minims, seminimims, or semibreves on the upbeat, or in dotted minims likewise on the upbeat. In this way the composition will be grave and appropriate to the style of the motet. If the work is for four or five voices, when all are singing together two or three should always hold still while the others (or at least one of them) move in the manners just described, and not in quavers and semiquavers, which would make the style madrigalian. But since I cannot be as clear as I wish speaking only, I present here an example in which you may consider all these things:

Do you see how while the bass moves the soprano begins by imitating its breve motion? And how while the middle part holds still the other two move? If only one part were to move, that too would be fine and answer to the proper ordering and to gravity as well. But if all the parts held still at the same time, that would not be the motet style or serve the required ordering, as I have said.

Hettore: I find that I have understood all this; please proceed as you wish.

Paolo: The style or manner (as we might call it) of the mass is like that of the motet as far as the movement of the parts is concerned. But it differs in its ordering, since in the motet you may compose the beginning of the second part as you please, as long as it conforms to the mode; but in the mass the beginning of its first Kyrie must be similar to the beginnings of the Gloria, Credo, Sanctus, and first Agnus Dei. However, if indeed I say they must be similar I do not mean they should have the same consonances, as would happen, for instance, if at the beginning of the first Kyrie the tenor and then the soprano sang *ut mi fa sol sol la* and the same thing happened without any variety to begin the Gloria and the Credo. I do not mean this at all, but rather that you use the same subject in different manners, once beginning with the tenor, then with the soprano, then with the bass, so that there is variety in the parts if not in the subject. If I give you an example you will understand more easily what I mean:

From this small example you can see that the theme remains similar but not the consonances; and this is as it should be. Now if the first Kyrie uses a theme from the beginning of a motet or madrigal or some other piece, the Christe should borrow some other theme from the same piece. You may choose from it any theme that is appropriate to the mode. You may compose the beginning of the second Kyrie as you wish, but at its ending you should use the theme that ends the piece on which the mass is based. You can see this in the mass composed on *Salvum me fac Domine* by Vincenzo Ruffo, in the mass composed on *Si bona suscepimus* by Jacquet, in the mass Don Pietro Pontio composed on *Vestiva i colli* in his Third Book of Masses, and in works by others. Likewise the ends of the Gloria, Credo, Sanctus, and last Agnus must follow the same theme and ordering as the end of the Kyrie. This is the ordering one should follow.

If you wish to compose a mass on your own subject you should follow the same ordering as if you had composed it on a motet or canzone. And you should call this mass *Missa sine nomine* since it is not based on any other piece. You can see examples of this in the Second Book of Masses of Jacquet, the First Book of Vincenzo Ruffo, and also in the Second and Third Books à 5 of Pietro Pontio.

One can observe also that most composers make the parts go together, note against note, at the words *Iesu Christe,* out of reverence and because of the gravity of these words. The same thing usually happens at the words *Et incarnatus est de spiritu sancto ex Maria virgine et homo factus est,* as you can see in Josquin and other composers whom I pass over for the sake of brevity. Now you understand the ordering you should observe in composing a mass on some other piece or on a subject of your own. If you are satisfied with all this, I pass now to speak of psalms.

Hettore: I am indeed satisfied; continue as you wish.

Paolo: If you wish to compose psalms (leaving aside the canticle of the Virgin Mary, that is, the Magnificat, and the Benedictus and Nunc dimittis), you will not be able to compose brief verses if you imitate the psalm tone through all the parts. This will make long verses, inappropriate to psalms. But you may imitate with one part or two, provided the imitations carry the psalm tone. And even if you began all the parts together you would not be criticized. And so that the middle of the psalm verse is apparent you must also mark it with a cadence on the mediation of the psalm tone. Also you must make sure the words are enunciated and understood, pronouncing them almost simultaneously in the manner of one of those songs called *falsobordone*. You can see this done by Adriano, Jacquet, and others; it is done thus so that the listeners can understand the words. If it pleases you, you may set the last verse of the psalm[3] in a more learned style, with a canon à 5. Now you understand the manner or style (as we call it) for composing psalms. And if you put some imitation in the psalm verses it must be brief. This brevity may be achieved in two ways: first, the theme may be short, with few notes; second, the parts may follow one another a semibreve or breve apart, but not more. All this in order to make the verses brief and avoid falling into the motet style, and because such is required by psalms.

Now I will tell you how to compose the canticle of the Virgin Mary, that is, the Magnificat. Even though it is truly a psalm, nevertheless it is one of the most solemnly observed psalms, so if you wish to set it it requires a more learned style in which all the parts imitate the plainchant or some other theme. It does not matter if one part begins one, two, three, or even four breves after another, as long as the parts begin in imitation. It is necessary to mark the middle of the verse with its own cadence on the mediation of the psalm tone. Composers usually imitate the psalm tone either with all the parts or with two parts while the others have other melodies, as you can see in the Magnificat in the first mode of Morales, that is, *Anima mea dominum*. Don Pietro Pontio followed a similar ordering in the Magnificat *Anima mea dominum* in the third and fourth modes, and other composers have done likewise. You should also make sure the parts have some melodies that leave aside the psalm tone, as long as they are in the appropriate mode; but at the end one or two parts should carry the psalm tone. Sometimes you might arrange it so that one part sings the whole plainchant, a very praiseworthy approach that has been adopted by many excellent composers such as Morales, Carpentras, Giovanni Contino, Jacquet, and others. Other times you might arrange it so that one part sings the first half of the chant and the other part finishes it, and this arrange-

---

3. The *Gloria patri* or Lesser Doxology.

ment too is praised. Or you can make it so that, reaching the middle of the verse with no one carrying the chant, one or two parts then sing the end of the chant; or that one part sings the chant up to the middle of the verse and then the parts introduce new melodies without imitating the chant; or that one part sings the whole chant while the others sing other melodies around it, which is the most learned and ingenious manner of all. All these various methods are used in setting the Magnificat, Benedictus, and Nunc dimittis.

The chordal style, with all the parts moving together, is appropriate for setting readings for Holy Week,[4] as it is for the Gloria of the Magnificat and the *Incarnatus est* of the Mass. In such works the composer should employ dissonances to make the music plaintive, as the words require. So that you may better understand this I will show you an excerpt from such a composition:

You can see how at the end the parts all move together and how the dissonances make the composition plaintive. It is admissable at times for one or two parts to move on their own in order to vary the composition; but they must do so with gravity, using semibreves or dotted minims on the downbeat or upbeat, and also some undotted minims. This makes the composition grave and sad, as the words require. The composer must choose a mode that is naturally sad, such as the second, fourth, or sixth.[5] It is true that the practiced composer can make his music sad or happy as he wishes in any mode, using slow or quick rhythms. But in choosing sad modes to express the passions of the words of the kind of works we discuss here, the composer will be esteemed of sound judgment; while if he did differently he would be reputed a man of little judgment who poorly understood the sense of the words. Now you have understood all that pertains to this sort of composition, and I will tell you how to make a ricercar.

The style of a ricercar should show long melodies with the parts entering far

4. The *Lamentations of Jeremiah*.
5. That is, the octave species A–A with D final, B–B with E final, and C–C with F final, respectively; or, in the conventional ecclesiastical ordering of eight modes, the plagal modes hypodorian, hypophrygian, and hypolydian.

from one another so that in playing it the individual melodies can be easily heard. One part or another must always be moving, even if there are only two parts. It is not proper for the parts to stop together on a semibreve (as one could do in setting the readings for Holy Week). Neither is it proper to begin two parts together, except when they have different melodies. And since you may not understand my speaking about this as well as if I showed you, here is an example:

You may repeat the same subject in various ways two, three, four, or more times, as you can see in the ricercars of Jacques Buus, Annibale Padovano, Claudio da Correggio,[6] and Luzzasco. You may also make a subject from plainchant in semibreves, breves, longs, and maxims. It is also allowed to proceed from beginning to end with the same subject or, if that does not please, to invent a new subject and repeat it as many times as you wish in the varied manner I have described. This is the way you should make a ricercar. Now I will speak of the madrigal.

The subjects of the madrigal ought to be brief, not more than two or three semibreves long.

Hettore: Why is this so?

6. Claudio Merulo.

Paolo: the reason is that if they were longer they would be more appropriate to the motet or the mass than to the madrigal.

Hettore: I understand; continue.

Paolo: I say also that it is appropriate for the melodies of the madrigal to move in semibreves and syncopated minims. You should also know that often the parts may move together, but with the quick motions of semiminims or minims. You must make every effort to follow the words. When they treat of harsh and bitter things, you must find harsh and bitter music. When they concern running or combat the composer must speed up. When they speak of falling or rising up you will make the parts in your composition fall or rise either by step or by leap. Thus Orlando[7] made the upper parts and then the bass rise up at the words "A lofty subject for my lowly rhymes"[8] in *Già mi fu col desire* from his First Book for five voices. And thus Cipriano[9] made the parts descend by fifths in the first part of his canzone *A la dolce ombra* at the words "That was burning down on me from the third heaven."[10]

Now you have heard some of the features of the madrigal. And if I have not said everything about these various compositions, which would be impossible, you will excuse me. At least I have hinted at the manner each sort of composition should have, so that with study you may perfect each one. Your judgment, then, will supply all I have omitted, taking from me the willing desire I have of satisfying you.

7. Di Lasso.
8. "Alto soggetto alle mie basse rime."
9. De Rore.
10. "Che'n fin qua giù m'ardea dal terzo cielo"; see Petrarch, *Rime,* no. 142, 1.3. The poem is a *sestina,* not a canzone, though musicians' use of such poetic terminology was frequently loose.

40 Thomas Morley

Thomas Morley, one of the leading proponents of the vogue for Italian and Italianate music in late-Elizabethan England, was born in Norwich in 1557 or 1558. At some time in his youth he studied with William Byrd, and in 1588 he was awarded a bachelor's degree in music at Oxford. Subsequently he became organist at St. Paul's in London and in 1592 entered the Chapel Royal. He died during the first decade of the new century, probably in 1602.

Morley is particularly important as a composer, arranger, and editor of secular music. He was largely responsible for the dispersion of light Italian genres, the *canzonetta* and *balletto,* in England, and his own madrigals, canzonets, and ballets are remarkable for the grace and freshness of their melodic invention. Morley also left many English services, anthems, and psalms, a number of Latin motets, and instrumental works for consort and for keyboard. He is chiefly remembered, however, for his book, *A Plaine and Easie Introduction to Practicall Musicke* (1597), one of the best organized and most useful of sixteenth-century musical handbooks. He dedicated it to his former teacher, Byrd.

Here Morley discusses the various secular vocal and instrumental genres that commanded so large a share of his creative energies.

FROM *A Plaine and Easie Introduction to Practicall Musicke*

This much for motets, under which I comprehend all grave and sober music. The light music hath been of late more deeply dived into, so that there is no vanity which in it hath not been followed to the full, but the best kind of it is termed madrigal, a word for the etymology of which I can give no reason,[1] yet use showeth that it is a kind of music made upon songs and sonnets such as Petrarcha and many other poets of our time have excelled in.

This kind of music were not so much disallowable if the poets who compose the ditties would abstain from some obscenities which all honest ears abhor, and sometimes from blasphemies too such as this, "ch'altro di te iddio non voglio,"[2] which no man (at least who hath any hope of salvation) can sing without trembling. As for the music, it is next unto the motet the most artificial and to men of understanding most delightful. If therefore you will compose in this kind, you must possess yourself of an amorous humor (for in no composition shall you prove admirable except you put on and possess yourself wholly with that vein wherein you compose), so that you must in your music be wavering like the wind, sometimes wanton, sometimes drooping, sometimes grave and staid, otherwhile effeminate; you may maintain points[3] and revert them,[4] use triplas,[5] and show the very uttermost of your variety, and the more variety you show the better shall you please. In this kind our age excelleth, so that if you imitate any I would appoint you these for guides: Alfonso Ferrabosco for deep skill, Luca Marenzio for good air and fine invention, Horatio Vecchi, Stephàno Venturi, Ruggiero Giovanelli, and John Croce, with divers others who are very good, but not so generally good as these.

TEXT: The original edition (London, 1597), as reproduced in *Shakespeare Association Facsimiles* 14 (London, 1937), pp. 179–81.

1. The fourteenth-century etymology of the term remains uncertain to this day.
2. "Other than thee [my love] I'll have no god."
3. "We call that [a point or] a fugue when one part beginneth and the other singeth the same for some number of notes (which the first did sing)." (p. 76.)
4. "The reverting of a point (which also we term a revert) is when a point is made rising or falling and then turned to go the contrary way as many notes as it did at first." (p. 85.)
5. "Is that which diminisheth the value of the notes to one third part: for three breves are set for one, and three semibreves for one, and is known when two numbers are set before the song, whereof the one containeth the other thrice, thus: 3/1, 6/2, 9/3." (p. 29.)

The second degree of gravity in this light music is given to canzonets, that is, little short songs, wherein little art can be showed, being made in strains,[6] the beginning of which is some point lightly touched, and every strain repeated except the middle, which is in composition of the music a counterfeit of the madrigal.

Of the nature of these are the Neapolitans, or *canzoni a la Napoletana,* different from them in nothing save in name, so that whosoever knoweth the nature of the one must needs know the other also, and if you think them worthy of your pains to compose them, you have a pattern of them in Luca Marenzio and John Ferretti, who as it should seem hath employed most of all his study that way.

The last degree of gravity (if they have any at all) is given to the *villanelle,* or country songs, which are made only for the ditty's sake, for, so they be aptly set to express the nature of the ditty, the composer (though he were never so excellent) will not stick to take many perfect chords of one kind together,[7] for in this kind they think it no fault (as being a kind of keeping decorum) to make a clownish music to a clownish matter, and though many times the ditty be fine enough, yet because it carrieth that name *villanella* they take those disallowances as being good enough for plow and cart.

There is also another kind more light than this which they term *balletti,* or dances, and are songs which being sung to a ditty may likewise be danced; these and all other kinds of light music saving the madrigal are by a general name called airs.[8] There be also another kind of ballets, commonly called fa las (the first set of that kind which I have seen was made by Gastoldi; if others have labored in the same field I know not), but a slight kind of music it is, and as I take it devised to be danced to voices.

The slightest kind of music (if they deserve the name of music) are the *vinate,* or drinking songs, for as I said before there is no kind of vanity whereunto they have not applied some music or other, as they have framed this to be sung in their drinking, but that vice being so rare among the Italians and Spaniards, I rather think that music to have been devised by or for the Germans (who in swarms do flock to the University of Italy) rather than for the Italians themselves.

There is likewise a kind of songs (which I had almost forgotten) called *Giustinianas* and are all written in the Bergamasca language. A wanton and rude kind of music it is and like enough to carry the name of some notable courtesan

---

6. That is, in repeating sections, in the manner of dance music (see Morley's description below of the various dance movements).

7. That is, would not hesitate to use parallel fifths and octaves.

8. The distinction Morley alludes to here between the through-composed madrigal and all other, strophic genres, collectively known as airs (Italian *arie*) would remain in force through the first decades of the seventeenth century. For an earlier writer like Girolamo Mei (see no. 41 below, pp. 207–11) aria was a formally neutral term, connoting something close to our "melody" or "melodic style."

of the city of Bergamo, for no man will deny that Giustiniana is the name of a woman.[9]

There be also many other kinds of songs which the Italians make, as *pastorellas* and *passamezos* with a ditty and such like, which it would be both tedious and superfluous to delate unto you in words. Therefore I will leave to speak any more of them and begin to declare unto you those kinds which they make without ditties.

The most principal and chiefest kind of music which is made without a ditty is the fantasy, that is, when a musician taketh a point at his pleasure and wresteth and turneth it as he list, making either much or little of it as shall seem best in his own conceit. In this may more art be shown than in any other music, because the composer is tied to nothing but that he may add, diminish, and alter at his pleasure. And this kind will bear any allowances whatsoever tolerable in other music, except changing the air and leaving the key, which in fantasy may never be suffered. Other things you may use at your pleasure, as bindings with discords, quick motions, slow motions, proportions, and what you list. Likewise this kind of music is with them who practise instruments of parts in greatest use, but for voices it is but seldom used.

The next in gravity and goodness unto this is called a pavan, a kind of staid music, ordained for grave dancing, and most commonly made of three strains, whereof every strain is played or sung twice. A strain they make to contain 8, 12, or 16 semibreves as they list, yet fewer than eight I have not seen in any pavan. In this you may not so much insist in following the point as in a fantasy, but it shall be enough to touch it once and so away to some close. Also in this you must cast your music by four, so that if you keep that rule it is no matter how many fours you put in your strain, for it will fall out well enough in the end, the art of dancing being come to that perfection that every reasonable dancer will make measure of no measure, so that it is no great matter of what number you make your strain.

After every pavan we usually set a galliard (that is, a kind of music made out of the other), causing it to go by a measure which the learned call *trochaicam rationem,* consisting of a long and a short stroke successively, for as the foot *trochaeus* consisteth of one syllable of two times and another of one time, so is the first of these two strokes double to the latter, the first being in time of a semibreve and the latter of a minim. This is a lighter and more stirring kind of dancing than the pavan, consisting of the same number of strains, and look how many fours of semibreves you put in the strain of your pavan, so many times six minims must you put in the strain of your galliard. The Italians make

9. Morley's naive definition is wholly misleading. The sixteenth-century *giustiniana* is a specifically Venetian form of the *villanella* that first appeared around 1560; the three singers, who invariably stutter, introduce themselves as old men in love; see Alfred Einstein, "The Greghesca and the Giustiniana of the Sixteenth Century," *Journal of Renaissance and Baroque Music* 1 (1946–47): 19–32.

their galliards (which they term *saltarelli*) plain, and frame ditties to them which in their mascarados they sing and dance, and many times without any instruments at all, but instead of instruments they have courtesans disguised in men's apparel who sing and dance to their own songs.

The alman is a more heavy dance than this (fitly representing the nature of the people whose name it carrieth), so that no extraordinary motions are used in dancing of it. It is made of strains, sometimes two, sometimes three, and every strain is made by four, but you must mark that the four of the pavan measure is in dupla proportion to the four of the alman measure, so that as the usual pavan containeth in a strain the time of sixteen semibreves, so the usual alman contains the time of eight, and most commonly in short notes.

Like unto this is the French *branle* (which they call *branle simple*), which goeth somewhat rounder in time than this, otherwise the measure is all one. The *branle de Poitou*, or *branle double*, is more quick in time (as being in a round tripla), but the strain is longer, containing most usually twelve whole strokes.

Like unto this (but more light) be the *voltes* and *courantes*, which being both of a measure are notwithstanding danced after sundry fashions, the *volte* rising and leaping, the *courante* trevising and running, in which measure also our country dance is made, though it be danced after another form than any of the former. All these be made in strains, either two or three, as shall seem best to the maker, but the *courante* has twice so much in a strain as the English country dance.

There be also many other kinds of dances (as hornpipes, jigs, and infinite more) which I cannot nominate unto you, but knowing these the rest cannot but be understood, as being one with some of these which I have already told you.

GLIMPSES OF OTHER MUSICAL WORLDS

41 Girolamo Mei

Girolamo Mei was born in Florence in 1519 and died in Rome in 1594. He received a thorough humanistic education from the Florentine philosopher Piero Vettori, whom he assisted in commentaries and editions of Aristotle and other authors. By 1551 Mei had begun the researches into ancient Greek music that would consume much of his energies in later life, but he seems not to have pursued these in earnest until after he settled permanently in Rome in 1559. There, from 1566 to 1573, he wrote his most important work, *De modis musicis antiquorum (On the Musical Modes of the Ancients)*; it was never published.

In this treatise Mei revealed for the first time the fundamental differences between the ancient Greek keys, or *tonoi,* and the modern modes thought until then to correspond to them. He recognized that the *tonoi* were not octave species like the modes, but rather transpositional keys by which the whole system of ancient pitches was shifted up or down. (Modern scholars agree with Mei's view and believe these keys took on the regional-ethnic names—Dorian, Phrygian, etc.—of the particular octave species they shifted into a central ambitus or octave.) Mei argued also that ancient Greek music was monophonic and that the nature of modern polyphonic textures precluded them from achieving the emotional effects of ancient song.

Through the 1570s Mei explained his views in a lengthy correspondence with Vincenzo Galilei in Florence (see no. 37 above pp. 184–89). The following letter is an early and important summary of the issues involved. The first two thirds of it (here up through the discussion of the ancient *tonoi*) were published posthumously in the *Discorso sopra la musica antica e moderna di M. Girolamo Mei cittadino ed accademico fiorentino* (Venice, 1602).

Letter to Vincenzo Galilei
(1572)

Excellent and my most worthy Sir:

. . . Concerning your queries I shall reply under several headings as distinctly and expeditiously as I know how, in order to be understood, and as succinctly as I can, so as not to be tedious. I shall do this in whatever order turns out to be most convenient, without any regard for whether you asked them earlier or later, in the first or the second letter.

I told Mr. Pirro[1] by word of mouth, as he gave you to understand, that I considered it certain that the singing of the ancients was in every song a single

TEXT: Claude V. Palisca, *The Florentine Camerata: Documentary Studies and Translations* (New Haven: Yale University Press, 1989), pp. 56–75. Copyright 1989 by Yale University; reprinted by permission. Translation by Claude V. Palisca. I have adapted and shortened Palisca's annotations.

1. This may be Pirro del Bene, who was a member of the Alterati Academy in Florence, to which Mei belonged. [Tr.]

air, such as we hear today in church in the recitation of the psalmody of the Divine Office, and especially when it is celebrated solemnly; although among the ancients the chorus of those who sang was of many voices, as occurred in the tragedies, where by law the established number was fifteen, or in the ancient comedies, where it was likewise limited, but to twenty-four. As for the chorus of the satyr plays, dithyrambs, and other hymns, it was customary in that religion for a large number to sing them together, but I have not been able to ascertain how many.

I have spoken of the chorus only; concerning the actors onstage, whether of the tragedy, the comedy, or the satyr play, or concerning those who sang solo whatever kind of poem, whether to the lyre, the aulos, or other instrument, such reservations are not needed, because, there being only one voice, of necessity it could not sing more than one single air. As to whether the air of the voice was the same as the air of the instrument that accompanied, and whether the notes of the air that the voice sang were the same as those of the instrument with respect to high and low pitch, to the quickness or slowness of the duration or rhythm—about this we shall discourse in its place.

What chiefly persuaded me that the entire chorus sang one and the same air was observing that the music of the ancients was held to be a valuable medium for moving the affections, as witnessed by the many incidents related by the writers, and from noticing that our music instead is apt for anything else, to put it colloquially. Now all this naturally must arise from the opposite and contrary qualities that are intrinsically characteristic of these two kinds of music; the qualities of ancient music being suited and by nature apt for bringing about the effects that it produced; those of the moderns, on the contrary, for hindering them. And these foundations, qualities, and principles must be natural and stable, not man-made and variable.

Now, granted that music, insofar as pertains to song, revolves about qualities of the voice and especially with respect to whether it is high, intermediate, or low in pitch, the idea began to form in my mind that principally in these qualities must lie the basis for its power; and further, that since each of these qualities of the voice is not the same, it is not logical that they should have had the same capacity. Rather, since they were contrary among themselves and born of contrary movements, it was essential that each should have opposite properties, necessarily capable of producing contrary effects.

Now nature gave a voice to animals and especially to man for the expression of inner states. Therefore it is logical that, the various qualities of the voice being distinct, each should be appropriate for expressing the affection of certain determinate states, and each, furthermore, should express easily its own affection but not that of another. Thus the high-pitched voice could not suitably express the affections of the intermediate and far less those of the low, nor the intermediate any of those of the high or the low. Rather, the quality of one ought necessarily to impede the operation of the other, the two being opposites.

On the basis of these thoughts and foundations, I began to reason that if in their music the ancients had sung several airs mixed together in one and the same song, as our musicians do with their bass, tenor, contralto, and soprano, or with more or fewer parts than these at one and the same time, it would undoubtedly have been impossible for it ever to move vigorously the affections that it wished to move in the hearer, as may be read that it did at every turn in the accounts and testimonials of the great and noble writers. To appreciate the truth of this conclusion more clearly and as if before the eyes, we may take up again the real principles and foundations mentioned above and first see where they lead us when accompanied by the other conditions that must necessarily be present. Then we should verify this conclusion against the authority of what can be gathered from what we read in those authors who left some notice of this ancient music in their writings.

It is a certainty that the high and low pitch of the diastematic, or, to put it otherwise, intervallic, voice is the proper subject of music, for these qualities are born of diverse and altogether opposite causes, the first arising from the rapidity and the other from the sluggishness of the movement that produces them. These qualities are proper symbols and signs of diverse and altogether contrary affections of the living being, each of the qualities expressing naturally its own affection. At the same time it is clear that affections are moved in the souls of others by representing, as if before them, whether as objects or recollections, those affections that have been previously aroused by these images. Now this cannot be brought about by the voice except with its qualities of low, high, or intermediate pitch, which nature provided for this effect and which is a proper and natural sign of that affection which one wants to arouse in the listener.

It is likewise very well known that pitches intermediate between the extremely high and the extremely low are appropriate for showing a quiet and moderate disposition of the affections, while the very high are signs of a very excited and uplifted spirit, and the very low of abject and humble thoughts, in the same way that a tempo intermediate between rapid and slow reveals a poised spirit, while a rapid one manifests an excited spirit, and a slow tempo a sluggish and lazy one. It is clear that all these qualities both of pitch and of time have by their natures the capacity to move affections similar to their own. Therefore the excessively high and the extremely low tonoi were rejected by the Platonists in their republic,[2] the former for being plaintive and the latter lugubrious, only the intermediate ones being accepted. These same people dealt the same way with meters and rhythms. Moreover, all contrary qualities, whether natural or acquired, are weakened by mixing and confounding and somehow blunt each other's force, equally if their power and vigor are equal, proportionately if not. From this it arises that each one mixed with a diverse one operates in relation to that force either imperfectly or very little. For if you

2. Plato, *Republic* 3.398c. [Tr.]

mixed equal quantities of boiling and iced water, both equally removed from being temperate, one by excessive coldness, the other by excessive warmth, not only would each have no effect, but both would be reduced to a middling disposition, not able by its nature either to cool or to heat. Only if a subject were inclined to one or other excess would it perhaps be able to operate one way or the other.

Now, since all the things proposed are indubitably true, it is necessary that the forceful effect in stirring affections which one reads that the music of the ancients had arose solely from those properties that had the capacity of stirring those affections when nothing contrary was mixed in that might impede and weaken their operative force. It was consequently necessary that all the singers sang together, not only the same words, but the same tonos and the same air with the same quantity of duration and the same quality of meter and rhythm, all of which things together were able to produce the effect that the artist strove for and to which he aimed in his mind to lead. And this could not be anything but a united and plain song directed at a single end through its natural and rightful means.

Up to now our discussion has been based on the natural principles posited above. But that this was in fact the method of singing, in addition to other arguments that could be adduced, the following in particular should be sufficient proof. Among those very learned and searching ancient writers who wrote expressly and diligently about this art (of whom between the Greek and the Latin I have surely read fifteen),[3] in none is there found any term that corresponds to any of those parts that musicians from one hundred and fifty years ago—when the music of our day is believed to have had its origin—until now call bass, tenor, contralto, and soprano. I leave aside for the present Plato, Aristotle, Athenaeus,[4] Proclus,[5] Pollux,[6] Vitruvius,[7] and others who have spoken of this discipline incidentally, if at length and rather copiously, for it was not their purpose to relate every aspect of it, as someone might well think and say. As to whether before that time people sang several airs together, as became customary, it does not seem reasonable to believe that this ever happened.

Add to this the fact that in the ancient writers there is no recollection of those consonances which our musicians call imperfect, such as the semiditone and ditone, the minor or major hexachord, and all those others of which their songs are full. Whoever wishes to discuss this matter properly cannot, or rea-

3. At the end of this letter Mei provided Galilei with a list of sources he had read. It includes, among ancient Greek writers, Aristoxenus, Aristides Quintilianus, Nichomachus of Gerasa, pseudo-Plutarch, and Porphyry. For the complete list see Palisca, *The Florentine Camerata,* pp. 75–77.

4. Athenaeus, fl. 200 C.E., was the author of the *Deipnosophists.* [Tr.]

5. Proclus Diadochus, Neoplatonist philosopher, fifth century C.E., wrote a number of philosophical treatises; but Mei probably had in mind as relevant to music particularly *In primum Euclidis elementorum librum commentarii* and *In Platonis Timaeum commentaria.* [Tr.]

6. Julius Pollux, second century C.E., *Onomasticon.* [Tr..]

7. Vitruvius Pollio, *De architectura libri decem;* on music, 5.4. [Tr.]

sonably should, believe that this could have arisen from any other cause than that they did not use them and therefore did not know them in their practice, and that they did not consider them because of their imperfection. The reason why they did not use them was that they all sang together a single melody, for they aimed at a goal altogether different from that of moderns and therefore did not have that need for them that our musicians do.

* * * * *

It appears to be clear enough, then, for the reasons given, that the music of the ancients was a single melody and a single air, however many or few voices were singing. It should not seem strange if it had such lively effects in moving the affections of others, as we read, when it was composed—as we would say—by a good master and arranged by an artist who had good judgment in the art and performed by skilled persons and suitable voices. For everyone sang one and the same air in one simple tonos and in the best airs with a small number of steps in such a way that with its descents and ascents the voice did not go at all beyond the natural confines of the affection that the words wanted to express. They used at the same time a meter or rhythm, whether fast, slow, or moderate, according to the meaning of the idea that they aimed to express. In this way they could not help but achieve most of what they were expected to do.

Nor should it appear at all out of line (as they say) or strange that the music of our times does not work any of these miracles, since it conveys to the soul of the listener at one time diverse and contrary signs of affections as it mixes indistinctly together airs and tonoi that are completely dissimilar and of natures contrary to each other. Since each of these things has, naturally, its own quality and force, capable of stirring and moving through its resemblance appropriate affections, this music cannot generally by itself arouse any affection. Indeed, no one who considers the matter honestly will have cause to think of this as appearing in its nature otherwise.

* * * * *

To all the things that have been said concerning our music, add the taste for continuous delicacy of chords and consonances and a hundred other superfluous kinds of artifice that the moderns have pursued as if with a gun (as they say), seeking to ensnare our ears. It is a supreme hindrance in moving the soul to any affection to be chiefly preoccupied and almost bound by these straps of pleasure, all things different from, if not opposed to, what by nature is necessary to an affection, because affection and moral character tend to be something natural, or at least they appear to be, and to have as their goal only to want to arouse the same effect in others. An example of this is when in a gathering some are weeping, others laughing, others conversing calmly, and others quarreling, while some dance drunkenly, and still others are doing other things, someone joins in who has no particular inclination to any of these affections; he will not be moved from his state except to be confused by the situation. If, on the other hand, someone joins a gathering in which everyone is lamenting or everyone is celebrating, only a great deal of preparation, both natural and spiritual, will prevent him from being moved and disposed in some way in keeping with these affections.

Consider further the supreme vanity of the use of many notes without any natural fittingness, whether considered in all its parts or together almost as a single corpus, or each by itself, something censured among the ancients by all men of judgment, among whom one does not hear perhaps any other complaint more frequently against the insolence and foolishness of the musicians of their times than that something is altogether unnatural, indeed, truly against every nature of affection. As anybody can hear, someone who laments never leaves the high pitches, and contrariwise someone who grieves does not leave the low pitches, unless a short distance, never crossing over into the intermediate pitches, which would not be suited to such a purpose. They would not trespass the limit, as we hear done in the airs of our musicians, which not only in the entire corpus of all their airs mixed together, but often in one only, whether soprano, tenor, or whatever it is, jumping now up, now down, through intermediate notes or directly, sometimes reach as much as an eleventh or twelfth.

Nor should we overlook the inestimable negligence of our musicians with respect to note values and rhythm in the various parts, whether each part is considered by itself or the entire corpus of them together. Extremely frequently, if not always, this is contrary to the nature of what would express the idea that the words signify, which arguably ought to be pursued beyond any other consideration. And this lacks any real distinction in each part; rather it differs haphazardly from one part to the other, since often the soprano hardly moves, while the tenor flies, and the bass goes strolling in slipper-socks, or, indeed, the other way around. How much imperfection this causes and how much it weakens the expression of the affections, through which the listener is moved to experience a similar feeling, does not require further explanation, for it is something that should be obvious to the little fishes, as they say, as well as to those who want to consider carefully the nature of each affection. For who is so dense as not easily to understand, if he looks around himself, that an infuriated person speaks hurriedly, and that the slowness of a suppliant's speech is different from the slowness of one who is calm? To this carelessness about tempo should be added their immoderate diminutions, starting from those notes called maxims and diminishing to those called sixteenth-notes, introduced without any reason or suitability to the natural movement of the voice.

On top of all these impediments nearly chief must be counted the disordered perturbation, mix-up, and mangling of the words. Thereby the power of the idea that may perchance be efficaciously expressed by them is not allowed to penetrate the intellect of the listener, as even the singers themselves can often recognize. The text, were it well understood, could by itself move and generate an affection in someone.

But what shall we say, besides, of that other unbecoming impertinence, that the soprano often sings the beginning of the words of a thought or repeats them, while the tenor is in the middle, the bass at the end, and the other parts elsewhere; or they are inconsistent among themselves in pronouncing the words? We cannot say, truly, other than that this too, along with the other conditions mentioned, drags behind the same standard—to distract the mind with diverse and, if necessary, contrary parts. This distraction means that all these points—as one may conceive them—strike helter-skelter and not on one center, not having thus sufficient value or force. Each one, being an impediment to the other, does not make an opening and does not penetrate, and thus does not stir an affection, the reverse of what the proverb tells us of the drop of water that, hitting the stone continually and unitedly in the same place, finally carves a hole in it.

· · · · ·

As to the marvelous effects of the music of the ancients in moving the affections and not finding any trace of this in the modern, if we wish to look with a straight eye at the matters discussed above, it may happen that we shall marvel no more at the effects, because our music does not have the same goal. This may be because ours does not have any means of accomplishing this as the ancient did, since it has as its object the delectation of the sense of hearing, whereas the ancient had the object of leading someone else to the same affections as one's own.

The project that I have been pursuing for some time is to seek to discover what the ancients intended by tonos—that is, Dorian, Phrygian, and the like—and whether these were the same as those that the moderns call first, second, third, up to the eighth tone. It did not seem to me from what I had read that this was possible, and today I believe that it is very certain that they are not the same. Those that our musicians call tones do not have the same conditions that we know those ancient tonoi had. If Franchino,[8] Glarean, and the other great geniuses among the moderns wished to restore to our tones the names of the ancient, better to make us believe that they are the same and call the even-numbered or plagal—instead of *second, fourth, sixth,* and *eighth—Hypodorian, Hypophrygian, Hypolydian,* and *Hypomixolydian,* and the odd-numbered—instead of *first, third, fifth,* and *seventh—Dorian, Phrygian, Lydian,* and *Mixolydian,* nevertheless, what our musicians call *tones* are nothing but simple diverse species or forms of the diapason and octave,[9] differing in height of pitch one from another only according to how they are found collocated in the order of the system, constitution, or scale—as others call it—of the steps or musical pitches. Now among the ancients the Hypodorian and Hypophrygian tonoi, and so all the others, arose from mutations of locus[10] that were

8. That is, Gafori.
9. On the species of fifth and octave of the modes see no. 34 above (Aaron), chap. 1, pp. 140–41.
10. That is, transpositions. [Tr.]

applied to the entire constitutions of pitches, whether of the diapasons or octaves or of other systems and constitutions, whether perfect or imperfect, when in the mutation of locus they became higher or lower in pitch than they were naturally accustomed to be in the common constitution or system. This natural or common constitution or system unaltered with respect to locus they called the Dorian tonos.[11] Its proper diapason or octave was the middle one, contained within the two disjunct tetrachords—that is, between the step the ancients called *hypate meson,* our E la mi, and the step they called *nete diezeug-menon,* our e la mi, inclusively.

•   •   •   •   •

The songs of Olympus and Terpander, so far as pertains to singing, were without doubt, in my opinion, a plainchant accompanied by an instrument, the lyre or kithara, which may be taken as the same, in the case of Terpander, because he was a kitharode, or a pipe in the case of Olympus, since he was an aulete. Although these songs in their airs did not seek out in climbing or descending more than three strings each—so simple and natural were they—nevertheless they were so beautiful melodically and of such excellence that they were never equaled or improved upon by those musicians who followed, despite the many strings they put to use. And this is evidently what Plutarch's words mean when he says of them: "τρίχορδα γὰρ ὄντα καὶ ἁπλᾶ διαφέρει τῶν ποικιλων καὶ πολυχόρδων—With their three strings and their simplicity, they surpass so much those intricate compositions using many strings that none could imitate the style of Olympus, and all who compose melodies for many strings and in several modes are left far behind."[12] Although they were made from three strings and were simple, they nevertheless excelled and outshone the varied and polychordal compositions of others. Not that they sang with three notes, that is, in three airs at the same time, or played, as we in our times have heard done sometimes by certain great players who have ingeniously played on a viola with a bow three or four parts and airs at the same time. A sure sign that the words of that noble author should be understood in the way stated and not otherwise may be—besides the truth of what they signify—that in that place the author praises the simplicity of those who used few strings in comparison to those who used many. None—for example, Timotheus, Philoxenus, and an infinity of others, with all their multitude of strings—could equal the songs of Olympus. Timotheus expanded his lyre to eleven strings, whereas up to Terpander and others like him it did not go beyond seven. For this alteration he was exiled by the Spartans as a spoiler and destroyer of the ancient

11. Mei announces here for the first time his important discovery, elaborated in *De modis musicis antiquorum,* that the Greek tonoi were not modes in the medieval sense, but keys used to transpose the central octave or natural system, called Dorian, to higher or lower levels of pitch. [Tr.]

12. [Pseudo-] Plutarch *De musica* 1137b. [Tr.]

music.[13] It is altogether beyond the realm of possibility that Timotheus played together at one time ten or eleven parts or airs on the same lyre.

· · · · ·

What the ancient musicians called *harmonia* in singing did not have anything in the world to do with consonances (as may be understood by whoever has some idea of the Greek language from the nature of the meaning of the word and its derivatives) but pertained to the composition of the air which was sung—that is, well adapted and suitably joined together according to the proper division and distinction of the intervals from one step to the other of a genus, which, whether used simply or mixed with others, was being sung or played.

The words or verse of Vergil: "Obloquitur numeris septem discrimina vocum"[14] do not mean, I believe, that Orpheus played seven parts on the lyre or was seconding or accompanying his singing of the chorus with consonances on the lyre, but that he with his lyre, which was made up of two conjoined tetrachords, which together contained only seven steps or pitches, as for example that of Terpander—and not like that of Timotheus or others which had a larger number—made it almost speak with his masterful and fitting accompaniment according to the melody, note values and rhythm of those who, in keeping with the habit of the choruses, danced as they sang. Here the poet's marvelous and deliberate care in this imitation should not be allowed idly to slip through one's hands. For, in order to make evident and to demonstrate that the playing of Orpheus had dignity, since it was customary to play the ancient rite πρόσ-χορδα,[15] that is, to play the same notes as those of the air that the chorus sang, he added: "Iam que eadem digitis iam pectina pulsa eburno."[16] In ancient times it was customary for the song of the chorus to be the principal part, while the instrument, almost like a servant, accompanied it, for human song was the real thing, whereas the accompaniment was its image. But then, under the pretext of carving a new path, musicians began to do the opposite—that is, to make the playing precede and the voice follow. We can read of many quarrels about this among the ancients, for with this mutation of custom they consented to having sensation become the principal and reason its subordinate. Because nothing else, in truth, would appear to have allowed the instrumental sound, invented to imitate the voice, to become the boss and to be obeyed by the voice in effecting the actions properly belonging to it, for nature gave the voice

13. Two sources for this story are Athenaeus *Deipnosophists* 636e and Pausanius *Descriptio graeciae* 3.13. [Tr.] Philoxenus (ca. 436–380 B.C.E.) was a composer of dithyrambs.

14. See no. 30 above (Gafori), p. 113, n. 7.

15. *Proschorda;* Pollux *Onomasticon* 4.63 defines this as the attuning of a melody to a stringed instrument—i.e., in unison. [Pseudo-] Plutarch *De musica* 1141b speaks of this method of accompaniment as ancient, before Crexus invented the method of accompanying with notes other than those of the vocal melody. [Tr.]

16. Virgil *Aeneid* 6.647: "striking them now with his fingers, now with his ivory quill" (trans. Fairclough). [Tr.]

expressly to man not so that he might with its pure sound, like animals which lack reason, express pleasure and pain, but so that, together with meaningful speech, he might suitably express the thoughts of his mind. Having reached this point, the corruption did not stop there. Almost content with this new status, it changed because of the march of time, and the manner of seconding the other became bastardized, to use this vulgar term. Whereas earlier one sang and played unitedly and always with the same durations and pitches, now the voice and instrument began not to correspond to each other πρόσχορδα— that is, with the same notes—but συμφώνως,[17] that is, with consonances and not with the same duration and measure, but with diminutions and *passaggi* and other such variations, all things imagined and thought up by the artists themselves in their ambition, all striving competitively to please most supremely the ears, without taking the intellect into account. This new allure- ment began to lead the soul astray from attention to the conceits and other imitations of the affections, almost enfeebling it with these excessive delicacies. Plato, in the seventh book of his *Laws*,[18] to counter these corruptions destruc- tive of the rational parts and characteristic form of man, orders with great diligence and commands that his youth never be taught any style of music in which there is any diversity or variety of pitches or durations between the sound of the lyre and the song composed by the poet, which is as worthy as the poet-musician who composed the air, for in ancient times musician and poet were the same person.

These corruptions became every day greater, especially after the introduc- tion of instruments with many strings, such as organs, spinets, harpsichords, lutes, and, in sum, all those that by means of many keys or many strings possess a large number of pitches. Whoever believed that out of this ultimately evolved this manner and custom of ours of singing together so many and diverse vocal airs would not have thought anything very far from the truth. For this, growing, as things pertaining to the arts do, whether useful or not, little by little grew so much in our times and became so extremely big, that this art, divorced from any care or law, has let itself become prey to the pure willfulness and power of its artists, without any more considered limitation or rule. Thus, through the ambition of each of them, the last not wishing to follow and approve the foot- steps and works of those who came before them, so as not to appear to confess almost by tacit consensus that they were inferior in industry or genius, it easily came about that these musicians precipitated themselves at breakneck speed, as they say, to discover always new styles and new forms of song. Soon their vanity gave rise to such a paradox that they tolerated that the words of their songs were not understood or that the sentiment that actually appeared in the words could not be felt. Thus we could not claim—almost to our shame—to

17. *Symphonos;* the term *symphonia* meant consonance, but only fifths, fourths, and octaves were considered consonances. [Tr.]
18. 7.812d, where Plato criticized those musicians who accompanied in the *symphonos* style rather than *proschorda*. [Tr.]

have been born rational; it delights us more to be without intellect and entirely subject to any pleasure whatever than to be truly human beings. But this discussion is beside the point. . . .

Rome, May 8, 1572

42 Fray Toribio de Benavente, *called* Motolinia

Hernán Cortés and a ragtag group of Spanish soldiers first landed at the place on the Mexican mainland they called Veracruz on April 22, 1519. On the following November 8 they entered, dumbstruck with wonder, into Tenochtitlan, the great floating capital of the tributary state of the Aztecs (or, more properly, the Mexica). Less than two years later Cortés's capture and destruction of the city was complete.

The military conquest quickly set in motion extensive efforts to convert the indigenous Mexicans to Christianity. Among the earliest missionaries in the Valley of Mexico were twelve Franciscans, the so-called Mexican Apostles, who arrived in June 1524. Fray Toribio de Benavente (ca. 1495–ca. 1565) was one of them. He took the name by which he is remembered from the Mexica themselves, who are said to have remarked at his strict Franciscan habit "motolonia"—in Nahuatl, "he suffers" or "he is poor." Motolonia learned Nahuatl well and studied Mexican society, customs, and ritual extensively. He numbers with his fellow Franciscan Bernardino de Sahagún among the keenest European observers of indigenous Mexico. Of his two chief works, the *Historia de los indios de la Nueva España* (1541) and the closely related *Memoranda* (1530s?), the first emphasizes the progress of evangelization after the conquest while the second is richer in proto-ethnographic detail. Though both treatises influenced writers on Mexico of the following generations—the reading that follows, for example, was taken over almost verbatim by Fray Juan de Torquemada in his *Monarchia indiana* of 1615—neither was published for centuries after Motolinia's death. The *Historia* first emerged in 1858, the *Memoranda* only in 1903.

Book 2, Chapter 26 of the *Memoranda* comprises one of the lengthiest and most specific accounts of Mexican sung ritual that has come down to us. Motolinia's evident admiration for the grace, skill, precision, and careful preparation of the native performers is shared as well by other early European spectators. Across the later sixteenth century such admiration would turn increasingly to condemnation and repression, channeling indigenous energies into European music-making and Catholic public spectacles while driving native ritual underground, where it seems to have persisted for a time in secret ceremonies of song and dance.

FROM *Memoranda or Book of the Things of New Spain and of the Natives There*

(1530s?)

BOOK 2

CHAPTER 26: ON THE MANNER OF THE NATIVES' DANCING, ON THE GREAT SKILL AND CONFORMITY THEY OBSERVED IN DANCING AND SINGING, AND ON MANY OTHER THINGS OF THIS SORT; SO THAT THIS CHAPTER AND THOSE THAT FOLLOW ARE NO LESS NOTABLE THAN THE PRECEDING ONES.

Songs and dances were very important in all this land, both to celebrate the solemn festivals of the demons they honored as gods, whom they thought well served by such things, and for their own enjoyment and recreation. For this reason they gave two names to their dances, as is explained below.[1] And because in each town they put much stock in these things, each chieftain had a chapel in his house with his singers who composed the dances and songs; and these leaders sought out those who knew best how to compose songs in the meter and verses they practiced. They prized most *contrabajos*, because in the houses of the chiefs they frequently sang in a quiet voice.[2]

Most often they sang and danced in the principal festivals, which occurred every twenty days,[3] and in other less important festivals. The most important dances took place in the town plazas; other times they danced in the patio of the chieftain's house (for all the chieftains had large patios), or in the houses of lesser lords.

When they had won some battle, or when they elevated a new chieftain, or when a lord was married, or for some other novel event, the music masters

---

TEXT: *Memoriales de Fray Toribio de Motolinia*, ed. Luis García Pimentel (Mexico: Casa del Editor, 1903), pp. 339–43. Translation by Gary Tomlinson. Where possible I have retained Motolinia's fluctuation between present and past tenses.

1. 2.27, where Motolinia gives the indigenous names for dance for recreation (*nehtotiliztli*) and for solemn, penitential religious dance (*macehualiztli*). The same distinction, though without Nahuatl terminology, is made by the Dominican missionary Diego Durán (1537–88) in his *Historia de las indias de Nueva-España e islas de tierra firme*, another important early source on Mexican song and dance; see Robert Stevenson, *Music in Aztec and Inca Territory* (Berkeley, University of California Press, 1968), p. 110.

2. Motolinia uses *contrabajo* to refer to a relatively high-pitched voice, not a low bass. The usage is confirmed by his discussion below of Mexican drums, where the higher-pitched *teponaztli* is said to serve as *contrabajo* to the lower *huehuetl*. See also Stevenson, *Music*, p. 98, n. 213.

3. That is, in each of the eighteen twenty-day months of the Mexican ritual calendar; to these 360 days were added five inauspicious or "barren" days, called *nemontemi*, filling out the solar year. Motolinia was one of the first Europeans to comprehend Mexican calendrical systems.

composed a new song, different from those celebrating the festivals of the demons or ancient exploits or past chieftains.

The singers decided some days before the festivals what they would sing. In the larger towns there were many singers, and if there were to be new songs and dances they gathered in advance so there would be no imperfections on the festival day. On the morning of that day they put a large mat in the middle of the plaza where they set up their drums. Then they gathered and dressed at the house of the chieftain; from there they came singing and dancing. Sometimes they began their dances in the morning, sometimes at the hour when we celebrate High Mass. At night they returned singing to the palace, there to end their song early in the night, or when the night was well advanced, or even at midnight.

There were two drums. One[4] was tall and round, fatter than a man, five hand-spans tall, of very good wood, well worked and hollowed out inside. On the outside it was painted, and on its mouth they stretched a well cured deer-skin. From the edge to the middle it sounds pitches a fifth apart, and they tune its pitches higher or lower in order to match it to their songs. The other drum cannot be described without the aid of a picture;[5] this serves as *contrabajo*. Both drums have a good sound and can be heard a great distance away. When the dancers have taken their places they prepare to play the drums and two singers, the best, act as leaders in beginning the songs. The large, leather-covered drum is played with the hands, while the other is played with mallets, like Spanish drums (however differently it is made).

The chieftain, together with other lords and elders, goes before the drums, dancing. These men stand three or four fathoms deep around the mat, and around them come another growing multitude that fills out the circle. In the larger towns more than a thousand and even more than two thousand take part in this central place. Around them comes a procession of two lines of dancers, young men, expert dancers. The leaders are two men chosen from among the best dancers; they lead the dance. In these two lines, by means of certain turns and graceful postures, they face sometimes their companions in front of them and other times those behind them. A large number of dancers, sometimes as many as a thousand or more according to the town and the festival, participate in these two lines. Before wars, when they celebrated their festivals with great abandon in the large towns, three or four thousand or even more would gather to dance; but after the conquest, when their numbers were depleted and growing smaller, only half as many danced.[6]

4. The *huehuetl*.
5. This is the *teponaztli*, a drum fashioned from a hollowed log laid horizontal and cut with an H-shaped slit. The two resulting tongues, of different pitch, were played with rubber-tipped mallets.
6. The indigenous population of the central valley of Mexico, estimated at 10–25 million at the time of European contact, declined steadily thereafter, especially because of smallpox and other diseases brought by the Europeans. By the 1620s it reached its lowpoint, approximately 730,000. See Sherburne F. Cook and Woodrow Borah, *Essays in Population History* (3 vols., Berkeley: University of California Press, 1971–79).

When they are ready to start the dance three or four Indians blow very lively whistles. Then they play the drums quietly, growing louder little by little. Hearing that the drums have begun, the people all hear the song and begin to dance. The first songs are sung quietly and slowly, as if composed in the soft hexachord. The very first concerns the particular festival being celebrated. The two singing masters always begin the song, and then everyone in the whole circle proceeds to sing and dance together. The whole multitude coordinates the movements of their feet as well as the best dancers of Spain. What is more, their whole bodies—heads, arms, and hands—are so synchronized, measured, and ordered that they do not differ from one another by even half a beat; whatever one does with right foot or left, all the others do at the same time and on the same beat. When one lowers his left arm and raises his right, all the others do the same thing at the same time. In this way the drums, singing, and dancing are perfectly concerted. Everything is so synchronized that one does not differ a jot from another, and good Spanish dancers who see them are amazed and greatly esteem the native dances as well as the great accord and feeling they display.

The dancers in the outer ring make (as we might say) a small beat, that is, they place two beats in the time of one, moving quicker and putting more work into the dance; and all those in this circle move in time to one another. Those in the middle of the circle dance to the full beat and move both their feet and the rest of their bodies with much gravity. Some of them raise and lower their arms with much grace.

Each verse or couplet is repeated three or four times, and the song is so well tuned that the singing, drums, and dance all stay together. Having finished one song—though the first songs seem longer because they go slower, not one of them lasts a whole hour—having finished one, the pitch of the drum is changed. Everyone stops singing (though not dancing) for a few beats. Then the singing masters begin another song, a little higher and livelier than the one before it. Thus they raise the songs and change the pitches and the notes, moving from a low one to a high and from a dance to a quicker step.

Various boys and children also dance—sons of aristocrats, seven or eight years old, singing and dancing with their fathers. Since their voices have not yet broken, they add much grace to the song. Sometimes they play trumpets and some little flutes, not very well tuned; other times they play whistles and certain little bones that give a loud sound.[7] Others go disguised in dress and voice, impersonating peoples of foreign nations and speaking their languages. These are like clowns. They go along cutting capers, making a thousand faces

---

7. For a glossary of Mexica organology see Stevenson, *Music*, pp. 30–85. For the instruments Motolinia mentions here see especially the entries *atecocolli* and *tecciztli* (conch trumpets), *quiquiztli* (wooden trumpet), *tepuzquiquiztli* (copper trumpet), *chichtli* (whistle flute), *çoçoloctli* and *tlapitzalli* (flutes). For pictures and further discussion see Samuel Martí, *Instrumentos musicales precortesianos* (Mexico: Instituto Nacional de Antropología, 1955).

and cracking a thousand jokes that make whoever sees and hears them laugh. Some of them go as old women, others as fools.

From time to time some of the participants leave to rest and eat, and when they return others leave. Sometimes they bring bouquets of roses and garlands that they wear on their heads and on their dancing costumes, which are made of rich robes and feathers; and in their hands they carry small, pretty feathers. In these dances they also wear many emblems and insignias that tell who has been valiant in battle.

From the hour of vespers until nighttime the songs and dances get more and more lively and higher in pitch, and the playing more and more graceful. It almost seems that they sing the air of some festive hymn that they have among them. And the drums get higher and higher. And since there are many people they can be heard at a great distance, especially when the air carries their voices, and especially at night. Then they burn many great torches, which is really a sight to see.

The Spaniards call these dances *areito,* a word from the islands.[8]

8. That is, the West Indies. Specifically, the word comes from Hispaniola, where Columbus first landed, and is derived from Taino.

43 Bartolomé de Segovia?

In 1524 Spanish explorers off the western coast of South America intercepted a boat heading north that was laden with precious barter goods. It was the first unequivocal evidence the Europeans had seen of a prosperous civilization to the south, and it ensured that further explorations would soon lead to contact between the Spanish and Inca empires. In 1531 Francisco Pizarro embarked for Peru; in late 1532 he used treachery to capture the Inca Atahualpa at Cajamarca and imprisoned him. Pizarro executed Atahualpa the following August, installing his brother Manco Inca in his place as puppet ruler. In November 1533, the Spaniards entered unopposed into Cuzco.

In the next decade, the far-flung and loose-knit Inca political system dissolved quickly under a succession of conquistador-governors who conspired to murder one another as well as the native Peruvians who rose against them, under Manco Inca, in 1536. From this chaos there survived few notices of pre-Hispanic life and society—indeed Inca traces are startlingly sparse compared to the relative abundance of information we have from central Mexico. The account here, the most detailed description by a European of an Inca celebration in Cuzco, is then all the more valuable. The harvest celebration witnessed by our author was called Inti Raimi, or Festival of the Sun. Its long avenue of living and mummified nobility and its full day of song, timed to the waxing and waning of the sun, are richly suggestive of the careful spatio-cosmological orientations that were basic, as recent researches have shown, to Inca worship.

FROM *Relation of Many Occurrences in Peru: In Sum in Order to Convey in Writing How These Kingdoms Were Conquered and Colonized*

(1553)

These things happened in April 1535 when in the valley of Cuzco they harvested the maize and other crops. Each year after the harvest it was the custom of the rulers of Cuzco to make a great sacrifice to the sun and all the *huacas* or shrines of the city. This was done in them and through all the provinces and the whole kingdom. It was started by the Inca[1] and consisted of eight days of giving thanks to the sun for the harvest just completed and praying to the sun for bountiful future crops. . . .

They brought out onto a plain at the entrance to Cuzco where the sun rises all the figures from the shrines, and they put the more important of these under rich and well wrought feathered awnings, which were a splendid sight. From rows of these awnings they made an avenue, with one row of awnings facing the other more than thirty paces away. In this avenue gathered all the rulers and lords of Cuzco, but no people of lower station. These were *orejones,*[2] very richly dressed in cloaks and shirts of silver embroidery with bracelets and disks of fine shining gold on their heads. They formed two lines, each of more than three hundred lords. It was like a procession with one choir facing another, and they stood very quietly waiting for the sun to rise. When the sun was partly risen they began to intone a song with great order and harmony.

TEXT: *Relación de muchas cosas acaescidas en el Piru en suma para entender a la letra la manera que se tuvo en la conquista y poblazón de estos reinos,* in *Crónicas peruanas de interés indigena,* ed. Francisco Esteve Barba (Biblioteca de Autores Españoles, vol. 209, Madrid: Real Academia Española, 1968), pp. 81–82. Translation by Gary Tomlinson. For a discussion of the account, see Sabine MacCormack, *Religion in the Andes: Vision and Imagination in Early Colonial Peru* (Princeton: Princeton University Press, 1991), pp. 74–79. Arguments in favor of ascribing the *Relación* to the obscure cleric Bartolomé de Segovia and against its earlier ascription to Cristóbal de Molina are made by Raúl Porras Barrenechea, *Los cronistas del Perú (1528–1650) y otros ensayos* (Lima, Banco de Crédito del Perú, 1986), p. 317.

1. That is, the ruler; *inca* in Quechua signifies a male of royal blood.
2. Literally, "big ears," so called by the Spaniards because of the large gold ornaments they wore in their ear lobes.

While they sang each one tapped one of his feet, like our singers of polyphony, and as the sun rose they sang higher.

A little way from these rows the Inca had his tent in an enclosure with a chair and a very fine bench. And at the beginning of the singing he rose with great authority and put himself at the head of the lines and was the first to begin to sing; and as he did, so did the others. After he had stood for a little while he returned to his chair, where he remained conversing with those who came to him. On a few occasions, from time to time, he went and stood with his chorus for a while, and then he returned.

Thus they sang from sunrise until the sun had set completely. And since until midday the sun was rising, their voices grew, and from midday on they diminished, carefully following the progress of the sun. All this time they made many offerings. On one side, on an embankment where there was a tree, there were Indians who did nothing but throw meat into a great fire where it was burned and consumed in the flames. To another side the Inca threw many llamas that the common and poor Indians scrambled for; this was a source of great diversion. At eight o'clock more than two hundred young women came out of Cuzco carrying large, covered pitchers, each new and identical to the others, containing a great quantity of *chicha*.[3] They came five at a time, in great order and synchrony, each group awaiting its turn. They offered to the sun many baskets of an herb they eat, called in their language *coca*, which is a leaf rather like myrtle. And they observed many other ceremonies and offerings that would take long to recount.

Let it suffice to say that, when in the afternoon the sun began to set they showed great sadness on account of its absence in their song and their bearing, and they worked to diminish greatly their voices. And when the sun set completely and disappeared from their sight they showed great wonder and, joining hands, prayed to it with deepest humility. Then they removed all the apparatus of the festival and took down the awnings, and everyone went home. They returned those figures and awful relics to their houses and shrines. And thus in the same manner they celebrated for eight or nine days. And you should know that the figures of idols under those awnings were the past Incas who had ruled Cuzco.[4] Each one was served by a crowd of men who all day long shooed away flies with certain fans made of swan feathers with tiny mirrors on them and by its *mamacona,* who are like nuns; under each awning there were twelve or fifteen of them.[5]

3. A beer brewed from maize.
4. I.e. their mummified remains, fundamental to Inca worship, called *mallqui* in Quechua, *bultos* by the Spaniards. See MacCormack, *Religion,* pp. 68–71.
5. The *mamacona* were the leaders of corps of women chosen to serve the sun. See ibid., p. 458.

44 Filippo Pigafetta and Duarte Lopez

In the 1480s, the Portuguese sailor Diogo Cão, searching for trade routes to Asia that would not cross lands controlled by hostile Turks, first came across the estuary of the Congo (now the Zaire) River. Explorers, missionaries, and merchants soon followed, and by 1516 the Portuguese crown had established the Kingdom of the Congo as one of its protectorates along the African coast.

Almost a century after Cão, in 1578, Duarte Lopez sailed from Lisbon to Luanda, a newly fortified Portuguese settlement. He spent the next ten years in the Congo, mapping its inland reaches and residing at the court of its Christianized ruler, Alvaro I. In 1587 he left Africa, in the office of Congolese ambassador, to request increased missionary efforts from Philip II, King of Spain and Portugal, and Pope Sixtus V. After notable misadventures, including storms that blew him off course all the way to the West Indies, he reached Rome in 1588. There he met Filippo Pigafetta (1533–1604), soldier, writer, explorer, and agent for Pope Sixtus V through many parts of the Middle East and North Africa. From Lopez's testimony and other sources, Pigafetta compiled his *Relazione del Reame di Congo et delle circonvicine contrade (Relation on the Kingdom of the Congo and the Surrounding Regions),* published at Rome in 1591. Though it saw only one Italian edition, the work was quickly dispersed across northern Europe. It was translated into Dutch, English, German, and Latin in the 1590s, the latter two translations serving as the first volume of Theodore de Bry's monumental collection of *Petits voyages.* The English translation was reprinted by Samuel Purchas in his own large compilation of travel narratives, *Purchas His Pilgrimes* (1617–25).

FROM *Relation on the Kingdom of the Congo and the Surrounding Regions*

(1591)

BOOK 2

CHAPTER 7: ON THE COURT OF THE KING OF THE CONGO AND ON THE CLOTHING OF THOSE PEOPLE BEFORE THEY BECAME CHRISTIANS; THEN ON THE ROYAL TABLE AND THE MANNERS OF THE COURT

•　　•　　•　　•　　•

The king of the Congo has a guard made up of Anzichi and men of other nations who stand around his palace armed in the manner I described before. When he wants to leave the palace they play the drums, which can be heard for five or six miles and let everyone know that he is coming forth.... The Mocicongos (as the inhabitants of the Congo call themselves in their tongue) ... do not keep any histories of their ancient kings or memory of past ages, not knowing how to write. They measure time by the phases of the moon and do not know the hours of the day or night, speaking usually thus: At the time of such a moon, such a thing happened. They measure distances not in miles or any such units but in the days it takes a man, loaded down or not, to get there. For their gatherings and celebrations such as weddings they sing verses of love and play certain strangely formed lutes. These are in the rounded part of the body and in the neck somewhat similar to ours, but the flat part, where we carve the rosette, is covered with a very thin skin, like a bladder, instead of wood. The strings are made from strong, polished hairs from the tail of an elephant or from certain threads from the wood of the palm tree. They extend from the bottom of the instrument to the end of the neck and are tied to pegs of various sizes affixed to the neck. From the pegs they hang very thin plates of iron and silver, of different sizes depending on the size of the whole instrument. These jingle in various ways, giving out an intermittent sound, as the strings are played and the pegs from which they hang vibrate. The players pluck the strings in good proportion with their fingers and without the sort of plectrum we use to play the harp. They play masterfully and produce a melody or noise (I know not which to call it) that delights their senses. Moreover—and it is a wondrous thing—with this instrument they signify the concepts in their minds and make them understood so clearly that almost anything they can put across in speaking they can also express by touching this instrument with their

TEXT: Filippo Pigafetta, *Relazione del Reame di Congo et delle circonvicine contrade*, ed. Giorgio Raimondo Cardona (Milan: Bompiani, 1978), pp. 161–64. Translation by Gary Tomlinson.

hands. To the sound and rhythm of the music of this instrument they dance in good measure and clap their hands.[1] They also play flutes and pipes artfully at the king's court and dance to their sound in a grave and restrained fashion, almost in the manner of a *moresca*. The common people use small drums and flutes and other instruments, which they play in a less refined manner than the courtiers.

1. The lute with metal jingles Pigafetta describes survives today in various regions of West Africa; for pictures see *Musical Instruments of the World: An Illustrated Encyclopedia,* ed. the Diagram Group (Paddington Press Ltd., 1976), p. 178, and *The New Grove Dictionary of Musical Instruments,* ed. Stanley Sadie (3 vols., London: MacMillan, 1984), s.v. "Lute," fig. 1f; for description of a related Nigerian instrument see ibid., s.v. "Gurmi." Pigafetta's fascinating reference to speech-like performances on this lute might at first blush seem to confuse it with the famous West African "talking drums," alluded to, at any rate, at the beginning of the excerpt. But caution is needed here; ethnomusicologists have noted that African musicians reproduce the intonations of speech on various instruments other than drums (see Anthony King, "Talking drum," in *The New Grove Dictionary of Musical Instruments;* also, more tentatively, J. H. Kwabena Nketia, *The Music of Africa* [New York: Norton, 1974], p. 188).

45 Matteo Ricci

From the earliest years of their order, the Jesuits dreamed of Christianizing China. But their first efforts met with no success; Francis Xavier, founder of the Jesuit mission in India and the first Christian missionary to Japan, died in 1552 while awaiting permission to enter Canton.

In the same year, Matteo Ricci was born at Macerata, Italy. Taught at Jesuit schools first in his hometown and later in Florence and Rome, Ricci traveled to Portugal in 1577 and from there to Goa the following year. Four years later, now ordained a priest, he arrived in Macao. He would remain in China until his death in 1610. From Macao Ricci followed a slow northward trajectory, through Zhaoqing, Shaozhou, Nanchang, and Nanjing, toward his ultimate goal, Beijing. Only in May 1601, after two earlier unsuccessful attempts, did he win permission to live in the imperial capital, where he stayed for his last nine years.

In the 1590s Ricci gained an intimate knowledge of Chinese language, literature, and philosophy, and in his missionary activity he pursued a method of accommodation to local customs and collaboration and debate with local intellectuals. This close contact belies the blank insensitivity to Chinese song and instrumental music evident in the excerpts that follow (contrast, for example, Motolinia's more positive tone in no. 42 above, pp. 217–21); perhaps such incomprehension reflects in part Ricci's general lack of musical training. In any case, the ultimate aims behind both Ricci's and Motolinia's accounts were the same: furthering Christian belief and identifying elements not reconcilable with it. Ricci reminds us of these aims in the final paragraphs excerpted here, describing how he turned the gift of a clavichord to the emperor Wanli into a means of proselytizing.

Ricci wrote his journals in Italian during his final years. The manuscript was translated into Latin and brought to Rome by Nicola Trigault, who published it there in 1615 as *De christiana expeditione apud Sinas suscepta ab Societate Jesu. Ex P. Matthaei Ricii . . . commentariis libri V (Five Books on the Christian Expedition to China Undertaken by the Society of Jesus. From the Commentaries of Father Matteo Ricci)*. Ten further editions in Latin, French, German, Spanish, and Italian appeared in the next six years, and Samuel Purchas included excerpts in English in *Purchas His Pilgrimes*. The excerpts here are translated from Trigault's Latin, the version that was circulated widely in the seventeenth century. His sometimes free adaptation explains the wavering between Ricci's own voice and third-person references to him.

FROM *Five Books on the Christian Expedition to China*

(1615)

BOOK 1

CHAPTER 4: CONCERNING THE MECHANICAL ARTS AMONG THE CHINESE

•   •   •   •   •

Musical instruments are quite common and of many varieties, but the use of the organ and the clavichord is unknown, and the Chinese possess no instrument of the keyboard type. On all of their stringed instruments the strings are made of twisted cotton, and they seem to be ignorant of the fact that the guts of animals can be used for this purpose. Their practice agrees fairly well with ours in the use of instruments to be played in concert. The whole art of Chinese music seems to consist in producing a monotonous rhythmic beat as they know nothing of the variations and harmony that can be produced by combining different musical notes. However, they themselves are highly flattered by their own music which to the ear of a stranger represents nothing but a discordant jangle. Despite the fact that they claim the first rank in the field of harmonious concert music, they have expressed themselves pleased with organ music and with all our musical instruments which they have heard thus far. Perhaps they will judge in like manner of our vocal harmony and orchestration when

TEXT: *China in the Sixteenth Century* by Matthew Ricci, trans. Louis J. Gallagher, S.J., pp. 22–24, 335–36, 376–78. Copyright 1942 and renewed 1970 by Louis J. Gallagher. Reprinted by permission of Random House, Inc.

they have heard it. Up to the present they have not had this opportunity in our churches, as our modest beginnings here have not yet reached that stage of development. . . .

I believe this people is too much interested in dramatic representations and shows. At least they certainly surpass us in this respect. An exceedingly large number of the youth of the land is devoted to this activity. Some of them form traveling troupes which journey everywhere throughout the length and breadth of the country, while other groups reside permanently in the large centers and are in great demand for private as well as for public performances. Without question this is a curse in the empire, and so much so that it would be difficult to discover any other activity which is more prone to vice. Sometimes the leaders of the troupes of actors purchase young children and force them, almost from infancy, to take part in the choruses, to lead the dance, and to share in the acting and mimicry. Nearly all of their plays are of ancient origin, based upon history or fiction, and nowadays few new plays are being produced. These groups of actors are employed at all imposing banquets, and when they are called they come prepared to enact any of the ordinary plays. The host at the banquet is usually presented with a volume of plays and he selects the one or several he may like. The guests, between eating and drinking, follow the plays with so much satisfaction that the banquet at times may last for ten hours, and as one play leads to another the dramatic performance may last as long again as did the banquet. The text of these plays is generally sung, and it rarely happens that anything is enunciated in an ordinary tone of voice. . . .[1]

•   •   •   •   •

BOOK 4

CHAPTER 6: THE LEADERS AT NANKIN SOLICIT THE COMPANY OF FATHER RICCI

. . . Let us here insert a word about Chinese music, an art that is of considerable interest to Europeans. The leaders of the literary class observe a solemn day of sacrifice in honor of Confucius, if sacrifice is the proper word. The Chinese honor the great philosopher as a Master, and not as a deity, and they are accustomed to use the word sacrifice in a broad and indefinite sense. This particular celebration is attended with music, and on the previous day they invite the Chief of Magistrates to attend a rehearsal of the orchestra, to decide whether or not the music will be appropriate for the occasion. Father Ricci was

---

1. On the music drama of the late Ming dynasty see "China" in *The New Grove Dictionary of Music and Musicians,* section III.1 (Colin P. MacKerras) and Kuo-huang Han and Lindy Li Mark, "Evolution and Revolution in Chinese Music," in *Musics of Many Cultures,* ed. Elizabeth May (Berkeley: University of California Press, 1980), pp. 10–31, esp. p. 16. The opera Ricci describes was most likely *k'un-ch'ü,* a florid style, accompanied by flute *(ti-tzu)* or sometimes lute *(p'i-p'a),* that thrived among educated classes in the late sixteenth century.

invited to this rehearsal and as there was no question of attending a sacrifice, he accepted the invitation. This orchestral rehearsal was arranged by the priests of the literary class, called Tansu, and it was held in a hall or rather in the Royal Temple, built to honor the Lord of Heaven. Father Matthew was accompanied by the children of the High Magistrate. The priests who composed the orchestra were vested in sumptuous garments, as if they were to attend a sacrifice, and after paying their respects to the Magistrate, they set to playing their various instruments; bronze bells, basin shaped vessels, some made of stone, with skins over them like drums, stringed instruments like a lute,[2] bone flutes and organs played by blowing into them with the mouth rather than with bellows.[3] They had other instruments also shaped like animals, holding reeds in their teeth, through which air was forced from the empty interior. At this rehearsal these curious affairs were all sounded at once, with a result that can be readily imagined, as it was nothing other than a lack of concord, a discord of discords. The Chinese themselves are aware of this. One of their sages said on a certain occasion that the art of music known to their ancestors had evaporated with the centuries, and left only the instruments.

· · · · ·

CHAPTER 12: FROM PRISON TO PEKIN BY THE KING'S COMMAND

. . . Later on, four of the eunuchs who played stringed instruments before the throne came, in the King's name, to see the Fathers. Playing on such instruments is considered to be an advanced art among the Chinese, and the palace musicians outrank the mathematicians. They conduct an elaborate school in the royal palace and they came to ask the Fathers to teach them to play on the clavichord, which was included in the royal presents. From being a casual student, Father Didaco had become very proficient on this instrument, and he went to the palace every day to give them a music lesson. It was at the suggestion of Father Ricci, made a long time before, that Father Didaco had taken lessons on the clavichord from Father Cattaneo, who was an accomplished musician, and in making the suggestion, he was looking forward to this very incident. The Chinese knew little or nothing about such an instrument, and Father Didaco had learned not only to play but to harmonize the various chords.

Contrary to the wishes of the Fathers, before beginning their lessons, the music pupils insisted upon going through the ceremonies, which are customary when a teacher meets new pupils, or rather when pupils select a new teacher. They asked Father Didaco to teach them with patience but with diligence, and not to become impatient if he found them slow to learn this art, hitherto unknown to them. Afterwards they went through the same ceremony with the clavichord, for an assurance of progress, as if it had been a living thing. Before

2. Probably the *p'i-p'a*.
3. The *sheng*.

long the Europeans were being entertained at meals and visited by some of the eunuchs in high position. Gradually they became known to the whole palace retinue with some of whom they formed permanent friendships. . . .

Each of the clavichord pupils was content with learning one piece. Two of the younger ones were apt enough at learning, but they waited for the others to complete the course, and so the time allotted for lessons was drawn out for more than a month. They were quite interested in having the pieces they were playing put to Chinese words, and Father Matthew took this occasion to compose eight pieces which he called "Songs for the Clavichord." These were lyrics, touching upon ethical subjects, teaching lessons of good morals and virtues, and aptly illustrated with quotations from Christian authors. These songs became so popular that numerous requests from the literati were received, asking for copies of them, and giving high praise to the lessons they taught. They said that these songs reminded the King that he should govern the realm with the virtues suggested in the songs, and in order to satisfy the demand for copies of them, the Fathers printed them, together with other pieces, as a musical booklet, written in European lettering and also in Chinese characters.[4]

4. On these songs and Ricci's use of music in his Christianizing effort see Jonathan D. Spence, *The Memory Palace of Matteo Ricci* (New York: Viking, 1984), pp. 197–200.

INDEX

Note: Numbers in boldface refer to pages where definitions for a term are found, or to the source reading passages themselves.